The Tome Partner

THE TOME TUNNEL

Andrew Harman

LEGEND

Published in the United Kingdom in 1994 by Legend
Books

1 3 5 9 10 8 6 4 2

First published in the United Kingdom in 1994 by

Legend Books
20 Vauxhall Bridge Road, London, SW1V 2SA

Random House Australia Pty Ltd
20 Alfred Street, Milsons Point, Sydney, NSW 2061
Australia

Random House New Zealand Ltd
18 Poland Road, Glenfield, Auckland 10,
New Zealand

Random House South Africa (Pty) Ltd
PO Box 337, Bergvlei 2012, South Africa

Random House UK Limited Reg. No. 954009

Typeset by Deltatype Ltd, Ellesmere Port, Wirral
Printed in Great Britain by
Cox & Wyman, Reading, Berkshire

ISBN: 0 09 928491 X

Dedication

A victorious thumbs-up, in no particular order, to
Maria, Gareth, Chris, Yvonne and Andy – the finest
amateur editors there are!

And a victoriously thumbed nose at Keri!

Contents

Prophecy for Fun

Ignoring the frantic cries of startled protest from the secretary, the thirteen-hole Prayer-Wear Boots of the Highest Priest smashed their way into the head office of the Bifurcated and Tubular Sundial Company Ltd and stomped onwards. Waving his arms in a dazzling blur of wild gestures (and neatly sidestepping the ricocheting oak door) the indigo-clad figure surged forcefully towards the latest cowering victim.

'Are *you* ready for the next life?' he demanded, surfing in on tides of faith, vast uncharted oceans of robes billowing from the high prows of his advancing shoulders. The High Priest's eyes smouldered with the passion of a man with a mission as he halted before the desk, raised his hands and adopted the traditional cruciformly imperious stance of St Lucre.

'N . . . not yet. You're early!' protested the little man feebly, his quill dribbling a trail of suddenly irrelevant ink.

'Does Death consult sundials? Do Demons keep diaries?' snapped the High Priest, rhetorically waving a long finger. 'Punctuality is not the concern of those from the other side. Or do you perhaps have foreknowledge of when your personal End is Nigh, eh, Naximanda?'

'I . . . I . . .' struggled the man, his pale eyes darting nervously behind his thick spectacles like a pair of terrified tadpoles in the final, trembling moments of terminal stage-fright.

'Are you prepared for *your* Appointed Time?' demanded the High Priest, his teeth sticking out like ancient grave-stones.

'N . . .'

'Post-mortal future secured?' snapped His Eminence,

Bharkleed the Fervently Exalted, freelance religious advisor and personal posthumous affairs co-ordinator, his white beard quivering with religious fervour as he lurched over the desk and pointed at the terrified ventricles of his latest victim's heart. 'Bags packed for the greatest journey of your worthless existence?' he growled, nostrils flaring with eager excitement. Bharkleed could sense the growing fear in the little man's body: see his victim's sudden attack of theological agoraphobia as his soul stared across the widening Plains of Eternal Damnation. The High Priest shrieked wildly, clapping his hands as Naximanda saw himself in the manner Bharkleed willed him to – as an irritating spot of scabby dandruff upon the pin-striped finery of Infinity's black-padded shoulders.

But Naximanda was scabby dandruff with a difference.

He had money. Pots and pots of it!

He wasn't the internationally renowned inventor of the best-selling self-illuminating 'Nocturne' sundial and founder of the Bifurcated and Tubular Sundial Company Ltd for nothing! But, sundials were one thing; souls, especially his very own, were an entirely different matter.

'If you died today, would you be a happy phantom?' trilled His Effulgence, Hirsuit the Very Enpedestalled, grinning manically over Bharkleed's colourfully trimmed left shoulder. Naximanda attempted to answer. And gurgled pathetically.

'Have you ever considered how long it takes to get a reservation with Charon?' asked His Eminence Bharkleed folding his arms and placing his bearded chin in his hand, one finger pointing subliminally hellward. 'And have you the faintest inkling of what one obolus is worth these days?'

The managing director's eyeballs trembled, his brow wrinkling like an exhausted and grossly understuffed corduroy pillow.

'Is rented accommodation cheaper in Hades if you're already cremated?' asked the third High Priest, His Emmolient, Whedd the Most Lubricious, rubbing his hands

2

oilily. 'And where are the hotest nightspots to be seen at if you're an upwardly mobile demon, eh?'

'As you can see, Naximanda,' said Bharkleed making the phrase sound more like a command as he stared deep into the twitching tadpole pupils of the little man and drew up a seat, 'there are hundreds, nay, thousands of questions to be addressed upon the event of your demise. I mean, have you ever heard of any person of a recently deceased nature rushing about changing his life savings into obuls just to pay Charon? You wouldn't believe how old fashioned he is, one obolus or nothing! And there's no other way over the Styx, let me tell you. Get it sorted before it's too late or you'll be really stung. See, between you and me, the exchange rates for the animationally challenged are absolutely shocking. Shocking! No securities, see? Bad credit risk.'

Hirsuit nodded enthusiastically, his expression displaying earnest concern and moved a menacing inch closer. Whedd smiled unctuously.

'That's why more and more people are turning to us for help in planning for what is, after all, inevitable.' An indigo-clad arm extended across the parchment strewn table towards Naximanda and flicked a card beneath his vibrating nose. 'There's only three things certain in a person's life – birth, death and the essentiality of making reservations.'

Naximanda shrugged a pair of extremely baffled shoulders. Conversations like this just shouldn't happen on Tuesday mornings.

'Let's face it,' continued High Priest Bharkleed, tapping the tip of the managing director's nose with the corner of the card until he took it. 'Death's an occasion that is far from stress free at the best of times without having to worry about details like reservations, monetary exchange, excess baggage allowance . . .'

'. . . ?' shrieked Naximanda's panicking eyes, looking up from the white rectangle in his hand.

'Oh! Didn't you hear? Thought *everyone* knew! Rhamyseehz the ninth. You know him, died a couple of years back, well he *really* got stung for excess baggage, I can tell you. It was all those horses, and servants, and wives. Half of them weren't dead! It's extra if you want to get into Hades if you haven't been dead for at least three days. Quarantine, you know. Really fussy about that, they are.'

'Wha. . . ?' struggled Naximanda opening and closing his mouth slowly.

'Still, good thing you can insure for that now, eh?' continued Bharkleed, his tongue licking across his angular teeth.

'Insu. . . ?'

'Vital. Never leave life without it!'

'But, what. . .?'

'. . . can go wrong?' interrupted Bharkleed grinning sharkishly. 'You just wouldn't *believe* it!'

'Double-booking,' offered Hirsuit over the High Priest's indigo shoulder.

Naximanda's eyebrows made a leap up his forehead.

'Double. . . ?'

'Happens more often than you might imagine,' said Bharkleed, joining his hands beneath his chin in an attempt at choir-boyish innocence, and fighting off an urge to flutter his eyebrows for added effect. 'Half a dozen demons off sick in Immigration, coupled with a sudden bout of enthusiasm by Pestilence, or dear old War being a bit trigger happy and the nice cosy windowseat you had booked has vanished. Along with your fare and your baggage, if it's been loaded. No use complaining. Can't do anything about it, except wait for the next free seat.'

'How long. . . ?'

'Who can say. Could be the next crossing, could be weeks, or centuries! That's the snag with Eternal Damnation. No hurry to get problems sorted, and without insurance they won't hold your accommodation. Let me tell you, you don't want to be homeless in Hell for a millisecond longer than you have to. If you think that nothing worse can happen to you once you're dead . . . well, then you'll have a *very* unpleasant surprise.'

4

'How?'

'. . . can it get worse? Yeech! You don't want to know,' interrupted Hirsuit, cringing as if imagining a series of unpleasant happenings at the absolute extreme ultra-violent end of the rainbow of stygian torment. He rolled his eyes.

'You don't need a *body* to have pain inflicted on you,' slimed Whedd, gloating as he grimaced over Bharkleed's other shoulder. 'Heard of people losing limbs in accidents and still feeling them burning, screaming with pain, years afterwards?'

Naximanda nodded, wishing he hadn't.

'Well, imagine that, over your whole body, every single sensitive bit, all the soft, delicate, fragile . . .'

'Whedd, please!' interrupted Bharleed. 'I'm sorry. My Most Lubricious Brother does become a little carried away at some points. I do apologise if he upset you. Just wasn't called for.'

Naximanda twitched and turned the colour of three-week-old spinach and blue cheese mousse.

'All this unnecessary unpleasantness can be avoided, see? No need to risk it!' Bharkleed grinned, leaning closer. 'How'd you like a guaranteed Happy-Ever-Afterlife in our specially built, all new Condominium for the Cremated. A multi-storeyed complex which takes the standard of Hadean accommodation into a new and golden age. Yes, you may be in Hell, but it'll *feel* like heaven. Interested? Join us today and we can offer you substantial peace-of-mind discounts for you and your family.'

'How do I. . . ?'

'Join the Most Elevated Church of St Lucre the Unwashed? Couldn't be easier. Simply believe,' answered His Eminence, Bharkleed the Fervently Exalted.

'What?'

'Believe,' insisted Bharkleed.

'Oh. What in?'

'The absolute and unshakable knowledge that by signing this piece of parchment you are entering into the most secure

5

business deal of your after-life, thus ensuring your safe and trouble-free passage to a place of ultimate rest,' said Bharkleed producing a large and ornately illuminated document and unrolling it before Naximanda. 'Brother Hirsuit, the Sacred Quill, if you please.'

'What's that. . . ?' began Naximanda staring at the parchment.

'Just to say that you have *heard* the Message of The High Priests of the highest of the Elevated Churches and that you have no questions, whatsoever.'

'Er . . .' hesitated the managing director glaring at the microscopically small print.

'Merely a formality,' oozed Whedd.

'It's not like you're signing your life away,' reassured Hirsuit.

Bharkleed pressed the quill into Naximanda's hand, crocodile smiling as he watched the latest conned convert scrawl his name next to the cross at the bottom of the sheet. In a flash it was witnessed, countersigned, blown dry and tidied away.

'You should be very proud of yourself,' said Hirsuit, smiling with just a few too many teeth. 'A great moment.'

The three priests, Bharkleed, Hirsuit and Whedd, stood and turned to leave.

'Is that it?' asked their latest convert. 'Aren't you going to pray for me, or anything?'

'Er . . . oh. No. We don't, er, do that now. Later,' answered Bharkleed over his indigo shoulder.

'Oh,' answered Naximanda looking crestfallen. 'Not even a few words of wisdom or blessing now. It's my first time for being born-again, see?'

Whedd swallowed and looked nervously at Bharkleed. Converts shouldn't ask difficult questions like that. None of the others had.

'Er. Very well,' said the Highest Priest, holding his hands out in a gesture of falsely pious blessing. 'For what *we* are about to receive, may we not have to wait *too* long.'

6

Was it Naximanda's imagination or did he wink at his colleagues at the end? Imagination, surely.

The six Prayer-Wear booted feet stamped urgently away as the managing director scratched his balding head, thoughtfully listening to the cheerful chanting of the priests. He almost envied them. They sounded so happy. If he'd had more imagination he might have felt they were killing themselves laughing inside and trying furiously not to let it show.

The tiny black and white pig struggled up the long muddy drag of Krill Street, Shirm, accompanied by spontaneous bursts of stifled childish giggling, the like of which is not normally associated with grown-ups. Especially if they are grown-ups of the cloth. It had definitely been a very, very good day and the three High Priests of the Elevated Church of St Lucre the Unwashed were grinning in the back of the pig-shaw with exceptionally unholy expressions of utter smugness, much to the confusion and suspicious unease of the driver.

'For what *we* are about to receive . . .' spluttered Whedd.

Hirsuit slapped his thigh as he exploded with pent-up mirth. 'Did you see his face?' he shrieked. 'I love it. I love it! The sucker believed you!'

'Brother Hirsuit,' said Bharkleed trying to look serious. 'I do not think we should be discussing important *religious* matters in such a manner.' He pointed covertly at the wagging ear of the pig-shaw driver, straining to snatch any of the pearls of gossip being carelessly hurled his way.

Fortunately for him he hadn't caught any details of the evilly corrupt seeds being liberally sown within the fleshy body of Shirm's rich and juicy financial centre. Even more fortunate that he hadn't a clue what havoc would be wrought upon their germination.

If Bharkleed had suspected that the driver knew anything incriminating he would have been a marked man – marked for Blessed Lieutenant Vher-Jah. Within a few short and extremely painful hours a real priest would be administering last rites to a glistening arrangement of most of his major organs. Artistically intriguing but utterly incompatible with life.

Bharkleed licked his gravestone teeth, grinning with relish as he thought of Vher-Jah's best works of persuasion – the man had such skill with a needle and hacksaw.

Outside of the environs of the panting pig, the driver and the cargo of three men, the population of Shirm lay blissfully ignorant of its impending financial and theological nightmare. This was mainly due to the fact that most of Shirm's inhabitants were non-human and spent their lives face down in the brackish slurry pit that called itself the River Torpid. And most of the humans were trying to haul them out with vast nets.

Bivalves and gastropods cheerfully gorged themselves with molluscan delight much to the overwhelming happiness of the men with the nets who worked for The Translittoral Mollusc Trading Company. The finest shellfish in the known world were harvested and exported from the whelk fields or drift netted from the vast, open limpet mines of Shirm.

But the three High Priests of The Elevated Church of St Lucre the Unwashed weren't drawn to Shirm by an overwhelming interest in numbers of shellfish. More a selfish interest in overwhelming numbers. Namely the profits of The Translittoral Mollusc Trading Company.

Tossing the pig-shaw driver three roats* for the journey and patting the sweating pig as they passed, the three passengers headed straight for the bar of the Swagger Inn.

'Three quarts of Hexenhammer, landlord.'

---

* Prior to what had become known in the Kingdom of Froul as 'High Summer' a person's wealth was measured in terms of the number of whelks he owned. However, following the now legendary eight months of searing heat and sweltering temperatures, even the most nasally impaired of investors was clamouring for a currency less eager to spontaneously biodegrade.

Thus was invented the highly treasured roat. A small disc of sun-dried river mud stamped with a dubious likeness of one of the heads of the remaining three Rotating Kings of Froul.

In a few moments three leather flagons of frothing dark ale appeared before the thirsty priests as they nestled in a dark secluded corner of the Inn.

'Cheers, men,' said Bharkleed raising his drink. 'Damn fine day, eh? Ha ha! More skipping lambs welcomed into our ever expanding fold of conned-verts! Our flock grows daily. How many new sheep are we about to fleece, eh, Brother Shepherd?'

'Fifteen top-grade clients this afternoon,' answered Hirsuit cheerfully, counting the clutch of parchments with difficulty in the gloom. 'All top-grade clients. Nicely fatted, heavy with the burden of far too much profit for their own good.'

'Excellent, excellent,' oozed Whedd around another mouthful of Hexenhammer.

'Let them enjoy their new-found devotion for a little while. Another week of extra profits won't hurt us,' said Bharkleed staring into the middle distance of a glisteringly bright, shining future of splendid auric opulence. 'Drink up, gentlemen! One week and phase two begins!'

As the last few flaggons of Hexenhammer were drained at the end of another undistinguished, drunken evening towards the end of the year 2526,* a bent and tired fossil of a

---

* Longer ago than anyone would admit being able to recall the top two echelons of Froulian society consisted of an Emperor and a total of thirteen Kings, one for each of the states. Following the untimely death of the Emperor after a suspicious accident involving him stabbing himself in five places whilst cleaning his favourite ten-inch hunting knife (the final slip of which lodged the blade tragically between his shoulderblades) the populace was forced to the polls. After countless unsuccessful and bloody elections to choose the next victim from the jostling *tredecim* of hopeful and aggresively defensive Kings it was decided that, for the sake of both civil peace and saving on hospital bills, each King would rule for one month in every year. The inconvenience of a calendar that slipped out of phase with the rest of the world was more than compensated for by the instant cessation of open hostilities and the closure of several hospitals.

And so peace reigned alongside the Rotating Kings of Froul for years and years and . . .

However, owing to a whole series of deaths, interstate wars, riots, monarchicidal invasions and family feuds, the number of Kings rapidly fell to three.

The Froulian Calendar is now one thousand four hundred and eighty seven years ahead of the rest of the world. And rising.

man struggled up a tiny spiral staircase on the far side of Shirm. His crimson slippers' bells jingled cheerfully, threatening to catch the faded paisley hem of his robe as he headed up for another night of TV.

Would it be a thriller tonight? he wondered, or some news? . . . bound to be bad news . . . maybe a mystery? You could never tell with Telechronologic Visions. The future held what the future held.

He took another bite of his cheese sandwich and struggled upwards. It was a battle he waged every night, armed only with a small beaten copper bowl of water, a drip-encrusted tallow candle, his divining licence, a small branch of laurel and hardy determination to see what the 'Tele' would show him tonight.

As the arthritic detonations of the prophet's aged knees vied to outdo the creaks of the not-quite-terminally en-beetled staircase, his ancient rib-cage hacked and coughed violently. Suffocated in the barrage of stale cheesy air the candleflame swooned, gagged, struggled to recover, then died. Swearing profusely and miscounting the number of stairs in the sudden dark he stumbled into the room, staggered over the pine coffin and collapsed in a heap of ink-splattered robes and a hail of curses. Years of nightly practice had finely honed this traditional outburst, giving maximum obscenity for minimum effort. The bowl of water, as it did every night, somehow managed to end up perched, more or less full, on a small three-legged stool and the sandwich spun into a far corner to huddle with some other ageing residents. Several million haemoglobin molecules snatched oxygen from the alveoli of Nostromo Kasein's panting lungs, like a shoal of wildly gasping catfish in a bloodbath.

He glowered at the coffin. It had been there for years. Tailor-made, silk-lined. He'd even been buried in it. Six times. He was the laughing stock of the Undertaker's Guild. Every time he walked past the Funeral Parlour he could hear them giggling, could see them pointing at him through the smoked glass. New recruits were sent round to measure him up, some weird initiation or something. Liberty! Cheek! Well, one of these days he *would* die just to spite them, *then* they'd be sorry. 'Who'd have the last laugh then, eh!' he grumbled to himself through the grey strands of his moustache, and dabbed water on his feet in the strict preparatory ritual he always followed. Quite why he did it he hadn't the foggiest idea, they never tell you *why* you do things in the 'Prophecy for Fun' correspondence course. In exactly the same way they don't tell you that you can't predict the time of your own death. Unless you've got a large cliff handy, but that's cheating. 'Prophecy for Fun!' Pah! Such a cheap trick to delay printing the answers to the last test until 3005. He wasn't going to waste his time scouring the libraries of the future to find out if he'd passed. And what about the title 'Prophecy for Fun'. Fun! *Fun!* If they'd so much as glimpsed some of the things he'd seen they wouldn't call it fun. Three years of witnessing the world explode in a swirling miasmic whirlpool of cosmic wreckage and destruction inside the comfort of your own skull, in full colour, night after night, *cannot* be described as fun. Grumbling and cursing colourfully as his knees crackled in osseous protest at being folded into a strange squatting position, he swirled the water in the bowl with a long gnarled finger and stared deep inside, like an arthritic heron waiting for a shoal of woefully misguided and careless chubb to offer themselves as a light snack.

It wasn't long before the water clouded over and swirling messages flooded through Nostromo's staring eyes, straight into his subconscious.

His hand shot out to one side, tore open a large book, flicked the lid off the ink-pot, twitched, snatched a peacock quill, and began scribbling wildly on the rough parchment surface of the open book. His eyes stared into the bowl, fixed, ignorant of the inky thrashing hand off to their right.

11

How long the scratchy scribbling continued he never knew, but it was deep into the night when the image in the bowl flashed static and shrank into a tiny spot in the centre. Nostromo collapsed in a panting heap, shaking the balding globe of his head, cursing the sharp singing note in his ears.

He stared dazedly at the ink-splattered book, spitting a curse through his broken teeth as he attempted to decifer the calligraphist's nightmare of twisted letters and shattered vowels. It was no wonder that he had constantly got three out of twenty for presentation. Tonight's message from the other side was going to take a *lot* of judicial interpretation and headscratching guesswork.

Now let's see:

> 'When the goatherd stumbles *splodge* on the key in the pot, the phoenix *blob smear* will. . . . in a hail of sandstorms, the eyes of *blurrrr* the dead *drip* will see the lo . . . th . . . of *slosh* the ancient *blatt* hieroglyph and the meek will cover their faces *splodge* a host of fi . . . cloaks.'

Or is it:

> 'Beyond the *splash* green floating island *drip* the red sphere will spin endlessly *blob* and fore . . . the yellow orio . . . power will *squirt* take the dogs of fortune out of their *splat* tanks after the gre . . . blood of the herring *sprinkle* turns milky.'

Nostromo scratched his head and looked worriedly at the three hundred and twenty five lines of piebald parchment.

A bloody mystery! he swore miserably. I hate mysteries! Especially messy ones. So damned vague. Could mean absolutely anything! Why bother? A whole week of blinking mysteries! Struggle up here, and for what? A shower of ink. Doesn't do my arthritis any good. What the hell've goatherds and floating islands got to do with the future? Bah! I wonder if those whelks I ate at the end of last week were all right. I know I was a bit greedy but . . . Oh no! Of course! It was the cheese sauce. Too much cheese sauce always gives me nightmares. Bound to be the cheese sauce . . .

Absently he flicked the parchment page back a few weeks, stared momentarily at the familiar ink pattern, screamed, snatched back to the latest soggy entry, screamed again, louder, and slapped his forehead. A repeat! A mystery *and* one he'd seen before. That's the trouble with TV, always repeating bloody mysteries!

Swearing volubly and sucking noisily at his false teeth, Nostromo kicked the coffin, shuffled out of the room and creaked down the stairs.

'Shan't pay my licence fee if they don't buck up their ideas!' he growled.

The recent period of far less than entirely accurate predictions flowing from the pen of Nostromo Kasein had lasted for far longer than anyone, including himself, could remember. However, this didn't mean that he wasn't possessed of the ability to watch TVs.

He would be one of the first to admit that publicly announcing one's very own imminent death, on six separate and widely differing occasions, did little to enhance one's reputation for faultlessly accurate foretelling. But – ask any prophet and they'd agree – it is notoriously difficult for anyone, except perhaps a highly determined and very depressed nutter with bare wrists and a glinting razor blade, to predict with any certainty the time of their own demise.

Unfortunately, due to age, overwork and his predisposition toward inhaling the smouldering, mind-expanding fumes of carefully selected dried herbs and ground leaves. Nostromo's TV reception was less than high definition. It was becoming increasingly difficult to winnow the genuine pearls of prophesorial wisdom from the swine of grunting, spurious ramblings tumbling from a drug-crazed mind close to the brink of senility.

It had been three years ago that he'd first noticed the

problem. He couldn't have chosen a more public time to lose hold of the apron strings of sanity than the after-dinner guest speech of the Ninety-Third Annual Prophet, Mystic and Psychics' Gala Charity Dinner of 2523. But, then, that's sanity for you. You take care of it all those years; protecting it from tortuous logic puzzles; shielding it from the Great Unanswerable Questions; running in the opposite direction when someone tries to hand you a small multi-coloured cube and ask you to rearrange it to get all the same colours on each of the faces, for fun!; and what does it go and do? Without a by-your-leave, or if-you-don't-mind, it ups and buggers off out of your head leaving you gawping at a room full of people staring at you as if you'd just predicted the end of the world.

At least, that's how Nostromo remembered it.

He shuddered as he recalled it all so vividly.

'. . . place that prophecy will hold in the public eye of the future is difficult to foresee,' he had said over the gentle clinking of the brandy glasses, his voice shakily hollow in the dark wood interior of the cavernous hall, 'but I'm sure one of you can help.' He paused and waited for the laugh. It didn't come. Instead, several large brickbats of hard stony silence were hurled from the floor. He fumbled with his crib notes, swallowed and struggled bravely on. Pretend it *wasn't* meant to be funny, he told himself unconvincingly. It's the only way!

'Of course, without doubt the single most important factors are, er, is, factors *is* the essential ability to communicate effectively . . .' Help! '. . . with the general public . . .' I don't like this game anymore . . . 'to bring about a greater understanding. Er, oh. Of the relevence of prophecy.'

It was then that it really started. Out of the corner of his eyes a pale green flashing began, as if someone was trying to attract his attention with an intermittent glow-worm on a stick. Then more joined in, glinting geometrically.

Uh-oh! he panicked, recalling what he had just eaten. Cheese, garlic, coffee, red wine and . . . chocolate. Ahhhhhg! Migraine!

14

He squinted at his notes but the flashing lights ploughed viridian furrows across his field of view, expanding, forming green glowing letters on his retina, spelling out words – a prophetic autocue . . .

'Latest update on End of World. Stop. Third August two forty. Stop.' He blurted in bewildered panic.

The Master of Ceremonies looked up from his brandy in alarm. This wasn't in the speech. He shouldn't be ad-libbing! Other guest prophets looked up from their after-dinner mints.

'Water rising uncontrollably. Stop. Stone trolls in market. Stop.' Confusion and alarm wrestled with Nostromo's forehead as the glow-words flashed at him. A migraine had never done *that* before. 'Atmospheric conflagration spreading. Stop. Plague. Stop.'

Suddenly the Master of Ceremonies realised what was going on. It was a prediction! A vision . . . and it sounded bad.

'Famine. Stop.'

The End of the World as we know it! His chair exploded backwards as he leapt to his feet, lurching for Nostromo's talking head. The third of August! It was August next month!

'White rabbit panicking. Stop. Alarm at lateness of hour. Stop.'

The Master of Ceremonies grabbed Nostromo's shoulder, whirled him round and stared into his unfocused eyes. 'When?' he screamed.

'Third August. Stop.'

'What year? Dammit man, what year?' he barked, 'This year? 2523?' His face was pale with panic. His strawberry mousse eagerly rising in his stomach.

'Confirm year. Query. Stop.' mumbled Nostromo.

'Yes, dammit! Confirm year!'

'Third August . . .'

'I *know* that! Year, *year!*'

'. . . Stop. Ten thirty nine. Stop.'

15

'Is that year or time?'

'Time two forty. Stop. Year ten thirty nine. Stop.'

The Master of Ceremonies shook Nostromo and swore colourfully. His strawberry mousse settled back to gently disgesting.

A few of the more-intoxicated members of the audience giggled hysterically as they heard this. Ten thirty nine! That was over fourteen hundred years ago. What the hell was this guy playing at? Predicting the end of the world fourteen and a bit centuries after the event! The panic evaporated suddenly, transforming itself into a cloud of startled anger directed accusingly at the perpetrator of the hoax.

Nostromo's vision was returning to normal as he rubbed his eyes and tried to recall where he was and what he was supposed to be doing. It was then that he noticed the malevolent look of do-you-take-us-all-to-be-idiots on the crowd's face.

He turned and ran . . .

Shaking in a cold sweat, three years later, he sat bolt upright in bed, clutching at his stomach.

'Bad dreams!' he whimpered. 'It *must* be the cheese sauce.'

Bugs in the dairy topping may have been responsible for Nostromo's bout of acute intestine-knotting flatulence; it's pretty unlikely, though, that a clump of rowdy *Escherichia coli*, no matter how furiously they flapped their flagellae and leapt around, could have had anything to do with what happened next.

Suddenly and very unexpectedly, the way things like this are wont to occur in novels, a memory chip of *that* Dinner shot out of the past, into his skull, avoiding his pituitary gland and buried itself in the clump of cells and stringy neurons that was his atrophied logic centre. It was only then, as he scratched his thinly thatched head, that a very peculiar, feeling overcame him. A feeling that, after all these years of missing the Bleeding Obvious's highly unsubtle clues and grossly overemphasised hints, it had finally got fed

16

up, exhausted, or both, and had just this instant yelled the answer in his ear, accompanied by banks of blasting sirens and retina-burning neons.

Nostromo Kasein felt extremely embarrassed. He'd heard that TV dulled the brain but . . . Terror ripped the bed-clothes off as he leapt from bed and snatched a large book off a nearby shelf. Rifling wildly through it he came to the entry on the Froulian Calendar System. He stifled a squeal, rolled his eyes into his forehead and counted backwards on his fingers. Then stopped, clamped his hands around his head and screamed.

It was times like these that made the privileged gift of prophecy at once gloriously exciting, fantastically fulfilling and highly likely to cause stomach ulcers, heart palpitations, hot flushes and fifteen or so other stress-related illnesses. All at once.

He shivered as he swore. It was two o'clock in the morning; it was dark; he knew the exact timing of the end of civilisation . . . and he was wearing pyjamas.

Just beyond the edge of the River Torpid, in the cold pre-dawn shadow of Mount Annatack, a small camp of men nestled. That is if eighty-five twenty-stone weightlifters, each sporting eight days' growth of beard, body odour and beer breath to match could be described as nestling. They had pitched camp late last night, and it showed. Weary after an all-day route march across leagues of cryptically marked wilderness, following the High Priest's Guidance, the exhausted gang had tossed tents on to the side of the hill, posted second-class guards and collapsed into a heap of snoring torpor.

If anyone had been brave enough, or sufficiently nasally compromised, to enter the camp and poke about beneath a random selection of covers it would have made interesting peeking. Boxes of highly coloured and beautifully printed parchments lay next to sacks of gold, candelabra rubbed wicks with pearls of chandeliers, and ornately carved onyx

17

Mah J'hreen sets rattled gently next to exquisitely glued-together shell animals. A typical week's Offerings from the Devotees of the Church of St Lucre the Unwashed.

Within a matter of hours, under the iron fist of Blessed Lieutenant Vher-Jah, this snoring camp would be a humming hive of activity as the parchment presses rolled once more into action stocking up on Certificates of Unquestioning Belief, readying the Envoy for the Great Conversion of Shirm.

Glistening and snaking like a predatory pinkish moray-eel out for the kill, the Lord Mayor's tongue flapped in concentration as he focused on the small pitted sphere before him. His mind was a blur of sluggish maths as he attempted to calculate its trajectory. Shuffling in uneasy adjustments, his thumbs interlocking around the raised club's handle, he glared in defiance at the distant bucket. Returning his gaze to the ball, and holding it fixed there as if to pin the object to the vast expanse of green floor-covering, he swung the club in as even an arc as he could muster.

At that instant the door was flung open and the stork-like figure of the Clerk flapped in backwards, tripped and was mown into the municipal green shag-pile by a panic-ridden prophet. The Lord Mayor turned in mid-stroke, concentration shattered, and screamed as the unpleasant sound of tortured verdant carpet was delicately counterpointed by the croquet ball's sibilant exit through a stained-glass cherub's navel.

'My handicap!' wailed His Worship, Wert Greadly, the eighty-seventh Lord Mayor of Shirm.

'Your worship, I, er . . .' squeaked the Clerk from the floor.

'How many times have I told you to knock!' shouted the oleaginous civic leader turning rapidly red in the face.

'It wasn't my fault. I . . .' pleaded the Clerk as the Mayor advanced, his club penduluming menacingly.

'Do you *care* about my handicap!' snarled Wert Graedly. 'All those weeks of extra training, wasted! Back to hoop one!

18

You *do* realise it's the Glenperegrine Croquet Open next month. . . ?'

'Yes, your civility, I . . .'

'. . . and Salivary Ballustrade will be there. You do *realise* that? Don't you?'

'Yes, your complaisance . . .'

'Then why didn't you observe Shirm Council Directive three five eight stroke six?'

'Sir?'

'Do I have to remind you every time? Knock!'

'But, your Worship . . .'

'Ahem.' Nostromo tapped his foot irritably and cleared his throat.

'It was him!' squeaked the Clerk pointing desperately at the prophet.

'This elongated stick-insect of yours told me to wait,' snapped Nostromo, stomping forward and waving an arthritic thumb over his bony shoulder. 'Wait. *Wait!* As if there was enough time!'

'Shirm Council Directive two five six stroke eight a) clearly states . . .' began Mayor Greadly attempting to rub several doses of the linament of local office into his frayed nerves.

'Don't you talk to me about bleeding Council Directives!' shrieked the irate prophet. 'Unless you've got one outlining how to panic at the End of the World. Eh?'

The Clerk winced as he stood and dusted a string of footprints off the front of his cloak.

'Mr Kasein,' urged the Mayor. 'Nothing was ever achieved by getting angry.'

'No? How d'you win wars, then?'

'Well, that's different . . . I mean . . .'

'Strategy,' interjected the Clerk, removing another dusty heelmark from a very delicate region.

'Yes, yes!' agreed the cellulitic dignitary. 'But we're not at war so . . .'

'Soon will be if you don't stop blabbering and listen!'

snapped Nostromo, circling his fists in the air. 'I'm not here for the good of my health, you know. It's *urgent*!'

'I'm sure it is, but do you have to be so, er, abrasive?'

'Would you listen to me if I wasn't? Eh?'

'But, of course. Your opinions are always readily received in this office. Shirm Council Directive six three three,' fibbed the Mayor through clenched teeth. The Clerk's mouth fell open at the shock of such a barefaced lie. Just wait till the Minister of Leisure heard *that* one, he thought.

'So how come I always seem to end up being frog-marched out of here between two nasty big . . .'

'Aha, aha,' hawked Mayor Greadly making the attempt at genuine amusement sound like a cat with a particularly stubborn fur-ball. 'A misunderstanding. Won't happen again.'

'Promise?'

'Promise,' oozed Wert, convinced he was winning.

The Clerk shifted uneasily, feeling like the private who wants to put his fingers in his ears in case the bomb he's holding happens to go off unexpectedly.

'Now, what were you in such a rush to tell us?' asked the Mayor.

Nostromo looked into the piggy eyes and said simply, 'There won't be any Croquet Open next month.'

'What? Why not?'

'Simple. There won't *be* a next month.'

'. . . !'

'There won't even be a next *week*.'

'Oh. Ha ha. Very good. You nearly got me there. This is another one of your end of the world things again, isn't it? When's it due this time? One thousand four hundred and eighty seven years ago?'

'Tomorrow!' snarled Nostromo cringing. 'It came to me last night.'

'Another vision?'

'A dream. It cleared up my prophecy!'

'It gets worse!' protested the Mayor. 'I shouldn't really ask, but what did it tell you?'

20

'Ten thirty nine *is* the right year! 1039 OG*!' squealed Nostromo.

'Oh, come on. We haven't used that for . . .' Suddenly Wert Greadly's face went ashen. 'Nearly one and a half thousand . . .'

'One thousand four hundred and eighty seven years,' interrupted Nostromo. 'I'm right. Two forty on the third of August ten thirty nine. Tomorrow!'

'Rubbish. This is just a cheap publicity stunt.' The Mayor strolled over to the wall and yanked on a long red bell cord.

'What are you doing?' protested Nostromo. 'You said you'd listen.'

'To opinions,' snapped Wert Greadly imperiously. 'Not the insane ravings of a publicity starved impoverished prophet . . .'

---

* Original Gravity. A crude calendar system.

It's quite well known that Infinity is big. Far too big to swallow in one go, that's for sure. But if you hack it up into lots of little bits it's alright. Much more manageable.

Scientists began by relying on absolute empirical methods for chopping infinity up. For example, the philosopher mathematician Gren Idjmeen measured how long it took for bricks to fall out of windows on sunny days. After spending lots of other people's grants he published the Original Gravity Calendar much to the delight of the vast majority of young male researchers. Despite the tiny drawback of being archaic in the extreme, based on the most dubious strands of tortuous logic and fundamentally impossible to synchronise with sundials or pub licencing laws it is still in everyday use. Almost certainly due to the full-colour pictures of lustfully naked maidens on deserted beaches.

Other calendars, however, were a little less glamorous. By counting the number of times which the famous Holy Rattling Rock of Say-Kho vibrated in the time he could hold his breath, doubling it, adding this to a larger integer, raising the result to the power of a third randomly produced six-figure number and dividing the total by his shoe size, Wroc Lhexx found that he could accurately define a period. Being a pioneer in his field he named this 'The First' and published a great many papers (sadly lacking decorative studies of female anatomy) explaining that by linking a whole string of firsts together one could invent an entire series of other larger periods.

It was only after discovering to his horror that the average day was made up of five hundred and twelve hours that he rechecked his calculation, altered the six-figure power and divided the total by fifteen and one eighth (in base nine) thus launching a new revised time period. This he apologetically called the 'The Second'.

'Hear, hear!' chorused the Clerk.

'. . . especially when I have important business to attend to,' he finished, stamping down the frayed divot of shag-pile and eyeing up a new ball.

'There's no point! You won't get to play!' squealed Nostromo hysterically.

It was hopeless. In a moment the door swung open and two enormous guards lurched in, knuckles inches from the floor. 'You rang, m'Lord?'

'Ah yes. Him. Out.'

The bouncer paused as the complex instructions filtered through far too many inches of skull, then he nodded, then grunted and then moved forward. Parallel processing was several generations above him on the evolutionary tree.

'You'll be sorry,' protested the prophet as he was forcibly hauled out of the council chambers between the two neanderthals.

'Er, guard. Slap,' called the Mayor as the door closed.

'Two thirty three,' screamed the hoarse throat of Nostromo. 'You'll see. Mark my words. It'll happen just like I said, tomorrow'll be the last . . . Hey, why are you stopping. Oh no, no. *No!* . . . Oowwwww! What d'you do that for . . . that's human rights abuse, that is . . . I'd see my lawyer if I thought it was worth it . . . owww.'

Wert Greadly's pink anguilliform tongue wriggled once more at the corner of his moist mouth as he lined up on the white sphere.

Some people will go to any lengths to ruin my training, he thought. What will they come up with next? The Lord Mayor swung his club.

A transient wave of sweet satisfaction coursed through the struggling body of Nostromo Kasein as a brief shower of glass was followed by the sound of screaming, pounding fists and a Clerk's forehead being forcibly and repeatedly pummelled against municipal green floor-covering.

Nostromo Kasein spat as he dragged himself out of a heap of

boxes, broken barrels and comprehensive selection of far less than savoury piscine entrails.

'Idiots!' he screamed at the receding backs of the Shirman Municipal Bouncers. 'This is the last day! Don't you understand? The End of Civilisation?' He kicked at a barrel and winced as he stubbed his toe.

The bouncers disappeared around the end of the alley.

The End of Civilisation! thought Nostromo angrily, they wouldn't even know where it began!

In a second Nostromo vowed not to be caught fiddling about while the world burned. He wasn't going out with a whimper, caught with his trousers down . . . unless. Hmmm, there was *always* that gorgeous brunette at the end of Krill Street. Hah! Go out with a bang! With her thinking it was me making the earth move! At my age?

No, he thought. If oblivion was out to get him, oblivion was what he'd get. He could hear several unopened bottles of Jag'd Anyuls crying for him. And if there's one thing that the prospect of being dead in the morning has the unerring ability to hone to perfection, then that's the ability to drink yourself utterly stupid.

'All right, you know what to do?' whispered Bharkleed twitching with excitement in the corridor around the corner from the Managing Director's office of the Translittoral Mollusc Trading Company. The other two High Priests nodded enthusiastically.

'Whedd, ready with your "vision"?'

The oily figure grinned, rolled his pupils up into the top of his eyelids and shook violently.

'Uurgh! Disgusting! Okay, that's great,' croaked the Fervently Exalted One. 'Let's go!'

Ignoring the protests of the secretary, caught off guard by a particularly stubborn cuticle which just wouldn't reveal her half moon, the three High Priests burst into Len Mulus' office.

'Are *you* ready for the next life?' demanded the one in the indigo robes.

23

'What?'

'Do you have your post-mortal future secured?'

'Miss Prision, do these gentlemen have an appointment?' called the MD.

'Do the forces from beyond book appointments?' snapped Bharkleed.

'Well, I suppose . . .'

'I can't seem to find one in the diary, sir,' squeaked Miss Prision, her disembodied voice floating around the door-frame apologetically. 'It could be a mistake, sir.'

'I don't pay you to make mistakes.'

'A sign of human weakness,' interrupted Bharkleed. 'A trait common to us all.'

'Well, I . . . more common to some than others,' countered Len Mulus from behind his desk.

'A very prophetic answer,' smirked Bharkleed.

'Why, you! . . . I thought it was rather good. How dare you come in here and start insulting me!'

'No, no, sir. It was a wise answer, very apposite.'

'Apposite to what? What're you *on* about?'

Hirsuit stifled a snigger.

Bharkleed took a deep breath and mentally smoothed the wrinkled boxershorts of his concentration, 'The next life,' he answered. '*That's* what I'm on about. What happens *after* the end of the world? Tell me, are you in a position to enjoy the advantages of immortality to its full? And have you thought of how you will pay for it?'

'Pay for it? You don't *pay* for it! I run a pension scheme. Other people pay for it!'

'Wrong!' chimed Bharkleed. 'Never heard of the Internal Market of the NHS*? Hmmm? And what the fuel bills for the Fires of Torment? Accommodation? Oh, and don't forget your entry visa.'

---

* The Nosferatean Hell Service. A hierarchical sytem of self-contained units designed, built and staffed with the express purpose of inflicting as much pain and discomfort upon its inmates as inhumanly possible.

'You saying you've got to pay if you want to pop your clogs?'

'Not as such, no. The actual cessation of normal animatory, cognitive and locomotory capabilities are entirely complimentary. Death's free. It's the bits afterwards that cost. Especially when places are at a premium.' Bharkleed could feel Len Mulus' interest growing. He could sense a question blossoming.

'Eh?'

It didn't quite have the inquisitorial edge that he had hoped for, but it was a start.

'Supply and demand! During times of peak demand, such as holocaust, plague, war, the *End* of the world etcetera,' Bharkleed explained, turning a chair round and folding his arms over the back of it as he sat facing the managing director, 'prices have an unfortunate tendency to move in an upward direction, leaving only those with the good foresight to be affiliated with the more lucratively furnished investment churches. Those in the position to enjoy to the full the new-found opportunities and experiences which this situation reveals.' He sat back and waited for the next interrogative thrust.

'But . . .'

Bharkleed held his breath. There was more, he knew there was more.

'. . . what's *that* got to do with me?' finished Len.

Bingo!

'I'm *so* glad you asked that.' And he was. 'Are you entirely certain that your time of departure will not coincide with that of a great many others? Statistically it is far more likely it will. In which case those with a fully enfranchised Certificate of Unquestioning Belief will reap immediate benefit in terms of transfer reservation, appartment selection and postmortem share management. Yes! Believe with the Elevated Church of St Lucre the Unwashed and your mortal savings will keep you far beyond your final retirement. Join today. You know it makes sense!'

25

'Well it certainly sounds fine . . . but,' began Len.

Bharkleed nodded and made a small gesture behind him.

At the given signal His Emmolient, Whedd the Most Lubricious whimpered gently at the back of the room, swayed a little and placed his hand to his sweating forehead. Len Mulus looked up in alarm. 'He all right?' he asked Bharkleed.

'Oh dear.'

Whedd rolled his pupils up into his eyelids and moaned a little louder, twitching once or twice for added realism.

'What's 'e doing?'

'I am most terribly sorry. Our Brother has these turns on occasions. It will pass, I assure you.'

'What's up with 'im? Is it catching?' asked Len as Hirsuit loosened the robes around Whedd's cellulitic neck.

'Oh no, no. It's simply a vision, that's all.'

'Wha—?'

'It's coming!' shouted Whedd, suddenly cutting across Len's question. 'The end. The end is nigh!'

'It's time!' said Bharkleed in an awestruck voice.

'Time? Time for what?' panicked Len, quite unsure why.

'His vision of the end,' explained Bharkleed, staring at Len's worried face, gauging his reaction. 'We all have one vision of the end.'

Whedd's eyes rolled feverishly. 'No!' he cried. 'Not so soon. We need more time to prepare them. Give us longer!'

'How long?' asked Hirsuit shaking Whedd in apparent genuine concern.

'Not enough,' groaned Whedd. 'Not long enough.'

Bharkleed pulled a large parchment document out of a pocket inside his robes and laid it on the desk in front of Len Mulus. The managing director's eyes were bulging with alarm as he watched the writhing High Priest in the throes of his 'vision'. A quill, freshly inked and ready for use, mysteriously appeared in Len's hand.

'How long?' yelled the MD. 'Tell me how long? I've got orders to fill!' Bharkleed's eyes lit up. Orders mean money.

'Twenty-two . . .' squirmed Whedd.

Bharkleed positioned Len's hand carefully over the dotted line.

'Years?' he fretted.

'Twenty-two . . .'

'Weeks?' His hand quivered.

'Twenty to three tomorrow,' blurted Whedd, thrashing madly before collapsing on the floor. Before he had hit the deck, Len's hand was already scribbling a scratchy signature on the parchment Certificate of Unquestioning Belief. A second later he had grabbed Bharkleed's hand in both of his and was shaking it with important earnestness as though there was no tomorrow, which in fact he believed was the case. 'You've saved me!' he cried. 'Saved me from eternal suffering. Thankyou, thankyou!' And with that he fled from the room to preach the news of the impending disaster to the rest of Shirm, to the rest of Froul, to the rest of the World whilst there still was a world capable of listening.

Bharkleed grinned and placed the Translittoral Mollusc Trading Company's bulging order book into his robe pocket.

Len Mulus' frantic apostolic exit, much to the absolute confusion of Miss Prision; was followed swiftly by a peal of raucous laughter and a clatter of chummily congratulatory back-slapping.

The blue touchpaper of Phase Two had been lit and was fizzing frantically towards the powder keg of victory.

Nostromo was half-way down his second bottle of Jag'd Anyuls and well on course for oblivion before he heard the screams through the dull alcoholic haze. Throwing his hands over his head and lurching for the window he yelled at the placard-waving madman in the street below.

'Ghowwawway!' he slurred raising the bottle.

The man spun round and yelled something incomprehensible about something ending.

'Theywohntbeleevyuh!' bawled Nostromo. 'Theydint-beleevemeeee.'

Still the voice ranted away.

'Shyutupangoawayy!' cried the prophet and launched the now-empty second bottle out of the window.

In the street outside of Nostromo's house a small ex-managing director ran madly about with a large hastily scribbled placard declaring:

THE END OF
THE WOLD
IS NYE

If, as has been suggested, language is indeed a virus then the virulent strain released that night by the High Priests of the Elevated Church of St Lucre the Unwashed was an immensely contagious one. Showing all the characteristics of a particularly nasty dose of herpes, it spread in seconds, homing in on vulnerable old women, fish-wives and gossips, setting their tongues wagging, infecting the gullible. By subtly altering its outer mask of lies with every reinfection, highlighting ear-pricking facts, introducing corroborative hearsay into its array of fiction it grew in strength, shunning the vaccines of categorical denial aimed its way, exponentially spreading the news of the end of the world.

And significantly enhancing the rate of conversion of followers pledging their faith and wordly goods to the safe-keeping of Bharkleed, Hirsuit and Whedd. Just as the High Priests had intended.

As the supposed final ever sunset burned into the blackness of night, half a dozen uniformed Shirman Municipal Bouncers stomped to the front of a heaving throng outside the Town Hall, parted and let through the furiously sweating figure of Mayor Greadly.

Something was happening. And he had to know what it was. Anything that could get this many voters together was worth knowing about. A bandwagon to be leapt upon or an uprising to be quelled? – he didn't care as long as it won votes! Keeping yourself in the public eye, that was all that mattered!

He greeted the travelling ministers, listened, turned pale, rallied well and in a news-worthy flurry of quill feathers leapt into the torrent of public opinion, instantly signing his very own personal Certificate of Unquestioning Belief. Inside he was gutted – no Glenperegrine Croquet Open. And after all those extra lessons!

Bharkleed's evil heart leapt around the walls of Shirm, cavorting and waving victorious arteries in a impromptu lap of honour, thrilling as Mayor Greadly signed and failed, as had all the others before him, to read Clause 7. Mind you, it wasn't too surprising since Clause 7 was in fact printed in beige letters, one sixteenth of an inch high, on the back of the Certificate. For the first time in his official life, Mayor Greadly's action actually gave the general populace a feeling of confidence. Within seconds, the Shirman Municipal Bouncers had stamped their thumbprints on dotted lines. Within hours eighteen long hundreds of pheasant quills had been worn to the quick by the droves of desperate Shirmans racing the approaching deadline, wrenching brightly coloured parchments from rapidly diminishing piles and hysterically thanking the crocodile smiling High Priests.

And all this time Bharkleed, Hirsuit and Whedd rubbed their greedy hands, gloating smugly at another victory.

Tomorrow would witness the red furrows of acute financial damage that the High Priests' Clause could wreak.

Tomorrow had better have a strong stomach.

As dawn rose on the final day of the world the populace stood in the streets staring skywards, struck dumb by the sight of the weather's meteorological swansong. Banks of orange clouds shot through with snarling veins of red; vast angry blue bruises of grumbling storm clouds spat tongues of lightning and trailed curtains of harsh grey rain; the deadly snaking tips of armies of swirling whirlwinds and tornadoes marched inexorably forward, tearing forests from hills, sucking lakes from their beds in cascading deluges of mud – all this and much more was missing.

A drizzly northwesterly breeze dribbled apathetically,

shrugged a brief squally shower and dropped a few bored millibars further into depression. As if one giant throat spoke everyone's simultaneous thoughts there was a tumultous gasp of utter anticlimax. That was the major problem with the elements – absolutely no sense of occasion.

All of the latest damp converts to the Elevated Church felt meteorologically cheated. Here they were, about to witness the end of the world as they knew it, feeling intensely smug about the fact that they all had their immediate post-mortem future sorted out, travel arrangements, accommodation, finance, visas and passmorts the lot, and it looked as if the possibility of the end of the world being heralded by a crackling pyrotechnic display of supernatural forces performed against a stunning panoramic backdrop of dazzling elemental prowess was as likely as a limpet learning to fly unaided. Backwards.

Throughout that final day the mood deepened as the forces of mundanity grew to fever pitch. Throughout Shirm groups fidgeted with frantic apathy and seethed with pent-up pointlessness. Why harvest tomorrow's limpets for all tomorrow's pasties, why wash the cart, or a million and one other things, when none of them would be here tomorrow?

Still, everyone felt sure something was bound to happen a bit later on. I mean, the End of Everything *had* to be something worth remembering. Didn't it?

In fact, that something happened at just after two o'clock. In the main market square of Shirm, a small pedestal mysteriously arose. Three heavily cowled figures dashed about it, lighting candles, sprinkling holy solutions, burning pots of thick, scented smoke. In short, busying themselves in ways designed to look at once devoutly religious and demonically industrious. The three figures gave the unequivocal impression, somehow, that they were struggling very hard to make final adjustments to a scheme in order to prevent something nasty and very final from happening. At ten past two, half an hour before time became an irrelevance, the tallest of the three figures began furiously ringing a large hand bell with all his might and yelling at the top of his voice.

'My people, my followers,' he cried. My trusting imbecilic mugs! he thought. 'Come gather round me, come stand before me, I have news to warm your cold, cold hearts. Despair ye not!'

Slowly, they came. Well, there was nothing better to do. In a few minutes a curious crowd had coalesced before the cowled triumvirate upon the pedestal.

The central figure threw back his hood in an overly theatrical gesture, stepping forward, revealing himself as His Eminence, Bharkleed the Fervently Exalted. At his side were Hirsuit and Whedd. Imperiously, Bharkleed raised his arms to stand in his favourite, crowd impressing, cruciform posture and declared, 'My people. My *beautiful* people. My heart is a battlefield of pride and terror, of honour and horror.' He wiped an imaginary tear from his eye and flicked it over the crowd. 'I have prayed to counter the forces of destruction, begged that you, my devoted followers, be saved.'

Butter them up, he thought. Grease their emotional palms! And they'll *eat* out of yours.

'It is too soon for the End. Too early to stop when there is so much of yours I still want . . . to enjoy. It is this that has kept my brothers and I awake all night on a desperate vigil, on a frantic search of ancient tomes, all in a last-ditch effort to save everything around us from a terrible destruction. But, I am sorry to say, nay terrified to admit, that I fear the task may be too great for our three tiny voices alone.' He sniffed audibly as if emotions within him were proving too turbulent to control. 'Only with *your* help may the end be averted. Are you with us? Will you try?'

A few voices murmured their feeble approval.

'I can't hear you. I asked will you try?' This time he turned his ear to the crowd, cupping hand to lobe as if listening intently.

A few dozen voices answered in the affirmative.

'Pardon?' he shouted and repeated the gesture.

More approval and a few nods.

31

'I can't hear you! Big shout now. Are you with us?'

Half a dozen shouts and a majority of positive grunts.

'Oh, come on. You can do better than that. Louder. Shout!'

A blasting response finally appeared, much to Bharkleed's relief.

'Excellent! Now we haven't much time so here's what I want you to do.'

He held his arm out in a straight line over the crowd, splitting them in half, and pointed to his left in a big expansive sweep.

'You lot,' he yelled. 'You are the world, and I want you to shout "save" as loud as you can. All right?' He pointed to the right. 'And you lot are the forces of destruction.' Some of the 'world' booed loudly at this point. It was going well. 'Now, forces of destruction, I want you to shout "destroy", all right. Everybody know what to do?'

The crowd roared its approval.

'Whoever shouts loudest decides the fate of the world. OK. Go!'

The whole of Shirm erupted in a massive shouting match. Cries of 'Destroy' fought with those answering 'Save', screams from the forces of destruction clashed noisily with the voice of the world, their compressions and rarefactions colliding, wrestling and shooting off at wild tangents. Sound waves met head on, rose together, clawing for more air space, higher and higher, until they broke in a fragmentary spray of white-water letters. And while the war of words raged, the three High Priests of the Elevated Church slipped down the back of the pedestal, picked up their bags of Certificates of Belief and headed out of Shirm, out of Froul and on to other pickings.

It would only be a matter of a few minutes before the shouting crowd realised that the End of the World had been averted. Then there would follow a huge celebration involving massive street parties, lots of food and even more drink. It would be a couple of hours before the first inklings of the feeling that perhaps, just perhaps, the claims about the actual finality of the predicted events were a little exaggerated. Within a few more hours people might begin to suspect that something about those priests didn't feel right and that maybe they ought to be asked a few gently probing questions, and only then, as had happened to so many other towns and countries in a swathe heading east in the wake of the three priests, only then would the townspeople realise they were missing.

With this shocking realisation, tripping hand in hand through the daisies of despair, would skip the dawning of a horribly sickening feeling that somehow they had all been taken for a ride.

Quite how far down a viciously potholed road of utter misery and absolute poverty that ride would take them would be illustrated in graphic detail in three days' time when the Envoy of Bharkleed, Hirsuit and Whedd came to call on Shirm, ready, willing and appallingly able to carry out the actions dictated in Clause 7.

It took three whole days before Nostromo Kasein finally accepted the fact that his prophecy had, thankfully, been utterly wrong. Cracking open his agonised eyes on the first morning, wincing with pain as blinding white light seared into his tender retina and collapsing into a far more comforting horizontal position, he had still to be convinced that this was in fact not the end of the world. He certainly felt far closer to something that was dead than anything even remotely alive. Even if that remotely alive something was having a really bad day.

Moaning pathetically, he closed his eyes and re-entered the state of willfully acute torpor that a particularly slovenly sloth would give its eye teeth for.

The next day he opened his eyes. It was only the fact that the five empty Jag'd Anyuls bottles hadn't been moved from where they had fallen – and that his head felt as if the bailiffs from the Thought Police were still trying to break in – that began to hint he hadn't moved. Had the world ended, pondered Nostromo through the most virulently screaming hangover of his life, then he felt certain that, no matter how gently it had occurred, he would not still be in the same spatial relationship to his bed, the walls and the five empty Jag'd Anyuls bottles. Therefore his prophecy was wrong.

Worn out by this slow-burning Roman candle of enlightened thought, his eyelids crashed shut and his brain closed down for another day and night.

At the same time that Nostromo was struggling up the slippery hill out of sleep for the third time, a group of very large men with some very sharp weapons were riding towards the outskirts of Shirm. Their jaws set, their tempers short and their bags empty, the Envoys of the Elevated Church of St Lucre the Unwashed approached to claim their dues. Dues arising from Clause 7.

With the sure and certain knowledge that he now *would* be playing in the Glenperegrine Open Croquet Tournament firmly planted in his one-tracked mind, His Worship, Wert Greadly, Lord Mayor of Shirm was determined to make up for lost practice time. White balls were scattered everywhere across the municipal 'shag-pile, each a testament to yet another distraction – the noise of his constituents. Thus, two sheafs of tightly rolled parchment stuck out from his ears, each a desperate attempt to prevent any further disturbances.

Amazingly it worked. He failed totally to hear the heavy clatter of horses' hooves on the courtyard outside; or the shouts of alarm as ten very large men in purple pushed past the Shirman Municipal Bouncers; or the sickening crunching of a brief fracas as their entry was unsuccessfully resisted.

For the first time in twenty years of local government power struggling, Wert Greadly was deaf to his door being struck by the screaming body of the spinning Clerk. The Mayoral club dealt a perfectly targeted ball, excited shrieks spinning from his tonsils as it homed in on the gaping mouth of the bucket, going to score! The first time!

With a flash of silent terror the Clerk arced over the Mayor's shoulder, overtook the ball and sent the bucket crashing into the far wall. A small stained-glass cherub breathed a sigh of relief and uncrossed its legs.

For a second the Mayor stood motionless, eyes wide with shock. Then he scowled, glared crimson, and leapt up and down on his croquet club screaming tirades of incomprehensible insults at the crumpled Clerk.

It was only when a vast purple gloved hand fell abruptly on his shoulder, turned him round and gently but firmly removed the earplugs, that the Mayor stopped.

'Greetings!' grinned the purple-clad figure of Blessed Lieutnant Vher-Jah. 'Offering!' he commanded in a tone of voice that sounded unused to eliciting a negative response.

'Offrng?' spluttered Wert, staring at the figure waving a vast brass plate under his nose.

The Clerk gurgled what he hoped sounded like an apologetic sort of gurgle.

'For the Elevated Church of St Lucre the Unwashed,' growled Vher-Jah.

'N . . . never heard of . . .'

'The priests, Your Worship,' whimpered the Clerk, timidly removing himself from the bucket.

'Eh?'

'This your signature?' questioned Vher-Jah thrusting a brightly coloured parchment at the flustered Lord Mayor still waggling the remains of his club precariously aloft.

'Could be . . .'

'Oh, well then, offertory time!' Nine huge heads nodded vehement agreement.

'But I . . .'

Vher-Jah's hand pointed to the plate and scowled. 'Clause 7 of the Certificate of Unquestioning Belief of The Elevated Church of St Lucre the Unwashed, signed by yourself not three days ago states, ahem, "In the event of the End of the World

35

(see Clause 6) being averted by divine intervention arising from an act of worship instigated by any member of the High Priests of the Elevated Church of St Lucre the Unwashed, or any subsidiary Church, social club or scout troop affiliated to the aforementioned Church, then all items declared usable by the High Priests (under Clause 6) for the Profitable and Secure Future of the foresigned in the Next World will be deemed as offerings to the Elevated Church and can be claimed at any time." ' Vher-Jah smiled at the Lord Mayor. 'I. e., now!'

'What? What?' squealed Wert. 'This is preposterous! What is Clause 6?'

Vher-Jah turned the Certificate of Unquestioning Belief over and said, 'Clause 6 states, ahem, "I, the foresigned, hereby entrust *all* my mortal-worldly belongings, savings, real-estate, stocks, shares, businesses, business premises and anything else of even remote value to the Estate and Office of the Elevated Church of St Lucre the Unwashed for the express purpose of using profits arising from these items to provide a managed fund for use in the Next World. This includes the End of the World." Is that clear enough?' asked Vher-Jah.

'But, what . . .' stuttered Mayor Greadly rapidly realising that soon he would almost certainly be ex-Mayor of Shirm.

'No "buts", mate. Bottom line. All this lot's ours. All right lads, load up.'

On Vher-Jah's command the other nine envoys, produced a large sack each and proceeded to remove everything from the room. This scene was repeated in various dwellings and business premises throughout Shirm at that very moment. Any resistance was dealt with using large sharp knives and the items were still removed under Clause 6.

After a few short but highly profitable hours, the Envoys of the Elevated Church of St Lucre the Unwashed, loaded their booty on to several large carts expressly looted for the purpose and rode out of an extremely impoverished Shirm heading east to continue their brand of stunningly lucrative conversion.

Bon Appetite!

Expertly dodging a familiar hanging string of glistening weed, swooping sharply to the right and performing a neat stall turn for the hell of it, the creature of the night slapped its way through the stale subterranean air of the secret passages. It knew the tunnels and dark runs, snaking and writhing below the Imperial Palace Fortress of Cranachan, like the back of its black leathery wing. It made this journey every day. Sometimes twice if there was a good headline.

Today could well be a two-trip day.

The bat arced to the left, wing-overed a sharp right turn, misjudged the corner, slammed into the far mould-covered wall and dropped the newsparchment from its mouth. Squawking and spitting vespertilious disgust it landed in a green and yellow puddle with a sound like a chamois leather in semolina. Then shrieked falsetto alarm as it saw the neatly rolled newsparchment teetering at the pool's edge. Flapping desperately it squirmed forward, leaping and snatching the latest *Triumphant Herald* from a terribly sticky end.

Far away, buried deep in the very living rock of the Talpa Mountains, four bony fingers drummed military tattoos of impatience on a burnished bronze throne. The osseous collisions rattled around the cavern, bouncing off casually stacked works of pilfered art, rebounding from precious missing heirlooms, careering off selected highlights of the amassed treasures of The Appropriator as he fidgeted irritably, waiting for today's newsparchment.

The bat scraped its wings cleanish, cursed the puddle, damned the tunnel wall, snatched the *Triumphant Herald* into its rodenty mouth and fell once more into the air with all the dignity of an airborne dishcloth.

The Appropriator scowled at a recently stolen painting of

some sunflowers and marvelled at its sudden leap in value. Amazing what the removal of an artist's ear could do to the art markets!

Just outside the main chamber the bat landed, panted for a few moments then began to writhe frantically on the ground, making a noise like something turning itself inside out. This wasn't too far from the truth. Its wings flapped madly, twitching and slithering; its stubby legs thrashed and squelched noisily, growing knees and sprouting greasy-looking trousers; its head turned from furry black to a cold, bald pale-blue; the front two teeth grew, the creature's breath whistling evilly between. In a few squelchy seconds the fruit-bat was gone.

Vlad Langschwein, vampire,* picked up the rolled news-parchment, shook the last few drops of slimy water from his head and stalked into the Appropriator's Throne Chamber.

'Where've you been!' screamed the Appropriator leaping from his bronze pedestal. 'Printing the damn headlines?' He snatched the *Triumphant Herald* eagerly from the talonish grip of the vampire's fingernails and pulled a face. 'Gack! You've been dribbling again! How many times have I told you not to carry it in your mouth?'

'Itssss qvicker by air!' snapped Vlad.

'It's disgusting! Can't be hygenic!'

---

* It is a little known fact that there are different grades of vampire.

Say the word 'lycanthrope' and instantly you think of a dark silhouetted figure howling at a full moon, turning into hulking great man-eating wolf, tearing about the countryside ripping innocent travellers to shreds in a wild lupine frenzy of uncontrolled horror. Well, I've got news for you, that isn't the way it is. Not all the time anyhow. You see, for every one werewolf, there are about a dozen werespaniels, five werelabradors, twenty to thirty wereterriers and utterly hundreds of werechihuahuas. But nobody hears about them. Every night people get attacked, but they never report it. Well, would you admit to having your ankle mauled by a faintly glowing green chihuahua on your way home from the pub?

It's the same with vampires. Only the really nasty criminals and heretics, when not in humanoid shape, come back as vampire bats. Only the serial killers, rapists and tax-collectors drink blood from sleeping virgins in their vespertilious form, flapping through conveniently open windows to sink their batty fangs into the porcelain expanse of a teenage neck. The majority have to make do with fruit. You don't believe me? Well, you explain that mysteriously shrivelled apple in the fruit bowl over there.

38

'Vhatt d'you vant? Qvick or clean?'

The Appropriator glared angrily from behind the black leather eyepatch, his one eye burning into the vampire. 'Just don't ever fly anywhere near me. I detest things that fly, things with claws and beaks and . . . above all pigeons!' He shuddered, wiped the newsparchment across the back of Vlad's jacket and unfurled it.

The Appropriator's face lit up with a thousand-lumen sneer of delight as he saw the headlines.

RINSE OF DEATH STUNS LAUNDRY
OVERNIGHT SOAK SET AT COLOUREDS MORTE

Scourge of Cranachan, The Appropriator, struck again last night . . .

He screamed joyously aloud as he read of his latest nocturnal doings, grinning manically as he recalled leaving the bobbing laundryman on the end of the clothes line, struggling to remove the boxer shorts from his mouth as the rope lowered him slowly into the coloureds' 40° overnight soak.

'He should have known not to cross me!' he shouted. 'When I want clean undies, I get clean undies! Don't people understand threats any more!'

'Acsssshunsss ssspeak louder dann vurdssss!' oozed Vlad.

'And I'm the action expert!'

'He who'sss visshhuss lassst isss visshuss longesssst!'

'Me, me!' shrieked the Appropriator. 'Fetch me the second edition of this scrofulous rag!' he growled waving the *Herald*. 'I need to know more of what my people think of me!'

Vlad turned and scurried off.

'And Langschwein!' shouted the black leather-clad figure. 'Walk!'

*

39

'Three groats on Kriller in the ten fifteen,' growled a voice that sounded like the whisper of megaliths in winter.

'Do yourself a favour, mate,' came the chipper reply. 'Crusher'll 'ave 'im in the second, just watch. On real top form at the moment, 'e is. Should've seen what 'e did to three o'them at once yesterday in a tag match. Shockin' it was. Paté.'

'I said "three groats on Kriller in the ten fifteen" and that's what I want,' snarled the voice in the tiny dark courtyard of back-street Cranachan. 'Had I wished to communicate a concept at variance with that, or had I been remotely interested in the current form of the so-called opposition, I would not have requested so clearly, "three groats on Kriller in the ten fifteen", would I?'

Despite the fact that the words were calmly whispered in well-pronounced Cranachan they held an air of pent-up menace heavier than an ocean of moray eels. Several of the more cautious punters moved warily away from the dark bulky shape with the granite vocal chords.

'N . . . n . . . no, ah-ha. See your point, squire. Three groats it is,' struggled the bookie peering at the figure in the shadows at the edge of the arena.

'And another three in the eleven thirty against Pugilator.'

The gathered crowd took a deep breath. In recent weeks, there had been no survivors against Pugilator.

'As an accumulator,' added the dark stranger calmly. Another flurry of deep breaths and itchings of questions. Who was this black figure? Did he know some inside information about Kriller's recent form? Should we follow his example?

The bookie winced. 'Accumulator, yes. Ahem, the odds for that are almost three hundred to one against, may I recommend . . .'

'Two hundred and eighty seven and a half to one against,' growled the seismic whisper, 'and no you may not recommend a thing. Your six groats.' A black gloved hand, encrusted with studs and knuckle caps, floated into the single

40

candle light followed by the humourlessly grinning face of Commander 'Black' Achonite of the Imperial Black Guards, his tongue glistening behind his tattooed teeth of office.

A sudden and rapid vacuum formed as the gathered crowd of Cranachan low-lifes flattened themselves out of reach in that moment of recognition. Commander 'Black' Achonite's reputation as the leader of the Cranachan Black Guard was legendary. It was he who had coined the Guard Motto 'Disagree and Die'. It was he who had introduced the official tattooing of teeth.* And it was he that had been the only person ever to be outright winner of the Cranachan All-Comers' Cow-Toppling Championships for five consecutive years.

'I shall await the outcome over there,' he growled, pointing to a small seat in the corner.

'As you wish, sir. As you wish. And good luck with your wager.'

'Luck does not enter into it. I have seen Kriller in action,' he answered as he stomped into the corner and sat waiting for the appointed boxing match. The crowd of onlookers warily returned most of their attention to the fight currently in progress.

The two assailants raised their vast clubbing weapons and circled each other in the arena below. Pugilator had already damaged his opponent's left eye, chipped the armour on his right shoulder and ripped a large chunk out of his fin. A thin

---

* Dental Displays of Rank and Honour among the Cranachan Black Guards served many useful purposes. They swiftly negated the need for sewing fiddly coloured squares of cloth to ebony-clad shoulder-pads – a practice which Commander Achonite found extremely suspect in an active security force, not only ruining the totally menacing stygian appearance of the uniform but also teaching his hand-picked men dodgy pastimes like sewing, threading needles and cross-stitching. He insisted vigorously, 'There are men . . . and there are those who like to wear coloured ribbons!'

Intrabuccal Rank Discrimination was a boon for discipline enforcement. Demotion within the Black Guards could be an extremely painful experience. One not easily forgotten.

Especially if you had a deeply ingrained fear of pliers inside your mouth.

trickle of blood oozed from the doomed opponent's panting gills.

The discovery of the six-inch *Crangon pugilatus* in the Eastern Tepid Seas four years ago had revolutionised backstreet gambling in downtown Cranachan. Shrimp boxing had long since usurped lizard-baiting as the national bloodsport. Competition was strong between the hundreds of unofficial league tables, the thousands of shrimp-breeding stud farms and the black market shrimp importers offering the backstreet services of horny crustacean stallions.

Suddenly a cheer went up announcing another victory for Pugilator. Black Achonite's emblemed molars grinned in the gloom as the odds against a win on Kriller crept up to three hundred and sixty eight to one.

He liked shrimp boxing, revelling in the senseless violence of two six-inch crustaceans mashing each other's brains to crab sticks for the voyeuristic gambling pleasure of a gathered audience. It was so refreshing.

And in a few moments it would be time for the ten fifteen. Muscling forward through the scrofulous clump of drop-outs, laying out cold a few that were too slow to move, Black Achonite secured his grandstand seat and settled down to watch Kriller versus Crusher.

It was all over very soon.

After a swift one-two to the side of his opponent's keratin carapace, a gut-wrenching belt with his tail to flip him over, and a final deep-cut follow through between the second and third plates Kriller destroyed Crusher. Black Achonite growled with joy at the masterful move, thrilling as Kriller's claws buried deep into the side of its opponent. It was then that he knew he was looking at a worthy opponent for the King's prize shrimp. Achonite simply *had* to have that deadly decapod.

'Read all about it! Appropriator strikes again. Latest art theft denounced in public. Read all about it!' shouted the newsparchment seller brandishing a copy of this morning's

Triumphant Herald above his head. 'Latest shrimp-boxing results. Full rundown!'

Behind the newsparchment seller a tiny, hand-size section of the wall moved, disappearing into the shadows on silent bearings. In a flash a gloved hand shot out, snatched a copy and vanished into the wall, resealing the invisible access hatch with only the slightest click.

Sounding like a small black leather bikini being shaken free of half a gallon of tomato ketchup. Vlad Langschwein flapped his way through the dark corridors of the Appropriator's Kingdom, the *Triumphant Herald* firmly in his fruit bat jaws.

Only two minds knew of this world of secret passages and treasure vaults snaking from sliding doors, tunnels writhing from swivelling entrances at the push of a sequence of stones, diving through mirrors . . .

Vlad slapped inelegantly on past the vast hoards of treasure, the weaponry, the money and the paintings appropriated ruthlessly over the last thirteen extortionate years. The generosity of people always amazed him – supplying countless invaluable family heirlooms for the intact return of valued pets or offspring. Strange how people seemed to prefer animals or children to priceless works of art.

The black-leather-clad figure of the self-styled Appropriator was sat upon an eighth-century gold throne, one leather gauntlet supporting his pointed chin as he sneered smugly at his latest enigmatically smirking acquisition, The Mohnaleesa. Across the far side of the cool underground hall a small fruit bat struggled its ungainly way forward, flapping inefficiently lower and lower until it crash landed, belly down on the shiny obsidian floor, skidding to a crashing halt at the Appropriator's feet. 'What time do you call this?' snapped the figure on the throne glaring out from behind his black leather eyepatch.

'Thhhhhorry, Thhhhhir,' spat Vlad changing back into his humanoid form, removing the newsparchment from his mouth and handing it over.

'Uuurgh!' snapped the inchoate figure, his leather armour creaking in irritation, 'How many times have I told you about your spit. You know you dribble too much!'

'Sssorry, but I vasss thinkink ssspeed vasss ov der esssssence,' whistled the vampire between his pair of pin-sharp teeth.

'Bahhhh!' came the reply as the Appropriator turned his attention to the parchment and started to read. Suddenly he exploded in rage, slamming his fist on to the arm of the throne, turning crimson and pointing wildly at one of the articles.

'Have you seen this? Have you! Look at it! What a *nerve* . . . Listen to this . . . just listen! "In a statement to the press Khar Pahcheeno, expert shrimp importer and owner of champion Pugilator had this to say about the loss of his painting the Mohnaleesa, 'this menace has gone too far, Punishing innocent animals for blackmail is the act of a coward . . .' " Coward? *Coward?* That animal was down-right vicious! How dare he call me a menace! What does he know about blackmail. It's an art form. Requires skill . . .' Vlad somehow turned a shade paler as he heard the tirade develop.

'. . . just wouldn't understand. Well, I'll show them. "Gone too far" have I. Don't know the meaning of the word. Well, tonight Khar Pahcheeno's going to find out how the Appropriator really punishes innocent animals!'

His face sneered in evil anticipation as he wrung the parchment between his hands, tearing the sketch of the man apart and crushing the article beneath his sharp spiky boots.

High in his gallery, above the seething, colourful chaos of the feast, the minstrel looked down as he strummed furiously at his lute. Idly he watched the laughing faces, red with mirth and ale, as his fingers spidered up and down the fretboard in dazzling scales and devilish chord shapes. One day, he thought idly as he nonchalantly augmented a seventh with an overlayed ninth, one day they'd actually pay attention. This galliard would be a hit if they would only listen. It's got everything you need for a good lute-song, love, hate and a bloody good key change in the middle. Miles better than this modern rubbish. Crumhorns! Pah! Syncopated clavichords! Never last. Give me a galliard and a flagon of mead any time. Real music, that's what we need . . .

Below him, fourteen motley-clad jugglers swayed dangerously in a very precarious pyramid. Three vast wolfhounds beneath the King's table stared at the oscillating heap with acute canine disdain. A vast sheet of flame raced roofwards, missing one of the enormous hanging banners by a scant inch, as a sweating fire-eater hicupped at precisely the wrong time.

And throughout all this feudal entertainment, the gathered diners continued to relentlessly gorge themselves towards total senselessness. It was a typical night in the Court of Cranachan. Vast acres of meat, forests of boar, vineyards of wine and entire lakes of duck were wolfed nightly by the invited guests. The King's favourites were always there, every important landowner, the full fat cream of the wealthiest citizens. All the King's most admired traits were represented, the callous, the corrupt and the filthy rich.

The pyramid of jugglers took another unchoreographed lurch forward sending a wave of terrified serving wenches scattering for cover. The King looked up, a bleeding leg of boar gripped tightly between his teeth. General Bateleur's sharply pointed nose flared in alarm as the tower lurched again. A flagon of wine poised inches from his open mouth, he stopped and stared, as the bottom row struggled to keep the upper storeys on the tidy side of equilibrium's boundaries. In the space of one badly judged footfall they failed.

The minstrel watched the jugglers' slick grins of professional showmanship plunge faster than a harlot's tarnished reputation, leaping overboard in sudden flight. Panic poured down the tower of jugglers, splashing the surrounding diners, drenching the air with microscopic particles of aerosol apprehension as, letting out a final arcing scream, the highest juggler succumbed to the forces of gravity. Unstoppably he soared monarchwards, arms outstretched, legs akimbo, wishing foolishly that his tunic had sleeves like the ladies of the courts', then maybe, just maybe, by flapping hard enough . . . .

The wish ended unceremoniously on a solid oak table, a gallon of gravy and a side of boar. Miraculously he was still alive. The banqueting hall was swathed in absolute silence as the juggler raised his head from the plate of gravy and stared into the black-tempered face of a very angry King. He tried to grin in his most disarming manner but somehow his face muscles wouldn't move. This is it, he thought, swallowing hard, Now I'm really for it.

The King scowled at the unexpected juggler on the table, ostensibly motionless but for the large glistening glob of gravy oozing down his nose making a bid for freedom on to his regal lap. His shoulders began to tremble as if an incredibly powerful and immensely localised earthquake had gripped him somewhere round the liver.

'I'm sorry, Your Highness, Your Regality, Your Worship, Sire . . .' grovelled the juggler, wincing as he removed a boar's roasted hind-quarters from a very private and personal place.

The King's face smouldered, his crown vibrating ominously on his head. All around was absolute silence. Even the fire roared quietly, crackling through held breath.

'. . . I really am most dreadfully . . .'

A unexpected lick of a smile whisked across the regal countenance.

'. . . I will see to it personally that . . .'

A snigger erupted from the King. His trembling abated.

'. . . it will not happen again.'

The King stared at the juggler squirming pathetically in the slowly congealing pool of gravy, opened his mouth and roared with sinister laughter. The sound was utterly unexpected, the crowd were stunned. The juggler was astounded, it looked like, miraculously, everything was going to be all right. The King was in a good mood.

'It's all right,' declared the King, his shoulders quivering as he saw the funny side of the situation. 'The whole matter will be forgotten in an instant.'

The juggler struggled upright off the table, his tunic browned, seasoned and thickening as it cooled. He bowed long and low, dropping a few choice vegetables as he spoke, 'Thank you, Sire . . . I really can't say how . . .'

'Oh, tush, tush!' grunted the King investigating his nails. 'Think nothing of it. Just report to the Executioner on your way out, there's a good chap. Guards, remove this man's head for me would you. Thankyou so much.'

The juggler's hands shot to his neck as he tried to scream.

'But Sire, it was an accident . . . It wasn't my fault!' he pleaded.

'Now, now, you've already entertained us quite enough for one evening,' said the King. 'Please, kindly leave now. The fire-eaters are getting restless, and there's the dancing girls still to come.'

'D'you want it on a silver platter, yur 'ighness?' croaked one of the Black Guards, glaring calculatingly at the juggler's head.

'No, no. One of the spikes on the castle walls will be quite sufficient.'

'Bu' they're all full up, Sire.'

'Oh dear, are they? What a shame. Well, just give it to the wolverines, then. They'll enjoy the gravy. C'mon, chop, chop! Now, where's the dancing girls? It's time for the dancing girls.'

The Black Guards dragged the gravy-trailing juggler out of a small side door, kicking and screaming.

'Wench!' shouted the King. 'Disfigure me that peacock!'

And with that the Ruler of the combined kingdoms of Rhyngill and Cranachan settled back in his dining throne and, the juggler already a thing of the past, prepared to watch the terpsichorean delights of his favourite troop of fifteen digestive crackers.

On the far side of the Talpa Mountains the sound of a very live and very wild boar charging the base of a tree could be distinctly heard, much to the terror of the three children who had scrambled up there several hours ago.

'*Told* you this was the wrong way, but you wouldn't listen!' snapped the little girl, glaring daggers at her brother's neck.

'It's the *right* way. Castell Rhyngill's just over there, it's a short-cut!'

'Oh, great short-cut! We're going to be here all night!' came the snarled reply dripping with sarcasm.

'That's not my fault!'

'Yes, it is! You went dashing off . . .'

'Are you telling me you wanted to *stay* there? Hogshead, tell her we couldn't have stayed there?' pleaded Firkin, utterly fed up with Dawn's incessant whining. 'Hogshead?'

Eight feet below, a round boy dangled temptingly above the livid boar, arms and legs wound around the thick branch. Hogshead's eyes were jammed shut, his mind, racing with terror, confusion and hysteria. Nothing made any sense any more.

A flash of white tusks glinted below as the frenzied boar collided with the trunk, attempting to shake them loose.

From beneath the crumbled wreckage of Hogshead's reasoning a broken finger of sense twitched. Memory fought blind panic as the wheels of sentience ground and spun within. His mouth twitched.

One hundred and fifty pounds of angry bacon pounded into the tree once more and Hogshead found his voice.

'A bo . . . A boa . . . A boar!' he shrieked and clung tighter to the branch. They were the first words he had spoken in fourteen years. In that instant the sandbags of understanding were ripped from the levee of memory and the torrents of recall burst forth. Images flashed in the heady froth, the most recent first: dashing from the sprinting tusks of a wild boar; materialising four feet above the smoke-wreathed remnants of a torched Middin, tattooed with hoofprints, trampled, destroyed; then the swirling, buzzing chaos of the time-flies wrenching them from the battlefield fourteen years ago, tugging, rewriting . . . replacing.

'Tell her!' snapped Firkin from above.

'Courgette!' whimpered Hogshead hugging the tree as his memory exploded with squirrel-haired recollections.

'No!' yelled Firkin. 'This idiot sister of mine!'

The boar hit the tree running and with a shock Hogshead realised that he wasn't designed for an arboreal existence. 'Dawn?' he cried as his fingers slipped.

'Who else?' snapped Firkin. 'Tell her we couldn't . . .'

'I remembered!' shrieked Hogshead.

'. . . have stayed in Middin!' finished Firkin as the tree trembled beneath the latest porcine onslaught. 'It's almost like she hadn't noticed Middin was a heap of ash. Burnt down. Torched!'

'There's no need for that voice,' snapped Dawn.

'But, it's true. It's all Klayth's fault!' ranted Firkin ignoring his sister and the boar. He snatched a burnt fragment of parchment out of his tunic and waved it angrily. 'He's got a lot of explaining to do! Why the hell did he torch Middin?'

'But it doesn't make sense,' protested Dawn thinking back to the times they had spent in Castell Rhyngill, playing in these forests with King Klayth. 'There's got to be a good answer!'

The boar pawed at the ground, snorted and charged again. Hogshead's fingers were numb.

'Yes! And Klayth's got it!' continued Firkin. 'I'm going to find out!'

'Oh? How? Run across the drawbridge yelling "Excuse me, Your Highness, but I wonder if you could be so kind as to explain why you ordered the mountain village of Middin, our home village, to be torched." '

'He can't deny it! Here's the proof!' insisted Firkin pointing to the parchment fragment which Dawn had found pinned to Middin's post. 'A declaration from the King, pah!' he shouted.

Dawn cringed. He was going to read it out again!

'Since you have deigned refusal to accede to the tithing agreements established in previous communications,' read Firkin, 'and since the time has now passed the zenith of that juncture, retribution shall be taken. All dwellings within one mile of the posting of this declaration shall be razed to the ground by torch. Let this be a warning for the future. Your ever loving monarch.'

The boar thundered forward, piggy eyes intent on dislodging something this time.

'Look!' insisted Firkin for the hundredth time, 'He actually signed it. He waved the parchment. Slightly charred but unmistakably, it said:

Your ever-loving monar . . .

King K . . .

The thick skull of the boar smashed into the trunk, sending angry vibrations ricocheting up the tree. With a strangled yelp Hogshead's grip failed. He scrambled frantically at thin air for a second, then plunged eighteen feet straight down. The boar received a severe concussion, a fractured rib and cut its lip on a tusk.

Suddenly six huge black-clad guards erupted from the surrounding undergrowth, hovered momentarily, then crashed to the ground pinning Hogshead and the boar down as surely as any avalanche in a vindictive mood, the biggest and nastiest-looking screaming, 'Poachers! Arrest them! Bring the pig as evidence!'

Firkin and Dawn screamed protests as they were shaken expertly out of the tree and leapt on.

'No poaching allowed!' bellowed the leader, scowling angrily at Firkin.

'There's some mistake!' he protested. 'We're friends of the King!'

'Oh yeah? And I'm the Queen of Shirm!' sniggered the

lead guard with the panache of a road accident. 'King's friend? Good one! The King don't *'ave* any friends! Speshly not runts like you! Take 'em away!'

'What do you think you're doing! Put me down!' shouted Firkin squirming against the iron grip of the guards. 'There must be some mistake!' he protested pathetically as he was bounced towards the castle dungeons along with the other two. 'There'll be trouble when the King finds out.'

'Oh yeah! An' how's 'e goin' to find out?' gloated the Chief Guard. 'You goin' to tell 'is 'ighness?'

'As soon as I see him, yes!' insisted Firkin.

'Only thing you'll be seein' is the end of a rope in a couple o' days' time!'

'What? What for?'

'Tramplin' the King's Daisies, er, excessive GBH . . .'

'GBH?'

'Yeah, hangin' offence.'

'But I didn't . . .'

'Yeah you did. We saw you, didn't we Uric? Grievous Bodily Herbicide, look at all them damaged blades of grass an' bruised leaves.'

Uric swung Hogshead happily and nodded enthusiastically.

'But you're causing more damage than us!' argued Firkin, staring at the crushed grass passing beneath him as he bounced on the pole, like a captured boar. 'Your feet are bigger.'

'Ah well we've got speshul permishion to be here off the King. Haven't we, Uric?'

'Why aye! Stands ta reesan, man! Security!'

Nodding happily, the six Black Guards swung their terrified prisoners towards a suddenly even more uncertain future.

In semi-darkness the four figures sat.

In gloom; in half-light and deep, deep silence, broken only by the nervous breathing of Khenyth the newly appointed

51

Chancellor of Rhyngill and Cranachan, they awaited the arrival of their Liege, the Ruler Victorious, His Regal Altitude, the King.

Khenyth tugged nervously at the collar of his Tunic of Office, recalling the all too recent public garrotting of the last Chancellor. 'Honest' Jim de Rottah had been found guilty of excessive underimbezzlement, faultless bookkeeping and not being a close chum of boxer shrimp breeder and head of the Cranachan 'Family', Khar Pahcheeno.

Khenyth's wary gaze floated with mortal nervousness over the complex arrays of armourments and weaponry arranged around the walls of the Conference Room. He stared at the ranks of halberds and columns of spears; glanced apprehensively across the swathe of swords and clutches of axes, and the plethora of pikes and battleaxes shining with muted menace. In seconds he had totalled their cost, in groats, roats and murder.

Abruptly the double doors to the Conference Room were flung inwards as the imperious figure of the King stomped in. His regal red cloak flapped behind him as he surged towards the vast slate throne behind the table. Even before he was seated, he was barking questions from behind his violently twitching handlebar moustache. The conference had begun.

'The minutes from the last meeting of OG 1039 were as follows . . .' began Khenyth.

'How many times have I told you?' bellowed the King, cutting off the Chancellor. 'Minutes are the past. I want to know about progress, about the future. Leave yesterday for the poets and historians, give tomorrow to me! Tell me something new, something glorious!'

'Tithes are running at a current rate of eighty-three per cent, your highness,' said Khenyth cringing beneath the razor gaze of the monarch.

'And. . . ?'

'And collections are mostly all right, Sire.'

'Mostly all right? I was under the impression that some "incentive" had to be applied to ensure complete, er, co-operation,' growled the King smiling evilly at the black brooding figure of Commander Achonite before staring fixedly at Khenyth.

'Well, yes, Sire. But it's all right now,' he finished limply.

'And. . . ?' growled the King once more.

'And?' whimpered Khenyth fondling his neck.

'Cost, man. Cost? How much did sending in the Black Guards cost and how are you going to recoup that loss? Bottom lines, man. Give me the bottom line!'

'Sixty-four guards for three days at three groats a day.'

'Bottom line!' fumed the King impatiently, slamming his fist on to the table, raising a pile of dust and a grin from Achonite.

'Four hundred and twenty-eight groats, Sire,' answered Khenyth.

'You charge a lot, Achonite,' smirked the King grinning at the Commander sitting almost invisible in the gloom, emanating malevolence from within his matt black leather armour. His helmet lay on the table next to him, glaring with only slightly less menace than the head it was designed to fit. An air of brooding military menace floated above his tightly cropped hair as he idly totted up the enormous mayhem potential of the wall coverings. He liked to know this sort of thing.

'The going rate for the internal market, Sire. Bigger land area to cover means higher costs.' Achonite spoke with a voice as ignorable as an avalanche.

'Good point,' agreed the King. Then rounding on Khenyth he shouted, 'So what are you going to do about it?'

'We have sufficient funds within the treasury to meet the labour costs incurred so I . . .'

'NO! NO! NO!' exploded the King, pummelling the table into submission. 'Wrong answer! Think man! Use your head or you will shortly lose it!'

'Er. Because the populace delivered a short tithe,' began the Chancellor falteringly, 'and caused us to incur an excessive, er, essential retaliatory expense then,' he swallowed. 'The cost should be recovered *from* the populace.'

'And?'

Khenyth's shoulders sagged. 'Raise the tithes, Sire?'

'By golly he's got it! Yes. Raise the tithes! Call it an administration charge if you wish but raise the damn things again. I don't see why we should have to pay for all this out of *our* pockets. It's hard enough having to collect the things normally without poxy, flea-ridden mountain villagers holding up the process. Issue a decree immediately. Raise the tithes at once! In fact back-date it. Twelve months! And cancel St Swindling's Day!'

'Yes, Sire. As you wish,' answered Khenyth, sweating.

'I do wish,' replied the King and then dismissed the Chancellor from his mind. He turned to Black Achonite and demanded, 'Tell me of your recent exploits. In fact, where were you last night?'

'I hear I missed an interesting display of juggling, Sire.'

'A little too much audience participation for my taste. They got a little carried away, lost their heads you might say.'

'Indeed, Sire,' chuckled Achonite, a sound not unlike that made by mating flagstones. 'I'm afraid I was detained on business, your Altitude.'

'Am I working you that hard?'

'Oh, no Sire. I believe I have found a rival to your little Thrasher. In fact, may I suggest a meeting later?'

'A rival? Ho ho! Indeed. I should like to witness this. My chambers early tomorrow!'

The Conference then turned to the more normal subjects of fascination and excitement that the King revelled in. Black Achonite's seismic voice recounted with immense relish the scattering of the villagers of Middin, the torching of the huts, luxuriating in the gory glory of the graphic retelling. The King's ears lapped up the tales of tyrannical activities, basking with gloating indulgence in the dancing reflected light of the crimson flames from the burning shacks, warming his evil heart by the heat from the campfires of barbarity. He

54

thrilled visibly as he heard of merciless deeds of 'essential law and order' carried out under the heavy-handed iron fist of his Black Guard. Thieves dragged through the streets by charging stallions, bodies torn to shreds by wild jackals before screaming crowds of onlookers for non-possesion of dog licences and public disembowellings for minor cart parking offences.

This, he thrilled as he thought, this is what being King is all about. It was good to be King. Dealing with the people's misery and abject destitution with the well-being of the monarchy uppermost in his mind. In amongst all the misery in the kingdom, the people needed to see a happy King.

With the relish of absolute wickedness seasoning his veins 'any other business of the day' was tucked into. Future plans and strategies were discussed, shouted about and eventually settled upon and organised, another back-dated tithe hike agreed on at eighty-eight per cent base rate and three hundred and four sundry taxes, including reading tax,* community tax†, hermit tax‡, thumb tax§ and carpet tax¶ were either introduced or tweaked in an upward direction.

---

* Reading tax. a) Persons about to read were charged at a rate of two-thirds of a groat per hundred words read per minute or seventeen and a half groats per book owned, whichever was the greater: and b) persons unable to read were charged a six groats per year education charge to attempt to teach them to read. Information regarding class times was written on notices clearly displayed in the Palace Library. (Entrance Fee six hundred and three groats.)

† Community tax. Anyone living in a community of more than two people was liasble to pay community tax. The value was arbitrarily decided by multiplying the score of five dice by the distance in leagues the community lay from the centre of Castell Rhyngill.

‡ Hermit tax. Anyone living alone for the purposes of religious solitude, inner healing or simply being unable to stand living in the flea-ridden, rat-infested whirlpool of depravity that is civilisation, was liable to pay hermit tax. The value was arbitrarily decided by multiplying the score from eight dice by the distance in feet the hermit lived from the centre of Castell Rhyngill. Payment of this particular tax was instantly on demand, in cash. As non-payment of hermit taxes was punishable by instant death it was not surprising that there were few hermits in Rhyngill.

§ Thumb tax. Any person found alive and in possession of one or more thumbs was liable to a tax of five groats per thumb per year. Anyone found to have wilfully removed one of their own thumbs, or have hired another person so to do, with the express purpose of reneging on payment of this tax was liable to a five hundred

Slapping his hands against his thighs some time later, the King and Commander Achonite left the Conference Room for a post-powertrip feast in the Banqueting Hall.

He laughed long and loud as he stomped through the corridors, staring with derisive scorn upon the heads bent in worship before him. The King was happiest when he was seen to be wielding his mighty hand of ultimate rulership.

Rulership spelt P-O-W-E-R.

Circling warily as the sun struggled skywards, the two armour-clad adversaries sized each other up. They were three rounds into the fight and already blood was flowing. A nasty gash oozed between two of the Royal Champion's chest plates. Glaring cold-bloodedly, eyes on stalks, antennae lashing the damp salty air, Thrasher lined up on Kriller. The Royal decapod had taken quite a beating. In fact, at present a more correct description would be 'Royal nonopod'.

Kriller lashed out with his left claw, grabbing Thrasher's antenna at the joint, forcing the Royal Champion to scrape uselessly at the bottom of the barrel, following up with a powerful sweeping tail-blow. Accompanied by a sickening crack and a bellow of rage from the King, Thrasher's antenna snapped.

Achonite stared intently into the barrel. 'Ah! I love the smell of seaweed in the mornings!' Kriller slashed angrily at Thrasher. 'I fear the Champion's days are numbered. And that number is up,' quipped Achonite through a tattooed grin, much to the King's disgust.

'A lucky break,' he snarled.

'Not for Thrasher, I'll warrant!'

The King squealed with shock as he watched Kriller

---

groat liars' tax and the removal of the other thumb. Any person found in possession of no thumbs would be slaughtered on sight.

¶ Carpet tax. Any person found in possession of a carpet or floor covering other than mud was liable to a tax of three groats per square foot.

remove another of Thrasher's legs with crustacean viciousness, then round sharply and lunge for the kill.

In a moment it was all over. The Royal Champion was scampi.

'Where did *that* come from?' snarled the King through a haze of anger. 'Why was I not informed? It could have got into the wrong hands. *I* have to have the champion!'

'It came from outside, Sire.'

'Outside! You mean they're breeding them outside?'

'Yes, Sire. Have been for years. Only recently have they got the hang of it.'

The King picked up the victor and held it in the palm of his hand, examining the new champion closely.

'Hmmm, not bad,' he said admiringly. 'who did you say bred this beast?'

'Slym Muphyn, lives in downtown . . .'

'I do not wish to know his personal details. Just send out an invitation to him for a place at the banquet tomorrow evening. I should very much like to meet him.'

Achonite looked suspicious. The King never had commoners at the same table during a banquet.

'Are you considering him for the new Royal Supplier?'

'Oh no! Perish the thought,' he said staring at the victorious crustacean. 'It's shell's far too thin.' And to prove the point, before Achonite's very eyes, the King clenched his gauntleted fist suddenly, grinning as he squeezed, the muscles and sinews standing proud on his arm as they crushed.

Wiping his hands a moment later he stared Achonite hard in the eyes.

'Kindly inform Pahcheeno to supply me with his finest, as soon as possible. I want imported stock. It is far superior and it allows me to spend more of the people's money.' He grinned, turned on his heel and marched out of the Fighting Room.

Achonite stared mournfully at the crumpled shrimp.

What a waste, he thought. That cost me twenty-five groats!

Deep inside the snug darkness of the pocket of Hogshead's tunic (which at present was deep inside the far less than snug darkness of Castell Rhyngill's poachers' prison) lay what to any cursory examination would appear to be a very normal, harmless slushy romance. However, on a closer inspection it would become apparent that pages thirty-five to one hundred and eighteen inclusive had been on the receiving end of a pair of extremely well adapted mandibles. Large curving things shaped over millions of preceding generations for the express purpose of chewing the lignin fibres of the parchment used in books.

Deeper still, within the cosy space which these jaws had hollowed out, something lurked. It wasn't a very happy something.

Had it possessed eyebrows they would have been angled in a hurt expression aimed at securing as much sympathy from as many quarters as possible. Had it owned a pair of lips they would have been trembling in the effort to prevent itself snuffling in an extremely undignified manner, and had it been endowed with a pair of arms they would have been rubbing furiously at its lower abdomen.

Ch'tin, the bookworm, had bellyache.

An extremely acute throbbing somewhere between a bad cramp and sheer agony. And rising.

Ch'tin squeaked pathetically as he writhed inside the book. He'd had stomach upsets in the past, there was the time when he'd eaten several hedges of privet, the occasion when he'd devoured a heap of partially decomposed leaf litter, and the hunger-crazed moment of madness when he'd tucked into a ream of political leaflets destined for canvassing in a local election. Some of those claims had really stuck in his throat.

But he'd never had a bellyache like this one. Well, maybe once before. But that was different, that had nightmares as well.

Nervously he recalled the last time, the voices, the swirling fragments of storylines released after he had tucked into Appendix IIIb of 'Ye Aynshent Almanacke of Conjoorynge, Magycke and Such'. How was he, an innocent bookworm, supposed to know that magical text books aren't just printed with ink, but the words are inkanted into the parchment using thaumatin dyes? Nobody tells you these things. Nobody warns you about it!

Ch'tin winced as another bolt of indigestion stabbed through his lower intestine. Somehow it felt horribly familiar.

But that was impossible.

Wasn't it?

The regular aerial dawn chorus chirruped, squawked and crowed its tuneless self across the snoring expanse of Cranachan, battering itself mercilessly against the unwilling ears of the sleeping residents, rattling them into wakefulness with all the subtlety of a pneumatic drill. A wedge of geese arced in, flared out and landed in their favourite morning spot. Over the years successive generations of howler geese had found that here, just between the soaring walls of the Imperial Palace Fortress and a curving expanse of roughly hewn cliff, was the most fabulous acoustic trumpet. The noise produced when four or five geese really let rip with their synchronised honking was legendary, especially when they managed to set up beats, reinforcing each new honk with the previous reflection, broadcasting cacophanous anserine howling to the surprisingly unappreciative Cranachanian slumberers.

Khar Pahcheeno uttered a blue string of choice curses, thrust his head under the pink nihilon sheets,* groaned and

* Nihilon. A finely woven material spun from the fibres derived from the copolymerisation of two compounds extracted from the decayed bodies of extinct worms, aphids and a comprehensive range of long dead sea-slugs. It was introduced shortly after the end of the now legendary Two-and-a-half-minute War and was an instant hit with the ladies of Cranachan who leapt into nihilon stockings in a big way, instantly discarding their older outmoded silk. After all, who wants to wear something extruded from a caterpillar's bottom.

rolled over. Dimly, through the haze of a few too many bottles of local red wine, he became aware of the fact that he was not alone. This in itself was not too unusual for Khar Pahcheeno. Being the most powerful and successful shrimp-breeder in Cranachan, and having fingers in many other far less legal pies, made the seductively persuasive presence of any number of nubile maidens far from uncommon. The lengths to which the daughters of any of the many not-quite-hugely-successful shrimp trainers would go to secure a better price for their father's next prize fighter, or the seductive skills of a desperate wife's attempts to shave a few feet off the mountain of debt her husband owed, were a constant source of lascivious delight to Khar Pahcheeno. After all, it was a very pleasant way to haggle.

This morning, however, there were a few things that awoke his finely honed sense of suspicion. Firstly, he did not remember inviting anybody in last night; secondly, the window was wide open; thirdly, the sheets were wet; and last, his companion smelt very strongly of fish.

Khar Pahcheeno's stomach churned as he pulled back the nihilon sheets. His eyes bulged in horror as he focused blearily on the scene before him. There, each of its ten legs neatly and callously removed, lying next to its own severed head, surrounded by two thin slices of lemon and a bowl of chilli sauce was the deep-fried body of Pugilator, the shrimp.

A small scrap of parchment was pinned to the headboard of the bed, and there, written in glistening fish sauce were the words:

BON APPETITE!

THE APPROPRIATOR

Of Swords and Stomach-ache

Sitting beneath a large lime tree, on a gloriously sunny day (as it always was), a young princess played with a small golden ball. Every day she walked the yellow path away from the pink and green pastel castle whistling the same tune as she did so. Each time, just as the sun sparkled off a very pretty bush she had the urge to skip, and each time, she never quite got round to it. She was the most beautiful of the King's three daughters and she knew it. Well, it *was* written in huge black letters at the top of the sky.

'Once upon a time the most beautiful of the King's daughters went into the wood . . .'

Bit of a giveaway.

She'd been playing with the little golden ball for a few paragraphs – you know, the boring ones where they describe the forest and the little slope, and the small fountain, and the well that was too deep to see the bottom of – when . . , surprise, surprise! . . . she fumbles an easy catch and watches with bored horror as it bounces away and dives into the well. Defying the laws of physics in an extremely irritating way, the ball actually sinks!

Then she begins to lament.

Every time, she feels extremely stupid lamenting over a blinking ball. I mean, Dad's the King, ask him nicely and he'll get another one for her. She could probably even sweet talk one of the toy-sellers if she tried. Beautiful princesses were supposed to be able to get away with anything. What's the point of being a King's daughter if you can't wangle a freebie now and then!

Still, lament it says in huge black story book letters, so lament she must.

'Oh! My pretty ball! Lost within the well!' And a few tears trickled down her rosy cheeks.

Yeuch, she cringed.

'Why weepest thou, O daughter of the King? . . .'

She waited for the familiar amphibian tones to bubble out of the well.

' . . . thy tears wouldst melt a stone's granite heart . . .'

And she waited.

And waited.

Her lamentation began to sound not a little forced. It shouldn't have to last *this* long.

'Pssst. Hey, froggy!' she whispered between staged sobs. 'Hey, come on!'

The surface of the well stayed perfectly calm.

'Oi! 'urry up!'

Another peal of half-hearted emotional outbursts of grief.

'Look, I can't keep this up much longer. Gimme the ball back!'

More aquatic reticence.

The beautiful princess stood angrily, hitched up her skirt and stomped over to the well.

'Oi! Greeny! Get out here and do your bit. C'mon: "Why weepest thou, O daughter of the King. . . ?" ' she yelled into the fathomless pit.

'Look, gimme the ball and we can all get on with it! Oh, you're not getting stroppy about working conditions again, are you? I know you get the crappy bits, sittin' all day in that pool, an' havin' to flop up those cold marble stairs. Tell you what, gimme the ball an' I'll not throw you against the wall so hard at bed time . . . deal? . . . whaddyou say?'

Nothing even flinched beneath the well's surface.

'Right, that's *it!*' she squealed, stamping her foot and shattering the glass slipper. 'Bugger! Props are going to hate me!' she cursed to herself.

'Five seconds to come out! . . . Five! Right I'm off to see The Editor. Prince, or no Prince I'm *not* putting up with you and your toady moods.'

62

She turned sharply on her intact glass heel and hobbled off grumbling angrily to herself.

Slym Muphyn, known to his exclusive circle of friends as 'The Mule', almost couldn't believe his eyes as a platter of steaming whelks was placed before him. Real whelks, imported all the way from Shirm! The King of Rhyngill and Crañachan spared absolutely no expense on himself. His banquets were legendary. Anything considered a delicacy, a luxury, an aphrodisiac or all three had to appear on the King's banquet menu. And if the tithes had to be raised to pay for it then that was the price the people paid for a happy monarch.

And as he kept reminding them, 'A happy King means that you live longer!'

Fire-eaters, clad in bright costumes, gulped evil-smelling liquid and tried their hardest to toast flies in vast sheets of orange death. Jugglers, now unsurprisingly unwilling to stray more than a few inches vertically, hurled their clubs, knives and flaming brands with exceedingly wary eyes on the King and the Council. Black Achonite gnawed on an enormous boar thigh, two huge wolf hounds salivating expectantly behind him. Motleyed jesters leapt and cavorted joyously, liberally whacking innocent gorgers with their inflated pigs' bladders. It was another peaceful meal.

'Been breeding boxers long?' shouted the King, boar fat dripping from his handlebar moustache.

Muphyn the Mule looked up from his whelks and pointed to his chest. 'Me?' he mouthed.

'Well who else breeds shrimps in this room, eh? How long?'

''bout two years, your 'ighness,' he answered, a whelk poised in mid air.

'And how many really nasty shrimps have you bred in that time?' yelled the King.

'Wha', champion material, like?'

The King nodded, his eyes smouldering strangely.

63

'Jus' the one, I'm afraid, Sire. Jus' Kriller. An 'e's bin sold.'

Black Achonite looked at the King's right hand and thought of his shrimp.

'Good,' said the King. 'Very good. Just as it should be. Enjoy the rest of your meal.'

Whether it was simply because he was the King Black Achonite wasn't sure, but there seemed to be an undertone of commanding finality in the way Khardeen had said that.

The shrimp breeder disrobed another whelk and shoved it into his mouth, thrilling as the heavy garlic butter exploded on his palate. Around him the plethora of banquet entertainers continued to scorch, hurl and strum in their several requisite ways.

Suddenly, Muphyn coughed and turned pale, his knife dropping from his hand, skewering the trencher of bread, pinning it to the table. His hands clutched at his throat as he turned first red, then yellow and finally a strange shade of puce. He panted, sweating then shivering, stood up, turned and crashed on to the floor in a short-lived twitching heap, pulling the plate of whelks over him.

'Oh dear,' said King Khardeen, scowling as the shellfish vanished over the table's horizon. 'Such a waste of good food.'

Achonite stared at the whelks before him and swallowed nervously.

'Fancy using whelks to poison someone!' added the King. 'They must have really hated him. Guards, get him out of here! Wench, unlace me that rabbit! And bring on the dancing girls!'

Achonite watched for a trace of remorse on the King's face as the body of Muphyn was removed. He knew that he hated competition but *that* was a little drastic.

In the far corner of the hall a squat figure, with slicked-back hair grinned in self-satisfied smugness and winked at the King. That was the best poisoning Khar Pahcheeno had ever carried out. Since it was a contract killing on behalf of the Crown not only was it perfectly free from any risk of further action, but it paid extremely well and it rid him of any competition on the boxer shrimp front.

Competition was something he could really do without right now. He cringed again as he thought of the body of Pugilator in his bed.

Then stood the realm in great jeopardy long while, for every lord that was harboured verily desirous thoughts of kingship. And all the lords of the realm, all the gentlemen of arms were sent for to attend at the Capitol upon pain of cursing. And the clergy set unto praying for some miraculous sign to determine whoforth shall be King. And when matins and the first service was heard to be done there had appeared a huge stone, standing four square and abbutting unto the high altar. Atop this marble stone, in midst the churchyard therof, was beheld an anvil nigh on a cubit high and therein was thrust a naked sword point firstwards. And in golden script, fair of hand and solid of meaning, was writ these words, thus: – Whoso pulleth out this sword, Exbenedict, from this stone and anvil, is the rightwise king born unto this realmdom.

And everyone was dead impressed.

And ten knights of puissance were purveyed rightwise quick and an annexed canopy thrown up forto heretofore protect and enshroud. And come Candymass day, the sweetest of days of yore, a host of gilded espadarilles tripped lightly toward that holy place, athrong with eagerness, alight with expectancy. And through the traipsing throng thrulled foot-hot a youth. Yeah, the young Halva, nourished varlet to Sir Khae, keen to enter the canopy of gules and verdure and withdraw Exbenedict. And brushing aside the sidedrops plunged he therein. And his voice was raisedeth high as he reached the stone and anvil and cried: 'Ha, bloody ha! Which joker's pinched the naffin' sword, eh? C'mon, where the blinkin' 'eck is it? 'ow am I supposed to be King if someone's 'alf-inched me bleedin' sword?'

And everybody shruggedeth their shoulders.

'Look! It's only me's supposed to pull the thing out. That's the way the story is! . . . Oh, no! No! It's not another rewrite is it? Right, that's it, that is it! I'm off to see the Editor. 'Le Morte D'Halva' Pah! It'll be 'Le Morte D'Editor' if he's rewritten me! I've got a contract . . .'

Throughout the lower levels of the Castell Rhyngill Prison Block a singly distraught scream escaped from a pair of female tonsils, crashing and echoing its panicky way into the deep dark gloom.

She stood there, in the pitch dark and . . . well, just stood there. It was very strange, one minute she was busy doing whatever it was she was doing and then . . . she wasn't. And now she couldn't remember what it was that she'd been doing in the first place. No, that wasn't right. It wasn't that she'd forgotten . . . she hadn't known in the first place, she was doing something now that she had *never* done before.

'Oh, come on darlin'. Don't play games.'

A voice sounded in the thick darkness. A dark voice oozing with brown teeth and lechery.

'C'mon, give it to me! You know you want to!'

With a deafening crash, and another terrified scream, she dropped the tray that she hadn't realised she'd been holding, scattering dry bread and water everywhere.

'Aw! What d'you do that for, lovey? I wanted that in here. I was lookin' forward to it. Nice bit of crust, yummy!'

She stared at the iron bars on the door as the figure swam into view of her dark adjusting eyes. How did she get here? And where was here?

Not possessing a classic Parathaumic Education in Temporal Rearrangement Phenomena, Courgette would have spent an awfully long time scouring the inside of her skull for any insight into the origins, name and taxonomy of the creatures responsible for shifting her away from that valley in the middle of the Talpa Mountains fourteen years into the past, without a by-your-leave.

Shaking with terror and scratching feverishly at her

squirrel-red head, she tried to remember what she had been doing fifteen seconds ago. She was looking down into a valley cheering as the mighty Cranachanian Army had been soundly defeated by a small group of youngsters and a very eager small brown marsupial.

She looked around in the dark for any sign of her companions, Firkin, Dawn and Hogshead. Especially Hogshead. Where had they gone?

Dimly she recalled a series of flashing lights, swirling images and a host of snatching hands grabbing at her body, pulling her away from the others. No, not hands, stronger . . . and smaller. And buzzing.

Time flies, the microscopic, quasi-sentient swarms of winged temporal messengers, commonly known as *Tempus fugit*, don't exist in *any* encyclopaedia, dictionary or reference book outside the Central Reference Library of the Guardians of Temporal Security and Continuity Errata Eradication. And even there, in that most responsible of chronologically hallowed arenas of learning, there is only one copy, which can only be read in very short doses, watched over carefully by several custodians. Security is essential. If a book like this were to fall into the wrong hands it would spell disaster for the antiques trade; the market would be flooded overnight with shoddy tapestries imported from centuries where labour was cheap. It would be the end for the stock market and venture capitalists; well, I mean who would invest in gleaming strings of companies *without* seeing profit and loss breakdowns for at least the next ten years.

The only breakdown that Courgette was likely to see in the next few minutes was mental. Had some passing stranger been kind enough to offer her a full and thaumaturgically correct explanation of the importance of her actions fourteen years ago in rewriting the victors of the two-and-a-half-minute war as the Rhyngillians, she would have been a small dribbling heap on the floor.

But as no explanation was forthcoming she settled into the

situation as best she knew how; clamping her arms around her bewildered head, she filled her lungs and screamed in the dark of the Rhyngillian Prison Quarters.

Swinging an enormous mallet in a sweeping arc the figure on the vast horse focused in on the ball. His steed frothed and steamed as its hooves gouged clods from the pitch, swerving and bearing down fast.

From away to his left a figure in black called, his voice booming across the polo pitch, 'Pestilence! Oi! Over here! C'mon man, pass!' And the crowd went wild.

Across the fifty-league line War turned, spurring his steed harder, scattering turf as he marked the Knights Templars, holding them off as Pestilence passed to Death. The black-cloaked figure intercepted the ball with his renowned accuracy, grinned fleshlessly and pounded toward the goal, cloak-tails flapping.

Pestilence shrieked desperate instructions to Famine as a Templar broke through War's defences heading straight for the charging Death. For a few apocalyptic moments it looked as if the Templar might tackle the grim reaper head on. Pestilence snatched at his reins, leaning hard into a tight sod-scattering swerve and dashed for the Knight. A wave of flailing arms swept around the stadium.

In the closing minutes of the final chukka of the Chapter Dimensions All-Comers Polo Championships Final, with the Apocalypse Four one goal down on the Knights Templars nobody saw the black cloud growing over Famine.

Hurling his red-crossed shield away and flattening himself to the sweating neck of his horse, the desperate Knight swerved scant inches around the back of Pestilence.

War roared a string of choice oaths and was glared at by the referee.

Death powered on, keeping the ball close to his steed's thundering hooves, powering in towards the goal. The capacaity crowd yelled hoarse encouragements. Could the Apocalypse Four snatch victory?

Black cumuli swirled and stacked above Famine as he galloped after Death.

Suddenly two more Templars broke rank, swinging out around War and powering up the field, mallets humming above their heads. The crowd erupted. Famine tugged on his reins and sped to intercept. In that instant the vast bank of black clouds solidified, seared pitchwards, struck Famine and was gone.

So was Famine.

Death was screaming for support, if he didn't get it he'd be offside, goal disallowed. War screamed, rampaging up the pitch in the closing moments as the referee licked the tip of his whistle, counting off the final seconds. Death swung at the ball from eighty yards out, smashing it in an ankle-high curve into the corner of the goal and missed. The whistle blew. The crowd went wild. The Apocalypse Four had lost! They had never lost!

Death turned, his skull creasing in anger. 'Where the hell was Famine! I could have scored if Famine'd been there. Famine?'

Where was Famine?

Courgette slouched miserably in the lower depths of the highly populated Castell Rhyngill Prison Block, the passage of time marked only by the water dripping from the ceiling. Questions, like the cockroaches on the floor, scuttled and chattered for attention. Her memory hopped and tugged at the worms of the past hiding in the green lawns of history, attempting to dig up some sort of an explanation. As she had carried out the duties which somehow she knew she had to, visions of the past had swum through her mind, glimpsed but hazy, tender succulent fish darting out of reach in cloudy waters flowing ever on under the bridge of bygone days. Each time it all seemed so much more distant. She knew for certain that she worked in the prison block and fed the prisoners with water and dried bread cooked by her father Val Jambon. A father she was never allowed to see. And she knew that it had been this way for the last eight or nine years. Every day.

Why did she remember a whole host of adventures? Hogshead, Firkin, Dawn, Klayth. She knew there was a Klayth. He was the Prince of Rhyngill and Cranachan. Why did she think that she knew him? She was certain that she remembered playing with him! She recalled distant places, Fort Knumm, Losa Llamas, the thaumaturgical physicists, the libraries of Castell Rhyngill, it was all so vivid! Why was she so baffled by all she saw around her?

Why did the word 'psychoanalyst' keep springing to mind?

Suddenly a host of yells, rattling keys and stamping feet hurled themselves into earshot as a heavy wooden door was unlocked and flung open. Six Black Guards were man-handling some new prisoners into the gloom of this underground world.

'Stop strugglin' ' shouted a large well-muscled voice.

'But there's been a mistake!' shouted a smaller, thinner reply.

'An' I keep tellin you, it's yours!'

'Euurgh! It smells in here!' squealed a small female voice. 'It's horrid!' Strings of memory were tugged in Courgette's mind.

'Don't worry, darlin'. You won't be stayin' 'ere for too long. Hah! Will they, Uric.'

A dark sinister giggle sounded in the gloom.

'Pheww! Good, I'm dot very good at holdig my breath,' replied the girl clutching her nose.

'I'm terribly sorry that you have to spend any time in here, but . . .'

'I should think so too!' protested the thin voice. 'The King will want to know why we were brought down here in the first place. It's shocking!'

'If you'll let me finish,' snarled the well-muscled voice. 'It should only be a few days. The Executioner's been off, see, bit of a cold, it's amazin' 'ow much a few sneezes can upset the balance on the gallows trap-door, you should've seen 'im

70

tryin' to set up four of 'em at the same time. Oh, it was sad. 'E's an artist, see? Loves 'is synchronised swingin'. 'Ey, Uric, remember the time 'e dropped ten of 'em in one session? Gorgeous it was! Five timed pairs workin' their way towards the centre, each one triggered by the feet o' the one before . . . poetry, sheer poetry. Crowd went wild! Well, you need hair-triggers for that sort o' thing an' y' just can't set it up if you're sneezin' all the bleedin' time.'

'So what?'

'Oh, sorry. Got a bit carried away there. Well there's a bit of a backlog, see? But, you're goin' to be dead lucky. You'll be dead chuffed when I tell you what 'e's plannin'. D'you think I should tell 'em, Uric?'

'Why aye. It's a reeel privilege,' answered Uric.

'Now, don't let this get out . . . oh, 'scuse the pun, but 'e's plannin' a five-triplet synchronised drop arranged in a triangle on the side of a pyramid. Oh, it's goin' to be beautiful. Anyway, I can't stand about chattin' all day. Got a few dozen acts of senseless violence to dish out before lunch. Get in there!'

There was a brief struggle, a few squeals, the slamming of a large door and the swift exit of six enormous Black Guards.

'Hope the weather stays good for the Executioner, ropes get a big sticky when it's damp,' said the Chief Guard as the door swung shut. 'It'd really mess up the symmetry if one of 'em didn't drop right.'

'Why aye, Reeeel sad,' agreed Uric.

With a gesture of vicious frustration, and a sneer to match, the black-clad figure of the Appropriator cursed richly as he screwed up the newly delivered newsparchment and flung it across the huge dark room below Cranachan.

'Reporters!' he screamed, glaring out from behind his leather eyepatch with seething anger. 'What do they know!'

'Haff dey ssspelt your name wronk again?' asked Vlad nervously.

'They think one of *his* rivals did it!' squealed the Appropriator, slamming his leathered fist on to the arm of the burnished bronze throne, 'It's a cover-up. They're trying to play it down. *I* murdered a national hero, and they're playing it down! What do I have to do to show them I mean business? Is it time for another murder? This time without the chilli sauce!'

'Who vould it be thissss time?' hissed Vlad through sparkling teeth wet with anticipation.

'Pahcheeno seems too thick-skinned for his own good. Perhaps a sliver of steel in the kidneys will teach him sense in the final ten seconds of his pathetic life!'

'Yesssss!'

'With that imbecile out of the way there'll be very little between me and my rightful position!' He leapt from his throne and ran out of the cavern kicking out at the newsparchment once more.

His mind raced through the past almost as fast as his feet through the halls and hidden corridors. He recalled his time as Cranachan Chief of Internal Affairs. It seemed years ago now. Before the war, that two-and-a-half minute fiasco! In OG 1025 it had all been going so well. He, Fisk, had been scaling the ladders of power with consummate ease and scrambling forever upwards. In a matter of months he would have been next only to the King. It was all arranged, all perfect! And then . . . War with that tin-pot neighbour over farming rights of lemmings. But to lose! It was too much. The last fourteen years he had spent in hiding, building up his own kingdom, his own power base, heightening his legendary reputation. But now, frustration was setting in. He had to move soon.

And that move would be murder!

Dark clouds gathered over the Market Square of Cranachan.

'Shrimp Wars about to start. Top breeders battle over

72

champions,' cried the newsparchment seller. '*Triumphant Herald* has all the details and pull-out shrimp recipe chart. A taste of murder! You sir! Can I interest you in . . .'

There was a flash of lightning, a cloud swirled violently like an elemental spin-bowler and struck the ground.

'Oh dear! Oh dear! I shall be too late!' came the flustered reply from a small figure taking a pocket-watch out of its waistcoat pocket.

'Sir? It don't take long to buy a copy!'

'Oh my earsh and whishkersh, how late it'sh getting,' murmured the pale gentleman and sprinted off in a strangely loping way.

The newsparchment seller rubbed his eyes and stared in shocked bewilderment as he watched the white rabbit sprint around a corner and disappear down a hole.

'I'm working too hard. Far too hard. Need a rest! Imagine thinking I could see white rabbits with a pocket-watch! How could he afford a pocket-watch?'

'Excushe me, my good fellow.' The rabbit had returned.

'Pocket-sundial maybe, at a push if he saved his carrots up but a pocket-watch? No chance!'

'Excushe me, my good fellow,' came the repeated saying, with only the slightest hint of a lisp as the mouth worked its way around the pair of enormous front teeth. 'I wash wondering if you could direct me to the river. I sheem to have become shomewhat dishoriented.'

The newsparchment seller stared open-mouthed at the white rabbit's clear pink eyes.

'A chertain alacrity in your reshponshe would be appreshiated ash the Duchessh doesh take on sho if delayed . . . Hello . . . Hello?'

The man behind the stall turned far too pale, rolled his eyes and disappeared in a crumpled heap behind the stack of parchments.

'Oh dear! I shall be far too late!' flustered the white rabbit and headed off in the opposite direction.

*

73

Far beyond the edge of the known universe, across the swirling vortex known as the Space-Tome Continuum, lie the Chapter Dimensions.

Several million years ago life began here in the normal way. You know, a slowly cooling planet, racked with volcanic activity, huge electric storms shorting in an atmosphere redolent with all the elements necessary for a fertile issue, consonants, vowels, phonemes, syllables all mixing and mingling in a thick literal soup. Oh yes, and a couple of vital ingredients only found in a few very rare spots. Transition metals of stupendous obscurity elsewhere, ficton and literanium were oozing out of the rocks and fissures in stunning profusion, giving rise, almost inevitably, to a host of ficton based life-forms. This multi-valent element could combine in thousands of varying ways with the other elements of the surrounding geography giving rise to diverse plot-forms, subtexts and, most importantly, complex multi-species storyline ecosystems. Every member of the Chapter Dimensions had its own place, its own bibliographic classification, its own essaylogical niche. Frog Princes fetched balls from ponds, magical swords sprouted miraculously out of stone anvils and Death, Pestilence, Famine and War regularly thrashed all-comers at polo.

At least, they normally did.

It was due to the fact that none of these things seemed to be happening that a huge crowd of angry characters had gathered amongst the marble domes of the Editor's Palace. Led by an irate non-King Halva, Sir Khae and an extremely miffed Wicked Witch of the West, the seething crowd had swarmed down the yellow tarmac road, wanting an audience, demanding answers. The ten flat rectangular guards at the gate, carrying clubs and looking important hadn't stood a chance. Especially when threatened by a smouldering dragon's nostril.

'Whoa, whoa! One at a time, please,' said the round bearded face of the Editor, smiling benignly down from the throne at the top of the table. 'I can't hear all of you at once!'

'I said, "Someone's 'alf-inched me naffin' sword!" '
repeated Halva as loud as possible, 'Exbenedict's gone!'

'Well . . .' began the Editor.

'. . . and my Frog's vanished,' ranted the Princess.
"Nowhere to be found, not hide nor flipper!'

'Well . . .' repeated the Editor.

'. . . and I've got ten thousand men, neither half way up
nor half-way down, in a right mess since the Grand Old Duke
naffed off in mid-order,' shouted a large man in a military
uniform.

'. . . I . . .' whimpered the Editor.

'Who's seen the spoon?' cried a small blue willow pattern
dish, her shoulders rocking in paroxysms of sorrow, 'He said
we should run away together! I've always wanted to elope!'

'. . . but . . .'

'I demand a replay!' snarled War.

The list of complaints grew. And all the time in the far
corner the forehead of a tall thin figure with a long whitish
beard, pointy hat and matching saxaffron robe, furrowed
deeper and deeper in concern. Something was very, very
wrong.

The more thaumically sensitive whiskers deep inside his
long nose quivered suddenly as a few threads began to part in
the eight-hundred-denier screen of the Space-Tome
Continuum.

A ladder snaked its way down the Stockings of Reality.

Squatting in rotting defiance upon the pale grey granite
jaw-bone of the Talpa Mountains, like a terminally caried
molar bracing itself to rebut another orthodontal assault, the
heap that was Cranachan lurked in a light northwesterly
drizzle. Reining in the horse as he crested the top of the pass,
the indigo-robed figured waited for his two companions to
join him. With the grin of a man who really enjoys his job he
stared out over the rough mountains. The rain meant
nothing to him, the shabby mouldering appearance of
Cranachan fooled him not. He was certain that the ranks of

75

followers of the Church of St Lucre the Unwashed would be swelled. He knew beyond a shadow of a doubt that there was oodles of dosh just waiting to leap into their ever capacious coffers. Cranachan had been in his evangelical sights for some time. Ever since he had heard the calling of souls eager to be unburdened of their filthy worldly possessions, crying out to share their wealth, eager beyond the bounds of fervent enthusiasm to make immensely overgenerous donations to St Lucre and his High Priests, Bharkleed, Hirsuit and Whedd.

And how did he, His Eminence, Bharkleed the Fervently Exalted, know that all this potential for financial worship and devotion existed within the bounds of Cranachan? Easy. The order book from the Translittoral Mollusc Trading Company of Shirm was in his pocket. An order for five thousand roats' worth of mixed whelks and limpets a month for overland delivery to Cranachan. Any place that spent that much on such shellfish pleasures had to be in need of a saviorual visit.

And in a few short hours they would be there. Ready to start again on another unsuspecting clump of mugs all too eager to believe in their particular brand of the afterlife.

'Ah, Brother Hirsuit, Brother Whedd,' said Bharkleed as his two colleagues joined him. 'Our next port of call.' He pointed across the rain-screened mountains and offered a little prayer. 'For what we are about to receive, may we not have to work too hard!'

Still wishing that he possessed a pair of even the smallest of arms with which to rub the gurgling, rumbling seethe of his stomach, Ch'tin groaned feebly within the folds of 'Lady Challerty's Loofah'. Sadly, it wasn't the appalling titular typographical error that was giving the ruminatory heart-ache, but something much, much worse.

And the voices had come back . . .

In the dark they came to him. The same, but somehow different from last time. Not snatched, random phrases of nonsense grabbed seemingly from the ether like a fevered radio ham with an attention span of fifty-five milliseconds, but actual sentences, full paragraphs, almost as if he had a lecture going on inside his tiny wormy head.

'Have you ever wondered where stories come from? What is the origin of legends, the well of folk-lore, who edited faery tales before the Grimm brothers wielded their collective quills? What if Hans Christian Anderson had been an atheist? Yes? You, sonny, you at the back with the pink and purple baldric? . . . no, no, "your mother's knee" is not the right answer. Yes, I know that's what she told you, dear, but it's wrong . . . yes? The lovely girl with the delightful orange wimple? . . . yes . . . mmmm. Oh no! Ha ha! That is the oldest misconception in the book, oops, 'scuse the pun. No. I'm glad you brought it up though. Hands up everyone else in here who thinks that people make stories up.'

Ch'tin writhed in abdominal purgatory whilst his head resonated with the lecture.

'See, dear, you're not the only one. Nearly everyone else thinks the same. You've all been taken in by those authors and writers and novelists. They are getting better at lying about it now. Er, you son, yes you. You didn't put your hand up then, is that because you don't think that people make stories up? It is! Would you like to share your opinion with us as to where stories come from . . . mmmm . . . yes . . . Oh no, no! I know that's what you've been told, but if you did leave an infinite number of typewriters with an infinite number of monkeys for any length of time you'd just get very inky primates! And an enormous dry cleaning bill!'

Ch'tin knotted his antennae in frustration as the voice continued.

'I can see that none of you have got the right idea, so I'll just have to tell you. Hang on I'll just sit over here and dim the lights a bit, make it look a bit more mysterious, there that's nice isn't it. D'you like that? Are you sitting comfortably . . .'

'Well, stories shouldn't be here really. They're a bit too dangerous, not quite stable enough to be allowed to mingle with this dimension . . .'

77

'Ch'tin!'

'. . . at's why they've got their own area, The Chapter Dimensions, to keep them away . . .'

'Ch'tin!'

'. . . nd stop them mingling too much with reality here and . . .'

'Hey! Ch'tin are you all right?' asked Hogshead peering into the folds of the book in his pocket.

'. . . really messing it up!' finished the lecturer.

Ch'tin shot suddenly awake and sat as upright as he could with such an inconveniently profound lack of buttock.

'You were making a real din there,' said Hogshead as Ch'tin stared about at the inside of the cell in bewilderment, 'Whimpering and groaning like there was no tomorrow. Bad dream?'

The bookworm nodded. 'In stomach have I hurts,' he added pathetically in this thin reedy piping voice.

'Serves you right for gobbling,' snapped Dawn.

Ch'tin frowned miserably, whimpered and curled up in the book again.

'Now look what you've done!' snarled Hogshead at Dawn. 'You've upset him!'

'But . . . how?' Dawn stared blankly at 'Lady Challerty's Loofah'. Something was definitely wrong with Ch'tin, he never let her get the last word without a serious argument.

'I don't know.' confessed Hogshead. 'I'm worried!'

'Worried? About the worm?' snarled Firkin rattling the cell doors ineffectually. 'What about us? Hmmm? Have you forgotten about being in here?'

'What's going to happen to us?' whimpered Dawn.

Firkin made a slicing gesture across his throat.

'What? For trampling on some plants?' trembled Hogshead.

'That's what the guard said! Don't you pay any attention! Grievous Bodily Herbicide! Oh, stop crying!' snapped Firkin.

'No!' she snapped, stamping her foot. 'I'm a little girl. I've got my rights! I've only got two days left and I want my fair share of bawling, sobbing and shrieking!'

'Can't you do it quietly?'

'Quietly? Quietly! You can't bawl quietly, doesn't work properly! No, no! What d'you want me to do, snuffle pathetically and gently dab my eyes with a little handkerchief? Pah, pah! Waste of time. I'm working up to let rip with a really good tantrum, leave me alone. You're a boy, you wouldn't understand!'

'Oh, please! I don't think I'll be able to stand this!' moaned Hogshead, rattling the cell door in hopeless experimentation.

'Well, why don't you try it. A good bit of raving hysteria'll probably do you the world of good!' snapped Dawn, redfaced. 'I mean, what else are you going to do? Dig a tunnel in two days? How about building a glider? Or storming the guards? What about chewing your way out? You thought *that* was a good idea before! Fat chance! It'll take a miracle to get us out of here! We are doomed, *doomed*!'

'Oh, don't say that,' began Firkin, pathetically attempting to comfort his sister. 'We'll be all right. We'll find a way out.' Inside he knew how corny it sounded. He wasn't a comforter, that was for wimps and cowards, he was a hero. Hogshead was better at that sort of thing. He knew what to say.

'Don't talk poo!' growled Dawn. 'We are trapped and in two days we are going to form a fifth of a synchronised hanging spectacular, and there's nothing you can do about it. Now if you'll kindly leave me alone, I've got some serious blubbering, unashamed mewling and frantic spluttering to get my tears into,' and with that, as if to order, her face turned a shade redder, her eyes screwed up, and like a peculiar new citrus fruit being squeezed mercilessly, she began to squirt everywhere.

'No, stoppit! Sssh, calm down. Hogshead! Oh, do something will you!' whimpered Firkin, feeling suddenly like an amateur plumber who turned the water on far too soon.

79

A loud resonant voice echoed from one of the other cells. 'Oi! Can the shriekin', darlin'! This ain't an 'ostel for 'ysterical wimmin wi' bleedin' 'earts!'

'I'm allowed to be hysterical if I want!' yelled Dawn as loud as she could. 'I shouldn't be in here!' She squirted a few more bawling gallons.

'Neever should I, but I'm not cryin',' answered the voice. 'If I'd made damn sure an' disposed o' my uvver partner, the way I'd thought of, then 'e wouldn't o' been able to grass me up! I'm jus' too trustin'.'

'Too stupid!' shouted another voice.

'Who said that? Who called me stupid?'

Dawn screamed on.

'I did! An' I should know!'

'Nobby? Is that you Nobby? What you doin' in 'ere?'

'Got dragged in yesterday by Achonite 'imself!' answered the disembodied voice of Nobby straining to be heard over the mewling racket.

'What for . . . go on tell me! Not let me guess. 'E linked you with the St Swindling's Day Massacre?'

'Blardyell 'arry, not so loud! I'm still in the clear f' that one!'

'Wha'? You really done it? Cor! I din't know!'

'Yeah, well, shutup!'

Dawn's eyes widened in the darkness of the cell as she realised that a) no-one was listening to her, b) the only sympathy she was likely to get was from Firkin, and c) something far more interesting was going on in the other cells.

'Did you do all fifteen o' them?' continued 'arry.

'Shutup!'

The rest of the prison was deadly silent, frantically eavesdropping. Dawn sniffled as she listened.

'At the same time?'

'Shutup!'

''Ow d'you get rid of all the blood? There must've been gallons o' the stuff!'

'Just lucky I guess. Now for the last time, shutup! D'you want to get me in trouble?'

'Ooh no! I wouldn't do that. You're a slebrity, a real star!'

Dawn was trembling as it suddenly hit her that she was surrounded by convicted criminals, responsible for a whole series of various felonious acts. Including mass murder. And he was called Nobby.

The first dark voice started up again, this time a little less forcefully, almost apologetically. 'Ahem. Er, Nobby? 'bout that thing I said before, y'know, 'bout doin' you in. I din't mean it y'know, aha, only jokin' y'know, er . . .'

In the gloom Dawn sniffed, took a deep breath and resumed her therapeutic screaming.

The red-and-white sale signs snatched at the stone troll's attention as she clumped through the largest of the cavernous shopping malls in the Chapter Dimensions. Suddenly a yellow and green stretch-lichen négligé waved frantically from the window display of Moss Bros. Almost before she had noticed she had veered across to the shop, tugging her son Chip at arm's length and plunged straight inside. She simply had to have it!

Snatching the négligé from the window she stomped into the changing rooms, ordering Chip to stay there and began to slip off her clothes.

Above the store a huge black cloud was growing, coalescing, thickening.

Chip kicked about boredly outside the changing rooms as blissfully unaware of the cloud as the next troll. His mother stripped off the last of her clothes, smirked and stepped into the lichen négligé. At that very instant the black cloud shuddered and plunged into the changing rooms, scattering clothes and debris everywhere, snatching a startled stone troll from admiring herself in half-price lichen underwear. And vanished before Chip's very eyes.

As if by magic the shop disappeared.

*

Paying as much attention to the secretary's cries of desperate protest as an entirely enarmoured knight would to a toothless chihuahua in a fit of pique, His Eminence, Bharkleed the Fervently Exalted flung open the door to the office of The Semi Automated Vermin Eradication Company Ltd, sole manufacturer and supplier of the Cranachan-wide famous 'Little Squisher Patent Rodent Remover'* and strode inside.

With acres of impressive indigo robes billowing violently behind him, Bharkleed stomped up to the desk and, pointing directly at the man behind it demanded, 'Are you entirely happy with your preparations for the other side?'

'Other side of what?'

'The distal side of that coil in which we are now entwined.'

'Eh?' grunted the Director.

'Are you ready for death?'

'Oh, yeah. Every day. The more the merrier!'

'No, you must have misheard. I said "death",' repeated Bharkleed looking exceedingly baffled.

'Yeah. An' I said "the more the merrier". I love a good massacre. What is this – a memory game? I'm not senile, yet.'

'Let me phrase it differently. Are you happy about death?'

'Yes,' replied the director, his arms folded across his chest.

'What?' spluttered Bharkleed. 'You can't be! Nobody is! That's what we make our living out of!'

'Well, *I* am. As a matter of fact I'm a fully ordained lay member of the warfarinnic monks of the Church of the Poisoned Mice.'

'What?'

---

* The Little Squisher Patent Rodent Remover consisted of two blocks of specially shaped locally quarried rock, labelled 'A' and 'B'. The instructions for use were as follows:– 1) Placeth ye yon block enscribed 'A' upon a surface of firm integrity and density,

2) Graspeth ye yon block enscribed 'B' with a goodly firm grip in ye right hand.

3) Placeth ye yon offending rodent in centralwise position upon ye block enscribed 'A'.

4) Bringeth ye yon block enscribed 'B' smartlyeth down upon yon block enscribed 'A' for swift and sure despatch of yon rodent.

'Yes! We meet every Tuesday. A large, and growing, body of like-minded devotees whose express purpose in life is to ease the passing of vermin to the other side.'

'Aha! You manufacture and distribute instruments of doubtless excellently efficacious rodenticide, but have you stopped to think of what will happen to *you* come your untimely exit from this great mortal cheesestore?' grinned Bharkleed with a demonically hungry grin.

'Me?'

'You!' answered Bharkleed. 'Have you got everything arranged for the final day? You, of all people should begin to appreciate the pain and hardship of passing over, having sent so many of our furry brethren to a swift end.'

'Well, it's one of those things I've never really considered. I mean it just happens to other people, doesn't it?'

'Up till now yes. But one day, not too far away, you'll find yourself in amongst a queue waiting to cross a certain river. And then you'll wish you'd met us earlier.'

'Oh yeah?'

'By simply believing in the Church of St Lucre the Unwashed your passage into the next world can be so much easier.' Bharkleed opened a glossy brochure entitled 'Death: A Hell of an Opportunity'.

'If I could just illustrate the evangelical advisory position which we can offer, I'm sure you will see why investing your belief with St Lucre will reap untold benefits in the next life.'

And with a subtly raised eyebrow of innocent curiosity another victim stepped on to the escalator of inevitability that led only one, certain way.

'Is your love-life slacking? Missing that first fresh sparkle of lust? Get back in the mood with 'alf a pound of aphrodisiac anchovies!' yelled a voice.

'You've wined 'em, you've dined 'em, now give 'em somethin' to really remember! Peet's Patent Passion Pudding! The dessert *not* to be trifled with!' answered another.

The market traders were in fine voice as they yelled and screamed their wild statements across the square, outdoing one another with claim and counter-claim, returning back-hand volleys of scathing insults when sales were lost, pouncing ruthlessly upon any innocent glance of interest and wrestling a sale out of it.

'New lemon-fresh window duck! Kills all known germs even under the balcony. Keep your street fresh, use a duck in your pail!'

Everything seemed to be on sale.

'Tense, nervous headache? Take all new Willow-bark and chew away your blues!'

People pushed and shoved their way between the stalls, struggling to move or fighting to stay where they were depending on the particular stall. Every day there seemed to be more and more here as other hawkers added their wares to the outer perimeter of the square, increasing the density like some growing organism, packing more people in.

As the morning wore on, hundreds of people swarmed into the square hoping to find bargains or something of interest, pushing and haggling, raising the noise and the temperature.

It was above their heads that the really interesting things were starting to happen. A black cloud was gathering, pulling itself together out of the other clouds in the sky, pouring itself down through the stratosphere like black bleach in a vast atmospheric toilet bowl. With it came a sticky electric feeling as the air shivered apprehensively, vibrated with nervousness and then quivered with the friction of fiction. It felt like a thunderstorm was coming, heavy and thick as if all the oxygen had turned to treacle, but nobody, even in their wildest dreams, could have guessed what was actually about to happen.

Electrical discharges earthed from above, glowing momentarily behind the vast black balloon of cloud before plummeting suddenly marketwards. The first stall to be hit ignited in a ball of sizzling anchovies, flinging sparking fish hundreds of feet into the air, scattering the crowd moments later as they turned into a torrential piscine downpour. The cloud grew, bigger and denser, expanding like a liqourice genie, until suddenly, as if alive, it raced to the ground, destroying several dozen more stalls in the impact, smashing feet into the ground, shattering the flagstones into a million fragments and hurling rocks high into the air. And there it stood for a moment, a giant gaseous column soaring skywards, swirling, pulsing like the ovipositor of some enormous nebulous insect, until, just as swiftly it retracted, disappearing through the hole it had punctured in the clouds.

And that was that.

For probably the first time in hundreds of years, silence fell on the Market Square as a few fragments of tarpaulin drifted gently earthwards and the stunned crowd stared at the wreckage of the stalls. Unsold wares were scattered randomly amongst the tangled prongs of canopy supports, shattered carrots and pulped tomatoes looking like a freshly splattered road accident, and a few sizzling fish spat and skipped as they cooled.

Apart from that everything was all right. Well, as all right as any bustling market would be had it just been stamped on by a vicious cloud that left a ninety-foot high solid stone troll buried up to its ankles in the very cobbles upon which it had been trading moments before.

The gargantuan troll stood utterly motionless wearing nothing but a delicately formed yellow and green stretch-lichen négligé and an expression of sheer startled surprise.

Fights for Women!

'Squads D and E to the left and right. A and B fore and aft. I want no one in or out of that thing unless I know about it. Understood?'

'Sah.'

'I said *understood!*'

'SAH!'

'That's better. Well go on then!'

In a moment a cascade of barked orders snapped out from the centre of the Black Guards and heavily muscled clumps of men dashed out into their designated places. Battered and mangled market stalls were snatched out of the way as the area was cleared of anything that could offer even the slightest hint of cover. Leagues of barbed string fencing were erected rapidly in a few highly trained minutes, curling away around the giant granite ankles like the spiky skeleton of a fossilised sand worm. In moments, cones of pikes gleamed in the afternoon sun, garrottes and spears fought for supremacy over catapults and oil cauldrons, and ball-and-chains clinked in quiet steel smugness next to the domed protection of shields and helms.

In short, they were ready for anything.

'All Black Guards in position and ready, Sah!' cried Captain Barak returning to the side of Commander Black Achonite.

'Good! Now we wait!'

Barak smiled proudly inside himself as he stood next to Commander Achonite. Outside he wore the arrogant half-sneer of command that he'd learnt from Achonite, the left upper lip curled just enough to show the dental emblem proclaiming his rank, the eyelids part closed so that the lower ranks couldn't see where he was staring and his nostrils quivering in studied readiness. He had to admit, he hadn't a clue why he twitched his nostrils, but it didn't half look good. Barak had once seen Achonite reduce a Vice-Captain with eight years' perfect service under his belt to a heap of spluttering tears in seconds, just by staring unblinkingly into his eyes and twitching those evil nostrils.

Despite his Cranachan background, Barak had progressed extremely well through the ranks of the Black Guard under a Rhyngillian flag, throwing himself into service with admirable fervour, hard work and the remarkably uncanny ability to be in the right place at exactly the right time. Barak flatly denied the long-held rumours that his fanatical devotion was in any way connected with a long-standing threat over the future of several of the favourite parts of his anatomy.

'Quite an audacious battle plan, eh, Barak?'

'Indeed, Sah,' he answered noncommitally. He'd achieved an awful lot by constantly maintaining an appearance of not too enthusiastic overeagerness. One of the things that he had discovered early on in his military career was the amazing amount of upwardly reflected power that can be shone on to any leader by letting them promote you into a position of authority that they are absolutely certain you neither wanted or would be able to survive in. Barak was especially adept at this.

'How did you see through their ruse, Sah?'

'Simple for a man of my military expertise, Barak,' answered Black Achonite staring up at the vast stone effigy newly planted in the market square. 'I've thought of this same scheme myself as a very shrewd attack manoeuvre, combining subtlety, flair and not a little showmanship for a stunning closing act of guaranteed victory. But not today. This is one attack that won't work! Before night is over there will be a bloodbath here! Besides, my scheme had far more style! I mean, look at that thing,' he pointed at the ninety-foot stone troll with scorn, 'it must weigh hundreds of tons. Now if they'd used my idea of a wooden goat to bring the troops in with, they would have saved themselves *so* much weight. Put wheels on it and the enemy might even bring it in for you. Must admit, though, I'd really like to see the catapult that fired that thing over the wall!'

Barak's head was spinning as he tried to figure the sense of the scene. Here was a ninety-foot stone troll that contained an advanced attack force of troops who, under the cover of darkness, while everyone was asleep, and assuming they had survived such a violent entry into Cranachan territory, would sneak out, murder the guards on the gate and allow the rest of the attack force to enter. As a plan it certainly had something. Although panache, flair and a certain sense of style were definitely *not* it. Idiocy was closer.

But an enemy was an enemy. There was something else that was bothering Barak.

'Sah? Forgive my ignorance if you can,' he began.

'Mmmm?' replied Commander Achonite, his eyes examining every contour for likely exits.

'I have been following all current relationships with surrounding Kingdoms, as is my duty, and I find myself standing here on the brink of another Black Guard victory girding my loins with valour, courage and, well, not a little utter confusion, Sah!'

' 'Tis not meet to join battle with a confused loin, Captain Barak. Why the confusion?'

If this was a new way of couching acute sarcasm within a sugar sweet coating laced with acid which Achonite had recently learned, it was very effective. Barak took a marginal step backwards and watched the Commander's hands carefully for any signs of diving weaponwards, as he nervously asked, 'Sah? Who are we being invaded by?'

'Ah! A sharp question, Barak. And one which will make this forthcoming clash all the more interesting . . .'

'Sah?'

Only now did Achonite remove his gaze from the monolithic effigy and look at Barak. Was it his imagination or had the troll appeared to look a little less, well, embarrassed when Achonite's military gaze had left it?

'D'you know, Barak,' whispered the Commander in a voice like mating burial mounds. 'I haven't a clue who we're fighting!'

From the far eastern end of the market square a cry went up, followed by a hand and an arm pointing skywards.

'What is it?' cried Achonite, staring for information.

The Guards pointed. The crowd of witnesses behind the rear barbed string trembled a little as another black cloud began to form.

'Clouds? Clouds!' growled Achonite. 'Stand to!' he cried. 'This isn't a weather class!'

'Sah?' whispered Barak, well aware that the Guard motto 'Disagree and Die' had a twin sister just as evil and just as ready for use. The phrase 'Contradict and Croak' ringing in his ears, Barak continued, 'A large black cloud preceeded the appearance of this first one.'

The atmospheric disturbance continued to grow, swelling visibly, expanding far faster than any normal cloud. Until suddenly, like its predecessor, it lashed downwards, plummeting thousands of feet in seconds, smashing into the ground raising plumes of smoke and rock.

'Ha! Missed!' growled Achonite smugly.

Vibrations rattled through the foundations of the very heart of the Talpa Mountains as, unseen by everyone, unheard by all, another several hundred strands of the Stockings of Reality laddered.

'Oh no, lad! Yon bewit goes through there!' chided the bearded tutor as the blond-haired Prince of Rhyngill and Cranachan attempted to kit out his tercel hawk for hunting. 'If you don't tweak it up tight he'll be off in a jiffy. Voom!'

'Look! This blinkin' thing won't keep his legs still!' protested Klayth.

'Ach! It's a tercel and they're *arms*! And what kind of a knot d'you call that!'

'Oh I don't know! Should the rabbit go round the tree then down the hole or is it the other way round?'

'You mean after all these years of teaching you can't remember how to fasten a bewit!'

'Yup! And this bit of string . . .'

'The leash?' sighed the teacher.

'Yes. I can't remember how to tie that to the jeremeys . . .'

'Jesses! They're jesses!'

'Same thing . . . oh! Stop flapping your blinkin' wings, you stupid bird!'

'Sails!' corrected the teacher slapping his forehead in exasperation.

'You serious? They're called sails? Where's it rowlocks and rudder?'

'Ha ha! Hilarious I don't think! Give it here or we won't get to fly it. Look at those clouds.'

Whilst the teacher wrestled with a flurry of leather and feathers Klayth looked up and tutted at the banks of black clouds gathering overhead. A rumble of thunder sounded.

'Are we going to catch something now?' pressed Klayth eagerly.

'I hope so. I'll show you what a tercel can do!'

Klayth's arm suddenly shot out and pointed towards the trees. 'Can it get one of them? Send it after that!'

He was pointing to a flimsily miserable excuse for a bird soaring elegantly into the trees with the aerodynamic panache of a mattress.

'Oh no! I don't believe it . . .' struggled the teacher.

'What?' asked Klayth. 'What is it?'

'I haven't been drinking today have I?'

'Not that I'm aware . . .'

'It's a borogrove . . .'

Suddenly a thing that looked something like a badger, not entirely dissimilar to a lizard and bearing a close resemblance to a corkscrew leapt out of the undergrowth spinning like a gyroscope and cavorted towards the sun-dial.

'Run!' screamed the teacher. 'It's a tove. And a real blinkin' slithy one too!'

In a second the tove was followed by a bellowing whistling noise with a kind of sneeze in the middle.

'What's that?' shrieked Klayth as a streak of lightning arced overhead. The tercel squawked.

As if to answer his question a clump of green pigs sprang from the undergrowth outgribbing furiously.

'Back to the Castle!' squealed the teacher. 'Them's raths and they're hungry! I can't believe it. It's not even four o'clock in the afternoon!'

In a moment the clearing was the exclusive haunt of a pack of happily outgribbing raths, slithy toves and a mimsy flock of long-legged borogroves.

Trembling only very slightly, the large knuckled hand carefully manoeuvred the final tiny stick into place on top of the others. Fifteen tiny effigies stood precariously on fifteen tiny trapdoors above fifteen fatal drops. Holding his breath, and trying not to quiver even in the slightest, the huge man tied off the final string with a slip knot, adjusted the other two strings and finally sat back to admire his work. He let out a sigh of relief and almost screamed as his whole delicately balanced fully working model quivered, shook and rattled as it tried to unseat at least one of the effigies. Mercifully it calmed down, settling back to its delicate equilibrium, holding back fifteen different large and extremely positive fatality potentials arranged in three arms of five, tiered up along the sides of a large pyrimidal stage. It looked glorious, and if 'Long Drop' Swingler knew an audience, especially a royal one, as well as he thought he did, it would be a real hit.

Grinning wickedly to himself as he poured out a large glass of Jag'd Anyuls he sat back and admired his genius. Nobody, in the entire history of capital punishment, had ever hung fifteen people at once before; especially not with a heir-archical triggering system like this.

Reaching up to a small peg behind him he pulled down a

large leather Balaclava and slipped it over his head. The smell of the animal skin worked its magic instantly, transforming him into Swingler, Executioner by Appointment.

'Your Highness, Ladies, Gentlemen, Children and other students of the Art of Creative Capital Punishment, welcome,' he shouted, rehearsing his part. 'Today, I have set up here an array to delight all you multi-rope fanatics, a scheme to thrill you advocates of parallel pendulums. Yeah, a splendid sequence of synchronised swinging, a jubilee of jolly gibbeting, a grand dangling gang of fellows upon the gallows.'

He took another sip.

'A roll upon the drum, if you please!' His hand reached out to the much-reduced handle linked to the three strings. This is where he'd get the crowd counting with him, audience participation was always important for a memorable gibbeting.

And then, as the final three figures were shouted out he'd grasp the handle, set his feet and finally pull!

The strings went taut, transferring the tension down to the three pins of the first victims, yanking them out of the trap-door and allowing gravity to take over. Three tiny bodies fell through three square holes, triggering the next three pins to be pulled, and so on. With each plummeting triplet Swingler's heart leapt with joy. It was so moving.

Tomorrow would see it performed for real! Before the admiring cold gaze of King Khardeen.

He couldn't wait!

'But are you *sure* it was a borogrove?' asked Surfeit later in the Cranachan kitchens as he poured another draught of tea for the terrified teacher.

'Sure? Of course I'm sure!'

'But, what's it doing here? I thought they were fictitious.'

'They are! And so's raths and toves. It's weird!'

The conversation ran over and over in Fisk's seething mind. He tried to understand it, tried to distil out the hidden agenda, the reality of it all. It evaded him completely.

One and a half hours ago, his ears twitching in acute curiousity as he squatted in the tiny passage behind the kitchen wall, Fisk had strained to hear every word that had been said. He had listened to almost an hour of mundanity before the conversation had shifted to the teacher's morning's hawking with Klayth, and boredom had changed to incredulity. Fisk always listened here after morning lessons. It was the closest to a real debriefing of all the tuition the next King of Rhyngill and Cranachan had received as he could get. Over the years he had been able to work out, and ignore, all the momentary flashes of romance with which the teacher was wont to illuminate his otherwise dull conversation.

At first, Fisk had considered the hunting expedition to be another flight of fancy. Then there had been the noises from the market square.

Fisk's black gloved hands tapped in extreme impatience on the arms of the eighth-century throne as he awaited the return of Vlad.

It wasn't everyday that sudden, unexplained explosions rumble through the fabric of the castle. It shouldn't take him this long to find out what caused this one. Fisk was seething with hatred. He hated the word 'unexplained', especially where it was attached to other things like 'explosion', or 'death', or 'robbery'.

Something was happening up there, something very strange. And he also hated the fact that he, once Chief of Cranachan Internal Affairs, and now, since the exile of King Grimzyn and his cohorts, the most powerful remnant of the once invincible Cranachan Empire, he was forced to skulk about in these passages and tunnels unable to find out such simple things as what was making huge unexplained explosions somewhere in the middle of the market square.

Well, all that would change. And soon. Once he found out how he could use this diversion to his advantage, he'd be there. His time would come again. A new arising would begin. A new era . . .

Bristling with excitement, a small fruit bat hurtled into the throne room, arcing tightly and pulling three g in a high-velocity wing-over turn. Pumping the air hard it sped forwards, raced around the back of the throne and screeched to a halt before the fuming figure of Fisk.

Accompanied by hideous squidging sounds the fruit bat's major limbs stretched, its wings melted, the black fur melded into a black suit and the bat metamorphosed into the slightly shabby figure of Vlad Langschwein.

'I wish you'd do that outside,' snapped Fisk. 'It is disgusting!'

'Sssssorry, Sssir, but I haff sssome newsssss!'

'About time too, you've been far too long. I could have waited for the *Triumphant Herald*!'

'Dat isss only publissshed tomorrow. Dissss happened momentsssss ago.'

Vlad then proceeded to explain in graphic detail about the troll in the market square and the second stabbing of black clouds far away towards the Talpa Mountains.

'Vhatt do you think it meanssss?'

Fisk stared at the floor, his chin deep in his gauntlet as he sneered thoughtfully.

'Keep an eye on what is happening up there and report on any further developments. I want to know *everything*!' snapped Fisk. 'Go now!'

'Yessss,' answered Vlad, standing and wrapping his cloak around his thin body in preparation for another meta-morphosis.

'Outside!'

'Oopsssss, ssssorry I forgot!'

'Cor, don't know about you, but I really need this!' said His Effulgence, Hirsuit the Very Enpedestalled, ignoring the gazes of intense suspicion as he necked the first half of a flagon of ale in a matter of seconds. His upper lip decorated with a veranda of froth, he gasped for air, and swallowed the second half just as rapidly, slamming the flagon on the bar of The Gutter and demanding, 'Same again, miss, I've got a thirst on!'

'Steady on, Hirsuit,' growled His Eminence, Bharkleed the Fervently Exalted, 'That's not behaviour becoming of a man of the cloth.'

'Look, I've had a hard day's con . . . er, preaching, and I'm blinkin' thirsty! It's about time I spent some of my cut!'

'I'm not denying it. Just be a little more discreet. We still have a long way to go.'

'Yeah! And I know somewhere I'd like to go,' leered Hirsuit as the barmaid bent to grab a pouch of pork scratchings for a regular.

'Where's Whedd!' snarled Bharkleed, scowling as he angled his wrist-sundial to catch any available light in the grim bar interior, 'He's late!'

'Always is! Why you recruited him in the first place I'll . . .'

'That's enough! People are listening.'

'Bah!' groaned Hirsuit, draining his second flagon and catching the barmaid's eye for a third. As she placed the frothing leather cup on a bar he leaned over and whispered, in his most becoming tones, ''Ere darlin', what're you doin' later? See, I've got some beautiful illuminated manuscripts I thought you'd like to 'ave a look at.'

'Oh! You men of the cloth, you're all the same!' she cried in mock disgust, thumping his shoulder. 'Manuscripts, you say? Well, makes a change from "Gravestones I have loved" or "Famous souls I have saved".'

At that moment an extremely red-faced barrel of a man dashed into the bar of The Gutter, robes flailing, and raced towards Bharkleed, panting desperately.

'It's about time you show . . .' began Bharkleed before he was shut off by the eager ranting of Whedd.

'You'd better get to the Market Square, quick! You won't believe what's going on! C'mon!'

'Who! Hold on, I'm having a drink,' protested Hirsuit, winking at the barmaid.

'There's no time!' babbled Whedd. 'It's a miracle . . .'

'What're you on about?' snapped Bharkleed, 'What's happened?'

'Come an' see. I saw it an' I don't believe it. It's huge!' Whedd was tugging at Bharkleed's sleeve. 'C'mon!'

His Eminence stood and followed the frantic Whedd.

'Er, see you later, darlin',' whispered Hirsuit before he was dragged out of the bar. Whedd snatched a small blackboard from outside The Gutter, tucked it under his arm and dashed off toward the market square, Bharkleed and Hirsuit hot on his trail.

For minutes he sprinted, dodging through crowds of people, ducking around sharp corners, hopping up and down as he waited for the other two to catch up, spinning round as if to catch his tail, reminding Bharkleed of a dog that he had seen in one of the Moving Magic Lantern Palaces in Shirm. Bharkleed was amazed, he had never seen Whedd move so fast for so long when it didn't involve food. Although, at this precise moment in time he would have been extremely hard pushed to guess exactly what this sudden bout of furious alacrity did involve. Even had he been given several thousand guesses and a few kilos of powerful mind-expanding drugs it's very doubtful indeed if he could have come up with the truth as it was about to unfold.

Several feet ahead of Bharkleed, Whedd vanished round the corner of a ramshackle building that was obviously designed by an architect who had never been introduced to the concept of the straight line or the right angle. Bharkleed followed and was confronted by one of the most awesome spectacles of his life.

Quite literally hundreds of people were standing motionless in the Market Square staring up at a ninety-foot tall statue of a particularly embarrassed-looking stone troll. Apart from the fidgeting of a large man in an impressive uniform, nobody moved. It was as if they were waiting for something to happen. The troll wished everyone would stop staring. She felt naked in only her stretch-lichen négligé, standing huddling like someone caught in the shower. If only they'd turn around she could run.

A scratching caught at Bharkleed's ear, grating irritatingly from the ground to his left. Whedd was scribbling on the stolen blackboard with a piece of stone he had found, carving a message into the black painted wood.

'What's going on?' asked Bharkleed. 'Did you drag me away from a quiet flagon of ale to stare at a brand-new statue of a troll? And not a particularly life-like one at that!'

'It's not a statue,' whispered Whedd, scratching away at the board. 'At least, I don't think it is! Well, I've never seen statues delivered the way this one was.'

'Eh? Stop talking in riddles will you! I've got a date waiting!' growled Hirsuit.

'It just came out of the sky!'

'What?'

'Black clouds, swirl, swirl, then whooomf. There it was! Doesn't it feel weird to you, like that place we went to a few months back, out in the middle of the moors, all those stones standing next to each other, what was it called . . . stone-hedge! This is like that, I bet you! It's a great opportunity!'

Bharkleed stroked his chin as he looked at the faces around him. They all wore the same expression, fear, wonder and irritation that they couldn't get their weekend's joint 'cause the market's shut!

All it would take is a little persuasion and they'd be new believers.

Who else could possibly be better suited to do the persuading than these three?

Whedd stood up and showed off his board.

Terrified by Trolls?
Scared by Spooky Statues?
Alarmed by the Afterlife?
Then Talk to ME!
Or Him!
And Him, too!

The Elevated Church of St. Lucre the Unwashed was about to benefit from this weird occasion to the tune of several hundred souls and all their worldly goods!

'Brothers, Sisters! Be not afraid of this monster,' shouted Bharkleed. 'For though it represents the End of the World, I am not scared, for I can walk tall and say "Get behind me, statue!" But I can hear you all asking, "How can he say that?" and "Why has he no fear?" and I say to you "It's because I know about the afterlife." Yes, I have a reservation on the other side, I have my passmort, my visa and my ticket is stamped. Brothers, sisters! Talk to me, come to me and I will give you that feeling!'

Whedd smiled in admiration: give him an audience and the smell of money and there's no stopping him!

'Sit down!' complained Firkin in the gloom of the cell.

'No! Not until I'm convinced there's no way out!' snapped Hogshead as he chewed at the door.

'You've been at it for hours,' growled Firkin. 'There's no way out!'

'Are you just going to give up?'

'What else is there to do?'

'Try and find a way out!' snapped Hogshead scratching at another panel.

'And you can shut up, too!' growled Firkin, scowling at Hogshead's tunic. 'I've had just about enough of your whimpering!'

In the warm dark interior of Hogshead's tunic pocket things weren't any better.

Ch'tin's digestive system was knotting and writhing in stunning flatulent turmoil. All the unfortunate bookworm could do was lie curled up groaning pathetically to himself. It was getting progressively worse, at times he felt as if his body were hovering somewhere between reality and nowhere, as if he were being dissolved into a million parts and then reassembled. And all the time he lay there and whimpered.

Hogshead rounded on Firkin. 'Leave him alone, he's not well!'

'What's up with him?'

'I don't know, stomach-ache, I think.'

Dawn pulled the book out the pocket and peered inside. The tiny green bookworm groaned and writhed pathetically.

'I think he needs to see someone,' offered Dawn, helpfully. 'He looks a funny colour.'

'He's always a funny colour,' groaned Firkin, miserably.

'You know what I mean . . .'

Suddenly, taking everyone by surprise, the small wooden panel in the door was snatched open and a lump of dry bread and a jug of water was shoved in.

Reacting more by instinct, and surprising even herself, Dawn leapt up and grabbed at the hand as the door closed.

'Wait, wait,' she cried. 'We need help. Get a doctor, there's someone dying in here.'

The hand struggled, writhed and fought to free itself. Dawn had both her hands around it, wrestling to keep hold.

'He's got the plague . . .' lied Dawn. '. . . and if you don't agree to help I'll hold you here until you get it too!' It wasn't a very good blackmail strategy, but she was under pressure and it was off the top of her head.

The hand tugged and fought still more.

'Hold still, or I'll bite your fingers off!' snapped Dawn. This seemed to work better.

'No! Don't bite me!' came a voice through the door. Hogshead's jaw dropped open. It was a girl's voice. 'Who's ill?' she asked.

'Ch' . . .' began Dawn.

'Courgette!' blurted Hogshead. Then instantly wished he hadn't. The first girl's voice he hears after arriving back in the correct time, except for Dawn, and he immediately thinks of Courgette. How desperate can you get? he thought.

'Er, yes. . . ?' came the voice.

'Courgette?' repeated Hogshead. 'Is that . . .'

The hand suddenly vanished from Dawn's stunned grip and was replaced with a green eye and a wave of squirrel-red hair.

'Hogshead? What are you . . .'

'How are you. . . ?'

'. . . doing here?'

'. . . doing?'

They both blurted and struggled to stare through the serving hole.

'Who's ill?' asked Courgette, recovering quickest.

'I think I am,' groaned Firkin watching the capering figure staring through the hole.

'Ch'tin, he's . . . You've got to get us out!' pleaded Hogshead.

'How? I, er, can't . . .'

'You've got to! Courgette, you're our only hope!'

'They've got good staying power, I'll give them that,' conceded Commander Achonite as he scowled at the vast stone troll. 'It'll be dark soon. They'll be out then! You'll see!'

Somehow Barak thought not.

He couldn't put his finger on it but as time trickled by he became less and less convinced that cooped up inside the granite creation before them was an army of eager troops ready to join battle. It could have been the abject lack of exits, or the peculiar sentient feel about the monolith (there were times when he had been convinced it had been staring nervously at him, crossing its legs to cover its vast modesty, almost as if it had been more surprised to find itself there than he had), or it could be that deep down he thought the idea of invading enemy territory inside a home-made stone troll was so stupid that nobody would try it. Or it might have been the sudden and violent seismic rumbling which began away over towards the Talpa Mountains.

With its epicentre at the exact spot where the second lashing cloud had recently hit, a regular purposeful pounding began. And it started to move. Towards them.

'Feel that!' cried Bharkleed from the far edge of the market square. 'The End is Coming! Here! Now! Ensure your safe passage to the other side, reserve your place on the trans-Styx express, join the Elevated Church today and revel in the relief of belief!'

'What is it?' whispered Whedd, hiding his alarm from all but his criminal colleagues.

'Haven't a blinkin' clue!' confessed Bharkleed, 'but it worked! Eyes down for a full house!' he added as a new wave of putative believers surged towards them, baring their souls, opening their hearts and unknowingly emptying their pockets, safety deposit boxes and high interest, long-term, index-linked savings accounts.

'Name?' asked Bharkleed, whisking a pristine Certificate of Unquestioning Belief out of his pack.

'Surfeit,' answered the terrified-looking man before the high priest.

'Address?'

'Third bunk on the left, dorm 4, Palace Kitchens, Cranachan.'

At the word 'Palace', Bharkleed's ears leapt erect, quivering like a diviner's rods that had just found a vast underground lake stretching away in all directions, scant leagues below his feet.

'Occupation?'

'Eh?'

'Job?'

'Yes, thanks.'

'No, no. What do you do? In the Palace Kitchens?'

'Oh, I see. Chief Pastry Cook.'

'Been doing it long?'

'Too long!' answered Surfeit leaning closer to Bharkleed. 'Far, far too long. I was there fourteen hours today. Didn't even have a coffee break. My feet are killing me – they feel like, well, something that's been stood on for fourteen hours without a coffee break.'

'Oh, that's terrible. Now about the afterlife?'

'. . . and that Turbot Gurnard, he's the Royal Fish Cook, he just sits on his backside all day gutting fish!'

'Shocking, shocking! But, what about the other side?' asked Bharkleed once more, hopes of finding any useful mileage out of Surfeit fading with the passing diatribe.

'. . . slicing up a blenny here, hacking up a swordfish there . . .'

'That's all dreadful, but it's *this* life. What about . . .'

'. . . and the things he does with whelks! Dreadful! Shouldn't be allowed . . .'

'Look, Mr, er, Surfeit, there are other people . . .'

'*I* should have had that job, you know,' blurted Surfeit suddenly, a fire in his eyes as he prodded his own sternum with angry vigour. 'Should have been *me* gutting the King's fish, filleting the Royal roach, poaching the monarchical plaice!'

Why me, thought Bharkleed, Why do I *always* get the nutters with an axe to grind?

'Yes, I'm sure it should,' murmured the High Priest in practised, non-committal placation, 'but, look on the bright side, it'll be the End of the World soon and that'll be all over, and you'll be able to relax in one of our specially commissioned condominiums for the recently cremated. If you're ready to believe, sign here!'

'I can prepare skeins of lampreys in half the time of that doddering buffoon . . .' grumbled Surfeit as Bharkleed cautiously guided his quill into his hand, into the ink and over the dotted line at the foot of the certificate.

'Sign. Here,' he whispered, and gave Surfeit's elbow a gentle shove.

'Eh, oh, ah yes . . . and won't *touch* boxer shrimps,' he continued as his hand absently scrawped across the parchment, 'terrified of them, you know. Terrified!'

'Yes, well. Bless you my son. The coffers of St Lucre will thrill to your donations. Next!' shouted Bharkleed into the pulsing throng of people, surging ever forward as the pounding grew ever louder.

'Prepare the men!' shouted Achonite over the other side of the Market Square, his voice thrilling with the excitement of the enemy approach. 'Head off their advance! We'll show 'em!'

Barak rubbed his eyes in surprise and stared again at the

giant troll. It was only out of the corner of his eye, but he was certain that he had just caught a look of relieved excitement flashing secretively across the enormous granite countenance.

Away towards the mountains the pounding grew in volume and intensity, accompanied by a vast cloud of dust, swelling as if some enormous whirlwind were whipping its way Cranachanwards.

'Er, Sah, don't think I'm being a bit picky or anything but, don't you think they're moving a bit fast for a fully laden army hell bent on attack?' asked Barak cautiously. 'I mean, if they carry on at that rate they'll be worn out by the time they get here,' he suggested, nervously watching the swelling cloud and Achonite's growing temper.

'Nonsense. It's nothing but the wind carrying their dust!'

Barak stared at the limply dangling flags above the Imperial Palace. What wind, he thought, there's more gaseous movement behind a flatulent lemming than in the stratosphere today. He was about to point this out when his thoughts were overtaken by Commander Achonite's barked order.

'Double the Guard on the Eastern Gate, Barak! Whoever they are, they are not coming in!'

A brief flurry of sedimentary worry flashed across the brow of the troll.

'Sah? Isn't this a job for the Combined Army? We are a security force, not a tactical military unit!'

'Nonsense. I'm well aware of our official role, but we're here, we're ready, and we'll succeed!'

'Very well,' agreed Barak, reluctantly setting to organising a doubling of the Guard. Inside he felt certain that the source of the tremors and the dust was not an army on the move. He glanced at the vast statue behind him, shook his head in bafflement and sprinted off towards the wall.

A flurry of confusion broke out around the three High Priests as Surfeit thought of something and pushed his way back to the front.

Bharkleed cringed as he saw the approaching pastry cook and furiously tried to look busy.

'Now I'm a believer,' said Surfeit staring at the side of Bharkleed's head, 'can I pray for something?'

'Yes, yes! Anything you like.'

'Oh, goody! I've always wondered how to get rid of Turbot Gurnard! Thanks!'

'No wait, you're not supposed to pray for . . .' shouted Bharkleed, but he was gone.

Mad, he thought, totally barking!

Black Achonite folded his gauntleted hands behind his back and stared out at the dust ball standard of the approaching menace, the thrill of battle rising in his heart, blotting out all questions, all suspicions that this was not of this world.

In a few moments Barak was directing Black Guards in all directions and charging up toward the Eastern Gate, scrambling up on to the wall.

As he reached the top he stopped and stared. The cloud of dust and vibrations was far closer than he expected it to be. There was going to be no time to organise resistance. Barak yelled to the half dozen archers that panted either side of him, 'Hold till you see the whites of their eyes, then give them all you've got!'

The cloud surged forward, the ground pounding as if a small island were out for a morning constitutional.

'Steady, men,' ordered Barak. 'Keep calm. We'll see them soon!'

He saw the source of the cloud sooner than he expected.

Sprinting desperately, as if the entire world were on its tail was one enormous figure, on a collision course with the wall. And not slowing down.

'Fire!' shrieked Barak unable to believe what he was seeing. 'Fire!'

Before catapults or siege tower repellants could be drawn up it reached the gate. Like a sprinter at the tape it ploughed through the bolted, triple-ply oak gate, flattening it and the two giant towers without blinking an eye.

104

'I said fire!' yelled Barak. 'Why didn't you?'

'You said "white's of eyes", Sir. Didn't mention nothin' about grey eyes, Sir.'

The thirty-foot baby troll surged on across the market square, its arms outstretched, trailing fragments of gate and tower, flattening anything that stood in its projectile path. The ninety-foot troll turned and smiled suddenly forgetting her near nakedness.

'Magma! Magma!' yelled the baby, spraying tears of lava in all directions. 'Magma!'

In a collision of tectonic proportions the juvenile smashed into his mother's shins and hugged them with acute seismic relief.

'Chip!' she yelled causing the ground to shake. 'Where have you been! I've been worried sick!' From one hundred and ten feet above the ruined cobbled surface of the Cranachan Market Square a vast slab of a stone palm began its accelerated decent towards Chip's granite earlobe. The watching audience cringed as the whooshing increased, shifting litres of air, surging punitively on. Suddenly, a smack that felt and sounded like some gods had been practising their continent-tossing skills, erupted from Chip's ear and echoed around the square.

'That'll teach you to get lost! Don't do it again! Now come on it's way past your bed-time!'

She snatched the youngster's hand in an earthquake of a grip and dragged the juvenile out of the market square.

'I've found my Magma!' squealed Chip, his ear throbbing redly.

Achonite stood and stared as the vast figures pounded through the rubble that was once the Eastern Gate.

'I don't believe it. There's no such thing as trolls. I wanted an army!'

'Stop whinging!' growled the troll, shaking a needle of a finger at her offspring, 'Or I'll *give* you something to whinge about!'

Unseen, a shadowy figure on the back of a panting horse galloped into the Market Square waving a polo mallet.

The gently snoring bulk of the prison guard snoozed in blissful ignorance of her presence as Courgette crept closer and closer. How her surging pulse didn't wake him as it pounded explosively through her terrified arteries, she didn't know. Maybe there was such a thing as good luck after all.

Having left her little leather boots at the end of the corridor and crept slowly and stealthily forward, Courgette's metaphorically frozen feet were now matched by a pair of real ones. She was now within feet of her target and every muscle was aching, threatening to snap as the strain showed. Inches away from her grasp lay the heavy iron ring that held all the keys to the cells. All she had to do was lift it from the guard's belt . . .

She crept a step closer, hardly daring to breathe, barely daring to move.

Suddenly, like a vast beached seal, the guard coughed, snuffled and twitched restlessly in his shallow sleep. The keys jangled on his belt, shattering the silence like a peal of bells hefted by a host of wild campanologists. Courgette's hands slapped to her mouth, her body clenching into immediate rigidity, her eyes green pools of terror. The back of the guard's heavy hand rubbed his bulbous nose noisily, he sniffed volubly, then settled down again. Whether it was seconds or minutes Courgette couldn't say but she stood for seeming ages before risking another movement, finally plucking up the courage necessary to grab the guard's belt buckle and begin to slip it undone. The stiff leather creaked as she eased the tongue back, desperately attempting to maintain an even pressure on the guard's stomach. There was no turning back now. In a moment the loop parted, the guard's girth relaxing visibly beneath her grip, her hand snaked carefully toward the treasured ring.

'Hello, darlin' ' murmured the grinning face of the guard in the dark.

'Ah! . . .' exclaimed Courgette, her hands guiltily grasping the belt.

'I wondered how long it'd be before you came. I've seen you making eyes at me.'

'Ah! . . .'

'It's always the same sooner or later. Bound to 'appen,' smirked the guard lecherously.

'Ah? . . .'

'You needn't have been so shy, love. Could have just asked for it! I don't mind. I blame the uniform myself. I know, I can't help it if I'm irresistable in all this leather!'

'Uh! . . .' grunted Courgette dropping the belt, letting it dangle at the guard's copious belly.

'Don't worry. I've got a special little cell that nobody knows about. C'mon it's private, nobody'll catch us at it!'

Surprisingly quickly for his bulk, the guard leapt up, snatched Courgette and dragged her off down the corridor, past three doors and then into an open cell on the right.

Puckering his lips eagerly, he flung her on to the well furnished bed and grinned filthily. After smoothing back his hair and checking the aroma of his armpits he considered himself ready for her.

'Oooh, darlin' Give us a kiss!'

Panic racing through her heart, adrenalin surging as the Black Guard approached, eclipsing everything, Courgette could think of nothing less kissable. A waft of onions invaded her nostrils.

This wasn't supposed to happen. This was supposed to be a simple rescue operation. In, steal the keys, out! Easy-peasy!

'Oooh c'mon. A big snog . . .'

No! No! Help! In a split second, she had turned and pushed, ducking under the rapidly approaching puckering bulk, rolling off the bed and dashing for the door. Flashing into the corridor she grabbed the door, slamming it shut with all her strength, thrilling with surges of relief as the mechanism rattled and locked.

'Hey, darlin'. Come back! Oi! Open the door. Hey, let me out! Don't you like me any more!'

She sprinted down the corridor, the mission a disaster.

The keys were locked in the cell, further out of reach than before.

She had to get outside and think.

How was she going to explain this!

'Courgette . . . you're our only hope!'

No, it's not fair!

In his time as a Travelling Sorcerer, Vhintz had seen a lot of very strange events. He'd initiated most of them and so he knew that even though something looked as if it were screamingly impossible and several kerjillion parsecs beyond the boundaries of probability, it did in fact have a very simple explanation, mirrors, sleight of hand, that sort of thing.

It was with this premise firmly in mind, in a puddle in a particularly undistinguished stretch of forest, that he was trying furiously to convince himself that he wasn't on the edge of a bout of absolute screaming paranoia. Over and over he was telling himself that the remains of the wasp that was splattered up the length of his black cloak *hadn't* zoomed out of the sky and deliberately stung him. He was also attempting to reason with himself that the root of the tree which he was now face down in front of, and the puddle he was lying submerged within, hadn't in fact worked in tandem to trip him into that position. And he was failing. Utterly.

Especially in the attempt to convince himself that the ancient leather-bound book, which was now lying on a leaf-littered patch of forest floor three feet away, hadn't, repeat, hadn't leapt out of his pack flapping its jacket like some deranged moth and spun round his head twice before deliberately firing an electric shock of several thousand volts through his left earlobe.

All right, so he knew it was a magic book. But it had never done anything like *that* before. He'd treated it well, never bent its spine back, never creased the top corner of the pages over, and never, ever spilled anything on it. Why would it want to do anything like that to him?

Vhintz hauled himself out of the puddle, stared warily at

the tree root and sat down with his back against a different trunk.

You're losing it! he admonished himself. Careful now! If you start mistrusting trees, where will it all end?

He brushed several gallons of muddy water off the sequin moons, stars, bolts of lightning and tacky enamelled signs of the zodiac that festooned his scruffy black hat and cloak, and fished four or five treefulls of damp leaf-litter out of his pack. Fortunately, none of the many vials and bottles of strange coloured potions which he carried around with him had broken. It would almost certainly have been most embarrassing if they had. There was only one vial in his pack which didn't smell as if it had been eaten at least once by a halitotic demon from beyond the grave, and the effect which that particular pot of love potion had on any mare's libido was legendary. It would not do Vhintz's business any good at all if he turned up anywhere either smelling like the bottom of a devil with bowel trouble or being hotly pursued by a herd of lust-crazed stallions. It was always a bit of a gamble what the welcome would be like for a Travelling Sorcerer; one backfiring spell left by a previous visit and it was entirely possible that you might find yourself bound and gagged and hovering above the local duck-pond before you could say 'Bring out your scissors!'

Vhintz, still baffled at quite how he had ended up face down in the puddle, stood and walked warily towards the large leather-bound book. 'Ye Aynshent Almanack of Conjoorynge, Magycke and Such', lay inertly in the leaves. It didn't really seem possible that it could have been capable of discharging several thousand volts through his ear. He picked up a stick and cautiously prodded the book's spine. Nothing. Not even the tiniest of sparks. He poked again. Nothing. Feeling confident he reached out and touched the cover. Feeling nothing unusual, he picked it up, dropped it in his pack and headed off towards the widely publicised hanging event of the year.

There was bound to be a good crowd at 'Long Drop'

Swingler's fifteen-gibbet hanging, and where one or more people are gathered together for entertainment, then so shall a Travelling Sorcerer attempt to ply his wares.

Positioned as it was in the small of his back-pack, Vhintz failed totally to notice the shimmering aura of corruscation that crackled and darted across the surface of the book.

In exactly the same way, fifteen miles away in a dark and dingy prison cell, Hogshead failed utterly to notice the shimmering electric blue field of tiny sparks that dashed over the surface of a certain bookworm writhing in abject discomfort deep within his pocket.

Unsurprisingly, they also failed to notice that as the distance between the book and the worm decreased, the effect squared.

Not many people knew about the inverse square law in Rhyngill or Cranachan.

Across the far side of the ridge of the Talpa Mountains the dust was settling over the ruins of the Market Square of Cranachan following the swift exit of several hundred tons of stone troll. Massive structural repairs would undoubtedly be needed before Cranachan could be returned to anything approaching security – as a hazily cowled figure on the back of a translucent polo pony was discovering, much to his amusement.

Precisely why Famine found himself in the Market Square of Cranachan when he should be approaching the final whistle of the Chapter Dimensions All-Comers Polo Championship, he hadn't the foggiest idea. But he was finding it fun! He was surrounded by people, real fleshy people, not novel bit-part players. Creatures with genuine appetites to play with!

With a flick of his wrist here, or a swing of his polo mallet there he could create vast waves of grumbling stomachs, screaming with curdling peptic voracity. Within minutes, queues of ravening hordes were pouring into the square making a starving bee-line for the kebab stall. And Famine loved it! He sniggered as he tickled dormant appetites into starving snack-attacks, he screamed helplessly as crowds salivated madly, dribbling like wild dogs at a bell-ringers' party . . .

Now if only he could make a deal with the owner of the burger bar over there.

What a perfect day! thought the tiny sparrow as it filled its little lungs for another chirruping blast of song in Rhyngill Forest. A wife and three eggs, a beautiful new nest in the best tree around, an important position on the Sparrow's, Tit's and Warbler's Residents' Committee and a wopping great caterpillar digesting inside his stomach. What more could a young and upwardly mobile cock sparrow want. Except for a good sing!

Unfortunately for everyone concerned, including the young girl below, furiously attempting to drown herself in a sea of turbulent self-pity, a *good* sing was the last thing this particular sparrow was capable of.

Disregarding this slight inconvenience, his ribcage expanded a few more fractions of an inch as the last vital microlitres of air were jammed into his lungs, then, bursting with vigour, joy and semi-digested caterpillars, he let rip. It was the avian equivalent of a frustrated bathroom opera star. Loads of volume, gallons of gusto and scant, if any, attention paid to lyrical exactitude, dictional phraseology or, worse, the microtonal delights of precise pitching. It would probably be written something like: 'Sqwok skworrrqk cherp. Cherpy churpy twit sqwaurrrrrk!'

Ranting, squawking and generally being irresponsibly cacophanous, the tiny creature was blissfully unaware of the seething knot of anger growing below it. It chirruped on, swathed in the blankets of rapturous unknowing, utterly oblivious of the fact that a hand was searching through piles of local leaf-litter to locate a small, hard and rapidly hurlable projectile. In a few short seconds the feathered foghorn would be totally unconscious.

111

Courgette's eyes seethed green anger as she launched the projectile with deadly accuracy at the irritating creature. It whistled through the air, striking the sparrow on the side of the head, knocking it flying from the branch in the arc of squawking expletives. Instantly the rock contacted feather, Courgette felt sick, quivering with the pent-up feelings of anger, frustration and confusion. She couldn't believe that she'd just done that. She had wanted it dead, just for an instant, nothing else had mattered. She had never felt that angry, well not since . . . not since . . .

Images of vast dripping teeth slicing down towards a running boy on a tree across a river flashed into her bewildered mind. She felt herself running, swinging a log, screaming . . .

Above her a small black cloud coalesced out of the stratosphere.

In the now silent forest, near her favourite well, she screamed out as she had then, 'Get away from him, you bitch!' Her arms worked, her momentum carried her forward and in a flash she struck the river nydd . . .

The cloud grew, swelling and billowing, spreading and darkening.

Her head collapsed into her hands as she remembered it all. She'd succeeded then, risking her life to save him from a forty-foot river nydd only to fail now. But now she was letting all three of them down. How could she tell them she'd failed . . .

Suddenly, with the quietest of sussurations, a lance of silver stabbed out of the cloud and raced groundwards. It gleamed as it plunged, slicing through the air, heading straight for the red head of turmoil thousands of feet below.

Courgette tried to figure it out. She had to be strong, had to use her femininity, she'd been suffering too long . . .

As if in answer to her unspoken prayers a cold blade of steel sliced into the ground between her knees with a twang and stood quivering almost as much as Courgette. She stared at the cross of metal, oscillating in and out of focus, unbelieving. Runes of ancient meaning glowed on the blade of Exbenedict, runes that should by now, if everything was behaving itself as it should have been, be in the hand of King Halva – the true born king of all the kingdoms.

Courgette stared. A sword had just fallen out of the sky and landed, literally, at her feet, at a time when she needed guidance, when she sought direction. It was a sign! It had to be! A four-foot gleaming metal pointer to guide her actions. Her guts quivered within, wrestling with themselves to stay calm. Then gave up. What the Hell! they squelched, Swords don't fall out of the sky every day. Let's get excited!

Wiping her eyes with the back of her hand she stood and grasped the haft, her guts now writhing in intestinal encouragement.

From the tangled mass of roots below a large tree a small sparrow blinked and shook its head in concussed confusion.

As her fingers encircled the handle, Courgette felt very, very strange. Where it came from, she would never know, but a hidden strength was suddenly unleashed from within, coursing out of the fictional sword, words like 'thrust', 'parry' and 'hack to bits' exploded into her consciousness. Her face lit up, in precisely the same way that your granny's would if you gave her a state-of-the-art, laser-guided, plasma-jet rifle, pointed it at the pack of little brats that had been bothering her over the last few months, and said, 'This is the trigger. Go on!'

Courgette heaved the sword out of the ground and, struggling under the weight, hefted Exbenedict aloft, pointing the gleaming blade skywards. The sun shone a beam of light through the high audience of white clouds, illuminating the figure standing suddenly strong, suddenly proud, suddenly important. The shower of golden rays picked out the stunning glory of the scene of transformation in the clearing, gleaming on her chin as it set strongly, reflecting off her shoulders as they flexed and strengthened from within, bouncing off the suddenly solid pair of shapely muscular thighs.

113

'Yea, verily! In truth 'tis a sign' she cried aloud, her voice dropping a good octave. I taketh up this blade for the cause.'

She thought for a moment, I carry a blade. I must be a knight. Yea, ye first Knight of Womanhood.

'I, Courgette, carry arms for the cause. I shall start a movement,' she shrieked. 'It's colours,' she looked at the flowers in the clearing through eyes alive with a new fiery spirit; a surging cocktail of defiance, let anyone stand in her way and she'd . . . she'd chain herself to some railings . . . just see if she wouldn't. 'It's colours shall be purple, white and green and it's rallying cry shall be,' she began to swirl Exbenedict around her head in ever enlarging circles, the power surging from the sword, 'Fights for Women!' she cried.

The delicate poppy that was Courgette had become a heroine.

'Fights for Women!'

Having crept stealthily through a small entrance into the Hanging Courtyard of Castell Rhyngill and attempted to gauge if there would be any hostility raised towards any Travelling Sorcerers, Vhintz began to set up his stall. He slotted poles together, adjusted shelf alignments and draped a large colourful placard across the top announcing his ability and skill in 'Paracosmic shoe-reheeling, magical scissor-sharpening and thaumic wart removal. All potions guaranteed, all ointments applied under warranty.' He then arranged all his vials and jars carefully along the stall shelf. And waited.

It shouldn't be too long before the expected crowds of people would begin to drift into the newly erected area. Vhintz looked up at the sky. It felt like it was about to thunder, as if the sky was laden with heavy black clouds hanging in readiness to drown everything below. He scratched his head as he stared at the clear blue sky, then scratched the back of his hand. His skin itched from head to toe.

114

Half a mile away, deep in the bowels of Castell Rhyngill's prison area, three children were also feeling very itchy. Absently they sat and scratched, assuming that the irritation was due to the environment of damp, insect-infested confinement. And the fact that they knew that very soon they would feel the final tightening of rope around their necks.

Had Hogshead peered inside the hollow book stuffed into his tunic pocket, he might have realised that their imminent hanging was not the worst eventuality.

In the time since Vhintz had set up his stall before the neatly arranged gibbets, eight more strands of reality's black stockings had snapped, adding their numbers to the rapidly expanding ladder ripping its way towards the elegantly turned ankle of fate.

In a tiny, dimly lit room in Cranachan, awash with dense plumes of smoke, three figures pored over a series of parchments and maps. Their heads bent in deep concentration, they spoke in hushed tones, discussing their current progress.

'But what about here?' asked the tallest one pointing at an area just inside the shadow of the Palace Fortress. 'How many have we got in there?'

'Only twelve,' answered the small fat one.

'But they're the ones we want! That's where all the money is!'

'No it's not,' disagreed His Emmolient, Whedd the Most Lubricious. 'I'll tell you where all the money is! We need to . . .'

There was a sudden knock on the door.

His Eminence, Bharkleed the Fervently Exalted glared angrily across the tiny rented room, panic flashing across his face, before flicking his gaze back to the pile of Certificates of Unquestioning Belief, then at the door again.

'Hide them! Quick!' he snapped, pushing the pile of papers towards Hirsuit. 'Nobody must see them!'

'Just a moment,' he called to the door, in as pious a voice

as he could muster, his eyebrows knitting fearful blankets of apprehension as thoughts begged for answers.

'Light that!' whispered Bharkleed throwing a large scented stick at Whedd. 'Fast! And get your hassock on!'

Knuckles contacted the door-panels again.

'A moment, please!' he said, stubbing out his hastily rolled cigarette and hiding the map of Cranachan.

'Matches? Bharkleed?' whispered Whedd urgently.

'No. You've got them . . .'

'Hirsuit? . . .'

'What . . .' he snapped looking up from the pile of Certificates being stuffed into a case.

The door was knocked once more, 'Hello?' came a rather quavery voice.

'Matches. . . ?' whispered Whedd, close to panic.

'No,' grunted Hirsuit.

The door handle was slowly turned.

'Chant!' urged Bharkleed. 'Now!' Had his brow been entered in a furrowing contest he would have beaten the expert teams hands down. Hirsuit, lost for anywhere to put his cigarette stub, withdrew it into his mouth and held his breath.

'Ommmmnnahhmmmohhh . . .' groaned Whedd gripping the joss stick in his hands, closing his eyes and swaying gently.

'Mmmmmm . . .' added Hirsuit.

The door creaked open. ''scuse me barging in like this,' said a tiny animated fossil of ageing womanhood, struggling under a tray of blue crockery and biscuits, 'but I heard you prayin' an' I was wonderin' if you'd like a nice cup of tea!'

'Ommmnaahee . . . ooh Mrs Servyette! Oh, that is so kind,' said Bharkleed oozing sincere gratitude and hiding his acute irritation as well as Hirsuit's last few seconds of frantically secreting the Certificates. 'How thoughtful. Prayer can be such thirsty work!'

'Would you like me to pour?' croaked Mrs Servyette, her hand hovering over the teapot like an arthritically circling vulture. Hirsuit started to turn red, smoke curling out under his lip.

'No, thankyou. Though we are men of the cloth we are quite capable . . .'

'Whilst I'm here would you like a nice piece of cake, your Eminence? It's just come out of the oven. I know how partial you clergyfolk are to cake.'

'No, thankyou. The biscuits are fine,' insisted Bharkleed guiding the frail old woman towards the open door, his oozing patience wearing thin. 'Now if you don't mind we've still got a lot of praying to do.'

Hirsuit turned crimson with a hint of green, like a confused traffic light.

'Of course. I'll leave you to it, then. But if you need anything . . .'

'Yes, thankyou, Mrs Servyette,' finished Bharkleed finally closing the door, wiping his brow and breathing a huge sigh of relief.

Hirsuit collapsed on to the table in a fit of coughing and a cloud of suddenly exhaled smoke.

'Now, where were we?' snapped Bharkleed, pulling the map out from under the acres of his purple robe and spreading it once again upon the table.

'Whedd was about to tell us what we should do next,' growled Hirsuit sarcastically between splutters.

'Ah, yes! Tell us,' urged Bharkleed.

'Well, it seems to me that we aren't doin' as well in this area as we should be because we haven't . . .'

The door was struck again, 'Hello!'

Hirsuit snatched at the pile of Certificates pulling them in an avalanche on to the floor below the table. 'Now what!' he mouthed.

'Just a minute!' answered Bharkleed, shrugging his shoulders desperately.

'Ohmmaahnnahhh . . .' began Whedd again.

The handle turned and Mrs Servyette wobbled fraily in. 'I just thought I'd bring you these,' she croaked waving a small box of matches, 'only I saw your candles weren't lit and I thought to myself "I wonder if they need a light," I thought, so I brought up the matches to see if you wanted them at all.'

'Thankyou, Mrs Servyette. That's very perceptive. You don't get the same atmosphere without everything lit. We'll use them, now thankyou, but we are busy.' Bharkleed snatched the box and bustled their hostess through the door.

'Are you sure you wouldn't like a nice piece of cake? I baked it specially,' cackled Mrs Servyette through the closing door.

'No! Leave us alone. We're busy! We, er, we've got a lot of souls to save!'

'Ooh, well could you save a bit for me?' asked Mrs Servyette as she vanished down the stairs.

'Yes, yes. Goodbye!' he slammed the door, then turned to Whedd. 'What were you trying to say?'

'We are missing one vital ingredient here. One thing which, if we had it, would give us the instant unanimous support of all the people of Cranachan,' answered Whedd.

The door was knocked and swung suddenly open, taking all three priests by surprise. Mrs Servyette stood with a bowl and a sponge in her hand. 'Er, I just had my oil anointing kit out and I was wondering if you'd like your feet doing?'

'What?' snapped Bharkleed.

'Urgh!' cringed Hirsuit. 'Sounds disgusting!'

'Go away!' snarled Whedd. 'Leave us alone! Stop disturbing us!'

'I take it that's a no, then,' said Mrs Servyette.

'Correct!' confirmed Bharkleed.

'Well, I just thought I'd ask, you know there's some clergy who like it while they're praying!'

'I'm sure there are,' Hirsuit closed the door and shoved a chair behind it.

'Whedd, please continue,' muttered Bharkleed.

'Er, ahem, yes. Look on the map. We've got a massive patch of support here in the poor sections,' he pointed as he spoke, 'but they're financially useless. We've got a fair

118

following in this medium bit and very little here, right where we need it. The filthy rich bit. The very centre that needs the most "cleansing"!'

'Well, we know that!' snapped Hirsuit. 'What's your point?'

'Look at this,' he pointed to the Imperial Palace Fortress squatting inside the Cranachan walls. 'Nothing!'

'Yeah? And . . .'

'Well, we need the support of someone important to start the ball rolling. Someone who's word is final . . .'

'Yes . . .' agreed Bharkleed, his eyes focusing intently on the map of the fortress.

'. . . whose opinion everyone follows, whether they agree with it or not . . .'

'I see what you mean. We need to see . . .'

'The King,' finished Whedd triumphantly. 'If we have him we'll get everyone else easily.'

Hirsuit nodded.

'I suggest, in that case,' said Bharkleed, 'a proposed motion of a Royal Visitation to persuade His Regality, King Khardeen of Rhyngill and Cranachan, that a lifetime of dedicated belief in the Elevated Church of St Lucre the Unwashed is the best thing he ever did!'

'Motion seconded,' agreed Whedd.

'Carried,' confirmed His Eminence, Bharkleed staring greedily at the small rectangle of parchment that represented the King's personal treasury and grinning wickedly.

'Anyone fancy a cuppa?' he added. 'All this greed is making me thirsty!'

It appeared that fifteen naked scarecrow slaves were lashed together in three rows of five, marching up and over a wooden pyramid in the Hanging Courtyard of Castell Rhyngill. Ropes linked the complex series of poles and supports in baffling arrays of tortuous rigging, connecting one trap-door to the release mechanism of the next gibbet.

'Long Drop' Swingler's heart swelled with pride as he saw

the masterfully crafted stage set for his executionary extravaganza and decorated with a series of terraces and gardens. He strutted forward to the master release handle raised high on its very own podium. It would be from here that he'd start the whole show. Just as the royal guest breaks the bottle across the prow of the long boat, giving it that extra moment of inertia to set it off down that slippery slope of inevitability, so he would release the lever before a capacity crowd eager to see justice done. He could almost hear the cheers now, the rapturous thrilling tumult as fifteen more souls passed over the great divide. And all in a few short hours . . .

Time to chivvy the guards along.

There was much still to do . . . prepare the cast, get them into the green room . . . weigh them carefully . . . and pray for the weather to stay fine.

Suddenly something caught Swingler's eagle eye – a change to his plan. This would not do! At the rear of the three final gibbets, three tall poles had been erected, with a flag furled atop each.

Swingler's blood boiled. What was the meaning of this? In a rage he leapt down from the release pedestal and stomped forward, seething.

'You, man!' he yelled at the top of his voice to a labourer up one of the poles. 'Yes, you! What is the meaning of these . . . these things? They're not in the original plan. What d'you think you're doing?'

'Er, sorry, guv. Don't know. I just put the things up,' answered the man up the pole.

'Well, take them down. Immediately! If not sooner!'

'Sorry, guv, but I've got orders . . .'

'Hello,' interrupted a little man who had suddenly appeared at Swingler's vast elbow. 'Er, may I be of assistance?'

---

* The green room. A high-security waiting-room specially built for collecting the cast of Swingler's multiple executions. Its name was thought to derive from the frequently witnessed greenish pallor adopted by several of the room's more sensitive occupants in the last few seconds before their final departure. It was thought to be brought on by a peculiarly acute type of stage fright.

'Who are you?' demanded the Executioner.

'Wyllyums, the site manager,' replied the little man rubbing his hands.

'Aha! Well I want to know what those three things are doing at the back.'

'Being assembled, I believe. And, er, who might you be?'

'The name's Swingler. You might have heard of me.'

The site manager thought hard. 'Swingler . . . Swingler, er, I . . .'

'Here's a clue,' growled the Executioner. 'I kill people!'

'Swing . . . oh! Sweet chariots! *That* Swingler. Ha! Er . . .' Wyllyums swallowed hard. 'I didn't recognise you without your mask! What may I do for you, sir?'

'What the hell are those things, for the third time of asking!'

'Oh! A little, er, addition of my own. Er, I'll, er, show you.'

He turned, gesturing furiously to the man up the flag-pole. 'On my word I want you to give Mr Swingler a demonstration. All right!'

The man nodded, scrambling down as Wyllyums took Swingler's elbow, walking him carefully away, horribly aware that in the next few seconds he might well be joining the other fifteen victims.

'It'll be linked to the feet of the final three, er, special guests,' the site manager explained, 'in the same way that the others are. Now, picture the scene, everything's going lovely, they've dropped in sequence, whump, whump, whump, nine down, we come to the last few, the crowd are going wild and, whump, whump, the last three pull the flags at the same time and . . .' He turned and waved, '. . . the flags unfurl.'

Three flags dropped slowly, fluttering in the wind, accompanied by a sickening silence from Swingler. The Executioner frowned as he read each of the words printed on the flags. Then slowly a grin spread across his face and a look of acute relief washed Wyllyums.

He liked it.

Swingler patted the site manager's head and sauntered off towards the castle. He looked back only once. It was going to be good. What a way to end. Nice touch. The King would love it.

The three flags fluttered proudly proclaiming, 'That's all folks!'

Creeping stealthily down the dark prison corridor, her jaw set firm, her attitude as solid as her thighs, Exbenedict clutched tightly, Courgette approached the cell where Firkin, Hogshead and Dawn were incarcerated. Without making a sound she eased open the hatch and, staring warily down the length of the corridor, whispered inside.

'Hail and well met! 'Tis me, good companions! I'm afeared I cannot remaineth long so listen with care, only once shall I uttereth this. Keys are unavailable, but hold, I willst gain thy freedom with certainty. A plan hatches. Remaineth thee alert and ready. Understood? ... Understood? ... Hello? ...'

Her brow furrowed in query as she bent low and squinted inside the hatch.

'Hail you? ... anybody there?'

A green eye stared through into the dark interior of the dripping damp cell, searching out every detail, investigating every corner. It was all there, exactly as she recalled, complete in every detail, except for Hogshead, Firkin and Dawn.

A flash of panic raced icicle fingers up and down the xylophone of her spine as the truth hit her. It could already be too late!

On the far side of the Space-Tome Continuum, in a small southerly region of high pointed mountains and deep, dark valleys, a creatured soared through the clouds. Its wings flapped in huge arcs, lazily shifting thousands of litres of air with each vast downdraught, propelling itself and its

122

passenger through the still blue void. Its long antennae and the spear-sharp tip of its fifty-foot tail casually twitched to an infectious salsa rhythm unheard outside the confines of its sphagnum moss earphone covers. On a whim, matching a devilishly clever keychange, it folded one scaly aerofoil section, momentarily tucking it behind its snaky neck, flipping on to its back and cruised on through the blue, the sun sparkling off the gold-encrusted skin of its serpentine belly.

'Aaargh!' squealed the rider, suddenly jolted alert, horrified to find himself clinging desperately to the tiny horns sticking out of the massive head. 'What are you playing at? Roll over, are you trying to kill me! I'm slipping! Roll over!' yelled Prince Khevynn, his face turning almost as white as his knuckles.

The dragon, grinning widely to itself as it mouthed ancient words to the song blasting through its ears, cruised on in nonchalant backstroke apparently heedless to its rider's cries.

'Turn over! I can't hold on much longer!' screamed Khevynn, gazing in horrified attention at the tiny silver snakes of rivers glistening between his dangling feet. Fear shot through his body as he felt his grip loosen on the ivory smooth horns, lubricated by the sweat forming on the palms of his terror-struck hands. He clung on desperately, the blood draining from his arms, the feeling ebbing from his already deoxygenated fingers. Another ounce more sweat on the palms . . .

'Turn over!' he screamed unheeded, model mountains passing below in n-gauge beauty. 'You can have extra carrots!' he squealed, hysteria edging his words. 'Double ration of paraffin!' a dash of panic. 'Extra oil for a month! Two months! A whole year! What have I done to deserve this? You utter, utter baaaaaah. . . !' He was losing control at precisely the same time as his grip, slipping suddenly free from the tiny horns and accelerating away from the dragon in frictionless free-fall.

Prince Khevynn screamed for three thousand feet, took a deep breath then squealed for another fifteen hundred, stopped and decided that it was about time to enjoy his last in-drop movie:– 'Prince Khevynn of Perht, my life in final flashes'.

Five thousand feet above the helplessly tumbling Prince, a slow saurian thought trundled through the dragon's vast brain. Three minutes ago tiny nerves in the serpentine neck had noticed the fact that the stress loading on its cervical vertebrae had lessened, indicating a reduction in the mass being carried. A loss almost exactly the same as that of Prince Khevynn and . . . whoops. The dragon opened one of his glistening eyes, removed the sphagnum moss earphones and looked around.

Five thousand three hundred feet below a small, prince-shaped speck tumbled rapidly groundwards. And it was getting away.

The vast golden dragon rolled, swooped and dived, chastising itself for getting so engrossed in the music. But it was that rhythm. So solid, man! Colossal spinnaker wings forced the golden reptile body in a frantic power dive, its talons flicked to the volume control, wishing it had a fast and furious rock track to listen to. A few screaming mandolins thundering major power chords to headbang to would be utterly splendid.

The Prince's mind, having re-run the silver spoon bit and the proud parents, was now thrilling him with the playing in the palace garden scene. The ground swam up towards him. Hurry up, he thought manically, let's get to the interesting bits. There isn't long!

The hundred-foot golden streak of aerial auric reptile lashed princewards, plunging fearlessly through cotton-wool clouds, flight-plans and air-traffic control only a vicious rumour.

A tedious croquet match trundled through Khevynn's mind. Is this the sum total of excitement in my life? he thought miserably as acceleration whistled in his ears. A bicycle shed loomed. No! spare me the first kiss, please! Khevynn shuddered with acute embarrassment as the little princess from next door puckered in what she hoped was a very endearing way.

Now the dragon was yards away, now feet, then it had flashed past, swooping underneath, catching the Prince before soaring skywards again.

'What the hell d'you think you're playing at, you stupid lizard!' screamed the Prince of Perht, shaking with rage. 'I've a good mind to stop your rations for a month. No, a year!'

The Prince's vast steed turned its glistening eyes apologetically on its master and looked as sheepish as a hundred-foot fire-breathing monster possibly could. It added a little mewling noise for good luck, just to show how really sorry it was, and flapped on, heedless of a tiny wrinkle in the sky ahead.

It was as if a magnet had been placed in the centre of a huge television screen, pulling the electrons off course, bending the lines of normality way out of shape. And it was growing.

'I might just take away your headphones!' he threatened and was suitably pleased when the dragon's ears pricked up in alarm.

The reality glitch expanded.

'Yes! That's what I'll do. Just to teach you to be more careful, I'll confiscate those headphones!'

The dragon whimpered.

'Come on,' insisted Prince Khevynn, 'Hand them over. I'm not taking any chances.'

The picture ahead went funny as the vertical hold on a small area packed up.

The dragon turned its head and tried the doe-eyed look again.

'I've made up my mind. Hand them over. You've been a naughty dragon! This might teach you a lesson,' scolded Khevynn firmly. 'No! You can't get around me like that. Stop it! I mean it. Give me them now!'

At that instant the dragon's tail brushed the area of instability, it squawked, glimmered in and out of phase with reality for a moment and then vanished.

The Prince screamed and plummeted groundwards once again.

'Er . . . about the headphones . . . I didn't mean it!' he squealed. 'You can keep them. Come back! I'll get you some new ones!'

The dragon was sucked out of the Chapter Dimensions, spinning and swirling as if in a whirlwind.

Prince Khevynn's mind closed the curtains on reality, respooled the projector and gleefully started showing 'Prince Khevynn of Perht; my life in final flashes II.'

'Oh no!' he screamed as he accelerated again, the silver snaking rivers larger than before, the tips of mountains already above him, the forest-clad ground whistling ever closer, 'Not again!'

'All right, my little darlin's! Time to go!' shouted Swingler grinning in the black leather Balaclava. 'Listen! They're cheering for you! They've come to see you! Doesn't that give you a thrill?'

There was indeed a trembling tumultuous cheering echoing around the Hanging Courtyard as the warm-up puppet act entertained the crowd. They screamed with morbidly fascinated delight as the crocodile snatched the baby and ate the string of sausages whilst the hunchback with the big red nose declared 'That's the way to do it!', promptly clubbing the policeman and the dog to excess. Quite what 'it' was and how repeated bouts of corporal hammering aided its performance was far from clear, but the crowd loved it and as the final curtain fell they were well and truly in the mood for a good hanging.

Dawn trembled in shocked horror as she finally understood that it was all going to happen. The realisation that her time on this world was rapidly coming to an end had only sunk in over the last few minutes when her height, weight and neck size had all been taken by 'Long Drop' Swingler and then she had joined a queue to be measured by a man wearing a long black coat and a tall, shiny black hat, who apologised profusely when he explained, 'I only do pine boxes in your size, dear. But, when you're six foot under it doesn't really make that much difference. If you'd booked in advance you could have had a mahogany or teak. In fact, if all of you had clubbed together I could have offered a good discount. You know, party booking! Free brass fittings!'

'Is there a "Long-drop" Swingler in the house?' shouted a voice obviously reading the name.

'Yes, that's me!' shouted the Executioner looking extremely menacing in the gloom, clad in his black death-cloak and matching leather Balaclava. 'What is it, I haven't got all day. There's a crowd out there waiting.'

'Urgent communication. Airmail!' The postman sniggered at his own feeble joke. All communications from outside the walls of Cranachan came by airmail. Pigeons hardly ever walk anywhere.

Swingler pushed his way through the seething mass of his terrified cast and stood towering above the postman.

'Give it to me, quick!' he snapped, his mouth outlined hideously by the black of the Balaclava. 'Mustn't keep the King waiting!'

In the far corner of the 'green room' a pair of ears pricked up at mention of the word 'King'. Suddenly Firkin wanted to hear what was going on. If Klayth was there in the audience, then all might not be lost.

Swingler fumbled with the tiny carrying tube in which the message had been carried, removed his huge gloves, and tried again. In a moment he had torn off the tube's cap and was straining to read the letters scrawled across the rough parchment surface. His heart leapt as he saw the red wax and blue ribbon of the Royal Seal. A note from the King, to him! Such honour. Firkin saw the seal, recognising it immediately.

Behind the Balaclava Swingler's face creased into a broad,

pride-filled grin as the massive tip of his index finger traced the words accompanied by the roar of an expectant crowd.

Firkin watched carefully, intent on gleaning any clue from the Executioner's reaction. It wasn't hard.

As Swingler's fingertip reached the end of the message his shoulders fell, weighed down by disappointment.

'Bad news?' enquired the postman. 'Do you wish to reply?' he added pulling a quill and parchment pad from his satchel.

'Trolls!' growled Swingler. 'Just an excuse to stay in Cranachan! I'll show him next time . . .'

'Is that your reply?'

'Twenty-one at one drop! That'll get him here, trolls or no trolls!'

'Anything else?' enquired the postman looking up from his parchment pad. ' "Your faithful servant"? Or "ever yours"? How about "Yours devotedly"? that always goes down well with Kings!'

'What?' growled Swingler, coming round from the disappointment, becoming aware of the postman again.

'Your reply,' the postman answered.

'What reply? Give it here!' Swingler snatched the pad, read the front page and tore it up in shocked surprise. 'Get out!' he snarled at the postman, 'or I might have a last-minute substitution.'

Firkin's mind was reeling. The King wasn't going to be here. That much he was certain of. But why Klayth was in Cranachan, with trolls, he hadn't even the faintest of clues.

'Curtain up!' shouted Swingler the Executioner to two guards as he pulled on his gloves again. If the King wasn't going to be there that was *his* loss. There was an audience waiting, a cast in here, the stage was set. 'The show must go on!' he cried as the guards began to haul on a pair of heavy-duty ropes. Cold, harsh light flooded in beneath the growing slit as it opened, catching spinning motes and startled scurrying spiders.

Outside the excitement climbed as a panel in the floor rose

slowly from between the first two gibbets in the middle row. The capacity crowd strained to see the first victims step out of the pitch-dark orifice into the evening sun. As the panel reached its full height the large familiar figure of the Executioner stepped on to the sloping platform, obviously grinning behind the leather mask.

'Hello, Rhyngill!' he yelled, punching the air in excitement. The crowd roared back its response.

'Are we ready to swing? Are we ready to drop? Well, I've got a great show for you all here this evening, let me tell you! We've got murderers!'

The crowd screamed.

'Rapists!'

Tumultuous applause.

'Accountants!'

Three young women in the front row fainted.

Swingler turned to the open entrance. 'Bring them out!' he yelled. 'Those about to drop salute you!'

'Ladies, Gentlemen, Children, our first guest will be a familiar face to you all, I'm sure. He's decorated our walls for weeks on Wanted posters, evaded the Black Guards' manhunts until finally being caught at the end of a four-night siege in a disused barn, put your hands together and give a big hand for the man you all love to hate, crop destroyer and cereal killer, twenty-nine-year-old Rhunt Plowsher. Come on down!'

Escorted by two guards, the first victim was manhandled out of the holding-pens and wrestled on to the trap-door below the first noose. As the ring of rope was placed over his head the crowd erupted with appreciation.

'Thankyou! Thankyou! And now, I'm proud to bring you a criminal who I will personally delight in seeing swing.'

At the back of the audience a red-haired figure crawled stealthily into a position from which she could see. She stared at the arrangement of the chairs, the aisles, the gallows and the release mechanism trying to work out the best way to attack.

'And now,' continued the Executioner, 'I'm sure you won't mind if I bring up another murderer. We've had this little chap in our custody for a few weeks now . . .'

Courgette cringed as she listened to the banal chatter of Swingler introducing his victims, all the time her hatred and anger growing.

Unbeknown to Courgette and the entire crowd, her anger was not the only thing to be rapidly expanding. High above the scene, a small black cloud was spreading from its modest stratospheric beginning, pushing vapour tentacles out into the sky from its source far beyond the space-tome continuum.

'. . . and finally, for all those children out there have I got a treat for you! Three delightful little monsters caught ruining the natural world, destroying the biosphere, willfully murdering the King's property. They breed vandals young these days! Anyway, I want a big hand for our final three guests – a big hand for our little triplets, all the way from the Talpa Mountains, let's hear it for the Middin Three, Firkin, Hogshead and Dawn! Come on down!'

Courgette tensed even further as the familiar figures were dragged struggling into the cool evening air and wrestled on to the trap-doors. An extra cheer went up as the nooses were slipped on and a small loop was tied around their ankles, attaching them to the three flag-poles, ready to drop their farewell message.

Everything was ready.

The cloud expanded still further.

Swingler swaggered towards his raised podium, milking these last few moments for all they were worth. In a matter of seconds he would release the biggest synchronised drop in history. One tug on the lever that connected the three ropes to the three trap-door release pins and a place in the history books was secure.

Suddenly the time was right. Courgette broke cover from behind a huge woman devouring a vast box of fluffy white popcorn and sprinted wildly down the aisle towards the podium. She whirled Exbenedict about her head like a deranged hammer-thrower on acid. Her purple cloak flapped behind her like the wings of justice, her white blouse enshrouding the purity of her heart and her green-clad legs pounding the steps, sprinting for truth. 'Fights for women!' she screamed, clearing the steps three at a time. Above her the vast cloud spat a gold dragon into the sky.

'Tuggeth ye that not, scumbag!' squealed Courgette racing towards Swingler as he grasped the release lever.

Shock shot across his face, mostly hidden by the leather mask. This shouldn't have happened. His big day, his big moment . . .

Hands from the audience pointed as Courgette bounded past. The hundred-foot gold dragon swooped out of the sky straight for the crowd.

Swingler's hands folded around the release lever, the three ropes tightening.

One of the crowd screamed as the dragon flared its spinnaker-like wings to control its descent and blasted a three-hundred-foot sheet of searing flame.

Courgette screamed, 'Pulleth ye that lever and thy shallst feel cold steel in thy intestines!'

The crowd erupted in panic as the dragon soared down behind Courgette, landing on the castle walls. People began to flee.

I never knew I had that much power! thought Courgette smugly as she watched the effect she was having on the crowd.

'Climbeth ye down from that podium!' she yelled.

'Never!' shouted the Executioner.

'Then prepareth ye to die!' she squealed, hurling Exbenedict as the dragon let out another blasting sheet of flame.

The crowd went hysterical, scrambling over each other as they fought to escape.

Wow! I like this, thought Courgette.

Exbenedict arced through the air, gleaming and flashing as

it flew on a deadly course that would strike the Executioner between his spleen and his gall bladder. Well, if he'd been standing four feet above the ground, half-way between the podium and the gibbets, it would have.

The ropes went tight. Swingler held his breath. The fifteen victims screamed and Exbenedict flashed through the release ropes spinning into a far gibbet. None of the trap-doors opened. Courgette dashed for the sword, snatching it from the wood as the dragon ignited another wave of hot panic throughout the arena.

Swingler yelled in impotent anger, wildly trying to knot the ropes as the purple-cloaked banshee raced for the back gibbets, Exbenedict swirling metal death above her head. In three flashes of razor steel Firkin, Hogshead and Dawn were free and being bundled off towards Rhyngill Forest, freedom and an insufferably smug Courgette.

St Absent the Regularly Forgotten

Deep within the lower intestine of the Imperial Palace Fortress of Cranachan one man was brimming with excitement. His heart was pounding as he lit another candle and set to polishing another pew. A low moan rumbled through the room, rising and falling randomly depending on the mood of its maker as he sang to himself and put the finishing touches to the humble interior of the chapel.

In a few short hours the Public Chapel of St Absent the Regularly Forgotten would receive its biennial blessing from the King. Every two years, King Khardeen ventured into the subterranean labyrinth that led to the chapel, murmured a few words of hollow holy support and never darkened the place again until the next blessing. It was a duty he hated for the simple reason that it seemed as pointless as it was archaic. Khardeen's life had no room for religion, he had no time for the namby-pamby worship of long-dead men who regarded peace and love to be the highest rewards, and were even prepared to stand on tall bare mountains proclaiming this, feeding the crowds with bread and fish, for free! Khardeen knew very well that the way to a man's heart was through his pocket. Those little round tokens with his head on held amazing power over the masses. The greater the difference between the amount the King had and the amount the great unwashed possessed, the greater the respect they were willing to show. Of course, this might have something to do with the fact that higher taxes meant he could afford bigger spears, sharper swords and wonderfully well-stocked torture chambers. Who needs the heavenly delights of religion when you can wallow in the down-to-earth honest criminality of extortion with violence? Fortunately, for everyone living in kingdoms with even the smallest stretch of coincident borders with Cranachan or Rhyngill, King Khardeen hadn't seen the limitless warfare potential offered by staunchly devout religious disagreement.

Pausing momentarily from the psalm in hand, His Virtuousness, the Really Reverend Unctuous III, sniffed gutturally, rolled the collected fluid around in the back of his throat and spat volubly on to the candlestick in his hand. As he removed the accumulated grime and candlegrease from two years' neglect with a long disused pair of holey undergarments, he resumed his vaguely tuneful psalm. Only three more pews and he'd be ready.

As he scrubbed and spat, the Reverend Unctuous became aware of a series of sharp clickings, moving in and out of phase, growing slowly in volume. It was somehow familiar, somehow recognisable. Something that he had last heard, oooh, about two years ago. It was, oh, it's on the tip of my tongue, I know . . . *footsteps*. That's it, footsteps, coming here!

With a jolt of panic he suddenly realised . . . They're early!

Three sets of purposefully striding footsteps marched towards the chapel door, their heels clicking on the cold stone. Reverend Unctuous, suddenly washed by the tides of apprehension, snatched the remaining three candlesticks from the pews, tucked them behind the yet to be christened, baptismal font, wiped his hands and stood in the aisle waiting for the regal knock. It was only in the instant that the footsteps halted outside the door with military precision that he realised his hands still clung to the ancient moth-eaten undergarments. Stifling a squeal he flung them away to one side and forced a nervously sheepish smile as the door eased itself open, followed by three gentlemen in long purple robes.

The Reverend Unctuous blinked at the strangers, hesitated, then bowed in a long sweeping movement.

'Your Highness! On behalf of St Absent . . .'

The figure in the centre didn't seem to conform to his

memory of the King, less handlebar moustache than he recalled, but then it was two years ago that he last saw him. A lot could happen in that time, a shave perhaps or even a new King. News never travelled so far down here. In fact neither did people, normally. One of the many things which Reverend Unctuous regularly prayed for was a congregation. Even one or two sheep to round up once in a while would be nice.

'. . . the Forgotten I would like to extend the hand of welco . . .'

'Ahem!' coughed the tall, purple-clad figure. 'That won't be necessary . . .'

Reverend Unctuous, still bent double, looked up, 'Eh? But I always welcome you like that.'

'I don't think so.'

'I do! You come in and I say "Your Highness! On behalf . . ." '

'I've never been here before,' said the tall stranger, grinning at his two companions and mouthing the words 'piece of cake!'

'Oh! I see! In that case. Your new Highness! On beha . . .'

'Reverend. Stand up please. No, grovelling won't be necessary. Er, there seems to be some confusion here. I am not, nor have I ever been unless it's true what you say about reincarnation, royal in the slightest.'

'But, what are you doing here? You haven't come to visit me?' spluttered the Reverend, turning a little pink around the collar as he stopped polishing Bharkleed's boots.

His Eminence nodded in his most practiced pious manner.

'You have! Oh, what a day! Visitors!' enthused the Reverend. 'And I'm expecting the King any minute now!'

'Really? Now that is interesting. Ha! Fancy that, chaps! The King, coming here!'

Bharkleed moved forward and, in the smoothest manoeuvre this side of Shifty Nick's Second-hand Cart Emporium, slipped his arm around Reverend Unctuous III's shoulder and walked down the aisle with him whispering, 'In that case, as one man of the cloth to another, I wonder if you could help us in our mission. As you have the ear of the King . . .'

His Emmolient, Whedd the Most Lubricious looked up at His Effulgence, Hirsuit the Very Enpedestalled and grinned. It was so good to hear a real professional at work. Judging from the look on the Reverend's face it wouldn't be long before an unscheduled audience with an unsuspecting King would just happen to be arranged. How sad!

In the hall was a mounting din.

Characters from all walks of the Chapter Dimensions were shouting, straining to be heard over everyone else, yelling to tell their story. Or, to be more accurate, to tell how their story wasn't what it used to be.

The Editor's forehead furrowed deeper as the shire-horses of concern hauled the ploughs of extreme worry across his brow. Tales of absence without leave piled ever higher. Thousands of them. Coachloads of damsels were being distressed far beyond the call of duty owing to the sudden lack of the heroes who were supposedly dashing to rescue them. Placards waved angrily, demanding hardship bonuses. Other heroes (notably a very, very piqued St George who had specially sharpened his sword, boned up on dragon anatomy and spent all the previous night polishing his armour to look his best for the Illustrator) were fuming with anger at being kept waiting for their missing adversaries.

Chaos reared its ugly head and everyone in the Chapter Dimensions wanted to know why. Not least a very be-draggled looking figure who had just staggered in through the vast marble arch and up to the Editor's three-piece suite.

The crowd parted, slowly unzipping to allow through the limping man, his clothes shredded almost to the limits of decency. Quite what held them on him was something of a mystery.

'You wouldn't believe what happened to me on the way home today!' croaked Prince Khevynn of Perht, collapsing

136

on to the Editor's suite, his voice aching with sheer exhaustion and not a little over-acting.

'Try us!' shouted the crowd.

'Let me guess,' grunted the Editor, shaking his head in weary resignation and shifting uncomfortably on the sofa. 'Your dragon suddenly vanished in mid flap . . .'

Khevynn looked surprised.

'. . . leaving you to fall several thousand feet through the air . . .'

The Prince's jaw swung slackly open.

'. . . only being saved by landing miraculously on a densely forested mountainside where the hundreds of branches broke your fall,' finished the Editor, moving a floral anti-macassar behind the bedraggled Prince.

Khevynn's eyes were wide with surprise, 'H . . . H . . . How did you know?'

'Just a hunch,' the Editor answered, staring at the several branches of conifer sticking out of the shredded remains of his flight tunic.

'The Editor knew! It's a rewrite!' cried a voice from the crowd.

'A conspiracy!'

'No! No, I . . .' began the Editor.

'He's selling us out for sequels!' raged the King of Hearts.

'No!'

'. . . and comics. . . !'

'I wouldn't . . .'

'. . . and Magic Lantern rights!'

The seething crowd waved their placards as they heard the King of Hearts shouting. 'We've all heard your views on street-theatre tie-ins and fantasy franchises with mummers and morris men. It's started. Literary sell-out! Script-napper!' he ranted.

Suddenly, the tall thin wizard with the off-white beard, pointy hat, owl and saxaffron robes stepped out from the corner where he had been listening with growing alarm. 'My friends, fellows in fiction,' he shouted, arms raised as if to calm a boiling sea, 'these events are far more serious than mere exploitation, what? Far more important than just rewrites!'

'What? Have you ever been rewritten? Do you know what it's like to have your world turned upside down, all the rules changed, everything scrapped and started again?' shouted Rumpelstiltskin. 'It's a real pain!'

'I'm sure it is. But this is worse! Believe me!' shouted Merlot (for it was he).

'This could mean the end of fantasy as we know it! If we don't do something soon, nothing will be abnormal again!'

'What are you on about? Have you been at those mushrooms again?' shouted an alchemist.

'Everything that everyone has said points to one thing. Characters are not simply misbehaving, refusing to turn up when they should, running away from arranged battles, and rescues,' said Merlot scowling at the doubters with his fiery gaze backed by the added power of Arbutus the owl on his shoulder. 'Face it! Characters are disappearing!'

'True!' agreed Arbutus.

A ripple of bafflement ran through the hall.

'What do you mean "disappearing"?' asked the Editor, tugging at his beard in utter confusion, leaning forward on his sofa.

'Vanishing! There, then not there! Pooof!' answered Merlot, wondering what it was they didn't understand.

'Where to?'

'Ahhh. The other side,' said the wizard pointing mysteriously.

'Other side of what?' queried the Editor, beginning to get a headache.

'The Space-Tome Continuum.'

The crowd exploded into hysteria. This couldn't be true. Could it? There was no way that old myth was actually accurate. Was there? Characters just couldn't be disappearing into . . . into 'reality'? Could they?

'There's only one explanation! A hole in the Space-Tome

Continuum,' yelled Merlot over the alarm of protest and barrage of literary criticism. 'And it's growing!'

'You're talking rot, wizard!' shouted the King of Hearts from the crowd. 'Evidence, man! Or I'll have you executed!'

'I'll give you evidence! What vanished first? Little creatures, frogs, rabbits . . .'

'Spoons!' shouted a small blue willow pattern dish.

'Yes, and spoons. Now we're up to hundred-foot gold dragons!'

'And stone-trolls!' yelled another voice.

'It'll be people next,' insisted Merlot. 'You mark my words!'

'But everyone knows reality doesn't exist!' cried a large spotted cow. 'That's like saying the world's round and orbits the sun, or the moon's not made of green cheese. I'm up there every day. I know!'

'It does exist! I've been there!' shouted Merlot.

'Me too!' agreed Arbutus.

'He has been on the funny mushrooms!' insisted the alchemist.

'Well, we've all *heard* about your mad trip,' shouted the King of Hearts, 'but you didn't send us a postcard, or bring back any souvenirs! Where's the sticks of rock with 'Souvenir from Reality' stamped through them. We didn't believe you then and we don't believe you now!'

Some of the more impressionable animals cheered. Especially the guinea-pigs.

'Wizard,' continued the King of Hearts after a swift jab from his wife, 'you're talking rubbish. This is all to do with exploitation of characters for monetary gains. It's the Editor's fault. I'm going to execute everyone until I get proof, and when I do. . . !'

'Off with his head!' shrieked the Queen of Hearts, quite losing any semblance of regality she may have had.

The King turned on his heel and left the hall in a flurry of angry placards. In a few moments the hall was empty, except for a worried Editor, a grumbling Merlot and Arbutus attempting to extract a mouse from the wizard's hat.

'Are you serious about this hole theory?' asked the Editor stroking his beard.

'Don't sell "Souvenir from Reality" rock,' muttered Merlot to himself.

'Merlot . . .' said the Editor.

Arbutus looked up from the mouse.

'But he wouldn't know, he's never been there, jumped up little . . .' grumbled Merlot.

'Merlot!' shouted the Editor.

Arbutus turned and bit his ear.

'Ow! What did you. . . !'

'Is it *true*? . . .' insisted the Editor.

'Eh? What?' flustered Merlot.

'This hole thing.'

'It's true.'

'Well, what can we do about it?'

'That's a very good question,' answered Merlot and shut up.

'Yes, it is, isn't it. Well. . . ?' prompted the Editor.

'I'm afraid that I would be lying if I said I had the faintest idea. If it carries on like this, though, soon there won't be anyone left in the Chapter Dimensions . . .'

Suddenly, with a deafening clatter of frantic hooves three horsemen charged into through the archway brandishing polo mallets and shouting.

'Where's he gone?' demanded Pestilence. 'Thirty seconds to the whistle and he just vanishes! We've lost the cup! First time in eight hundred and . . .'

The Editor slapped his hand to his forehead and groaned wearily.

'Famine?' he hazarded under the murderous gaze of Death and War.

Pestilence nodded. 'Damn right! Best striker we've got and he just . . .'

'It's kind of a long story,' confessed the Editor. 'Have a drink while Merlot explains?'

Death dismounted as the Editor pulled two bottles out

from under the table. 'Red or white?' he asked, displaying the labels and smiling nervously. 'Just leave your mallets and horses by the door.'

Merlot shook his head. Why me? he panicked. Why did I have to have this mouth?

'Listen!' cried the eagerly excited voice of His Virtuousness, the Really Reverend Unctuous III, cupping his hand to his ear.

'What is it?' asked Bharkleed.

'Footsteps!'

'Excellent! Right on time. Just what I like to see in a monarch,' said His Eminence the Fervently Exalted. 'Places, everybody!'

In a moment the three High Priests of the Elevated Church of St Lucre the Unwashed had lined up shoulder-to-indigo-shoulder beside Reverend Unctuous in the tiny store-room sized chapel of St Absent the Regularly Forgotten.

The reason that this chapel was exactly the same size as a store-room large enough to store fifteen long hundreds of goose feather quills, fifty-five dozen reams of letter quality parchment and three state-of-the-art lap-top printing presses, was entirely due to the fact that up until ten minutes before the first feathers were due to be put in, it was going to *be* a store-room for storing fifteen long hundreds of goose feather quills, fifty-five dozen reams of letter quality parchment and three state-of-the-art lap-top printing presses.

It took a lot of grovelling, a very large amount of money in an offshore bank account and a brand-new bright red Fraree sports cart, each, for the architects (Messrs Heeth'n, Blasfeamer and Hypperkryt), but eventually an exceedingly impoverished Reverend Unctuous III finally secured his very own place of worship. After dedicating the chapel amid a blaze of fevered public apathy, and hurling wide the doors to a surge of raging underenthusiasm, Rev. Unctuous III wondered if, perhaps, he just may have chosen the wrong saint.

Forty-four years later he was still wondering and awaiting his first genuine worshipper. He tried to console himself with the fact that perhaps the population of Cranachan was so at peace with themselves that they didn't really need the warming comfort of religion's soothing security blanket.

Yeah, sure. The other one's got brass bells on . . .

Ah, well, he thought, at least the King comes to visit regularly. Okay, okay, so it's once every two years and he probably looks forward to it with as much relish as an ingrowing toenail, but it's regular.

And due any minute.

The footsteps grew louder. Two pairs of them. One confident in its forceful metre, the other more apprehensively running to keep up. Suddenly, they stopped and the harsh sound of a ceremonial stick pounding on oak rang through the tiny chapel.

The Really Reverend Unctuous III caught his breath, straightened his vestments and apprehensively opened the door, bowing long and low as he did so.

'Your highness! On behalf of St Absent the . . .'

'Yes, yes, yes! We know all that nonsense,' snapped King Khardeen breezing in to the tiny aisle, closely followed by a worried-looking man, clutching a small, clinking bag and wielding a large book as if it was a shield.

Bharkleed smirked with arachnid smugness as the juicy bluebottle of Kinghood approached his overtensioned web. Hirsuit and Whedd grinned crocodile smiles.

King Khardeen stomped up to the altar, absently flung several drops of water over it from a small brush offered by Reverend Unctuous and cursorially muttered. 'On behalf of the Royalty resident in Cranachan I hereby, oh, what is it? What is it, man?'

'Er, renew the decree . . .' offered the nervous man, his brow wrinkling as he hoped that it was correct.

'Yes, yes! Decree to allow St Absent to be Regularly Forgotten and, oh, blah, blah, same as last time, right! That's all that done!'

Reverend Unctuous' brow ruffled as he tried to work out why that hadn't sounded right.

The King turned to the man hiding behind the book, 'Chancellor . . .' he barked.

Bharkleed's ears, eyes and consciousness leapt on the word, running it to ground like a pack of rabid dingoes. Chancellor! Remember that face.

'Chancellor! The bag!' growled Khardeen, scowling at the small sack of gold in Khenyth's hand. 'C'mon, haven't got all day! There's a flogging at two! And I don't want to be late. That first thrash is *always* the best!'

Khenyth cautiously handed over the bag and carefully opened the book.

'As a token of the Monarchy's continuing respect,' began the King boredly, 'for the devotional practice of, er, oh. Look, I can't be doing with all this official theological nonsense seeing as I had nothing to do with it all in the first place. Here's your grant as usual. Five hundred and . . . and. . . ?" Khardeen clicked his fingers angrily behind him, demanding a response from the terrified Chancellor. 'Five hundred and. . . ?'

'F . . . Five hundred and ninety-five gold pieces,' answered Khenyth referring to the book, his voice quivering as it echoed in the cold, dark chapel.

Bharkleed licked his lips. Gold *and* the Chancellor, things were looking up!

'Now then, Rev,' growled the King, stroking his handlebar moustache and staring leoninely at the suddenly frail-looking man of the cloth. 'It's a difficult world out there, you know?'

Reverend Unctuous nodded. 'Oh, yes, your Highn . . .'

'Spiralling costs, you know. Onward and upward, ever upward. The requirement for keeping the peace with our neighbours is growing almost daily. What with the cost of huge banquets to keep them sweet . . .'

'Oh, yes, Sir.'

'. . . massive tournaments with the best knights to enter-tain them afterwards . . .'

'I do agre . . .'

'Dowries to buy, er, marry off their daughters . . .'

'Oh, yes, Sire . . .' A flash of disbelief crossed the Reverend's face. Bharkleed listened to the string of lies with rapt interest. He knew exactly what was coming. It was so refreshing listening to a fellow professional.

'Also, closer to home,' continued the King maintaining his droll but somehow fascinating tone of voice perfectly, 'there's the continuing need for new investments.'

'Yes, Sire, I quite agree.'

'Building repairs . . .'

Unctuous nodded.

'New education programmes . . . Do you know, it's amazing, the youth of today are so sadly lacking in the essential disciplines of warfare.'

The Reverend's face dropped.

The King assumed a confessional look of sadness. 'Education's not what it used to be. D'you know, kids today'll swear blind that caterpults eat cabbages and turn into butterflies! And a bowlass is something for putting in a girl's hair! Shocking!'

'Yes, Sire, I do underst . . .'

Bharkleed quietly smirked in admiration. The King of Cranachan was a ruthlessly consummate liar. It couldn't be long before the punchline.

'So, as you are always telling me, Rev., charity begins at the Palace. The King slapped the priest on the shoulder in a way that just wasn't too violently threatening. 'I'm sure you won't mind that I've had to approve a huge increase in Palace rents. Just to pay for all these dreadful banquets and new education and stuff.'

'Oh, I'm sure you've considered this carefully, your Highne . . .'

'Ooh, yes. Very. Hours of soul-searching. That's why I'm giving you a special tenth of a per cent discount rent, starting in five years' time.'

'Oh,' grunted Reverend Unctuous, his face drooping with acute fiscal disappointment.

144

'What do you say to that? Generous, eh!' growled the King, tightening his grip around the priest's neck, his words entirely at odds with his ruthlessly threatening scowl that inhabited his monarchical face.

'Yes, your Highness, erchhh, very . . .'

'So glad you approve! In that case, you owe the Crown Palace Rental Scheme, er . . .' Khardeen clicked his fingers again.

'Five hundred and ninety-three gold coins,' supplied Khenyth the Chancellor.

The King snatched the bag from the bewildered Reverend and flicked two coins at him, bouncing them off the holy forehead. 'Your change! And don't spend it all at once, Ha ha!'

The Chancellor marked off this transaction in the book, turned and followed in the wake of the King as he headed for the exit. Reverend Unctuous scrabbled about on the floor, searching for the two gold coins that would have to last another two years.

It was then that Bharkleed made his move, suddenly appearing out of the shadows, oozing as he greeted the King.

'Your Highness. It is *so* refreshing to see a Kingdom's Leader happy in his life's work . . .'

'Who are you?' barked Khardeen.

'So many other Monarchs-in-arms are burdened with the weight and worries of rulership . . .'

'What do you want?'

Bharkleed stared hard at the King and continued ignoring his questions, well aware that, as with power-mad royalty throughout the known world, it was the only way to hold his attention.*

---

* Bharkleed had learnt this lesson after a particularly strenuous 'meeting' with Princess Copula of the Nhubyle Peoples of Southern Hedon.

Some countries are run as monarchies, a King or Queen rules; some are theocracies, the church rules; Southern Hedon is an orgiarchy, lust rules.

Commanding the country according to strict Disciplinarian Orgiarchal Guidelines, Queen Fornicula the Insatiably Rampant insisted that the immediate introduction of carnal punishment would halt the rising wave of crime on the

'So many Heads are scared of what the future will hold . . .' he continued. 'But not you. Am I right. . . ?' said Bharkleed slapping warmed oil on the back of Khardeen's ego and grasping its shoulders firmly.

'Er . . .'

'*They* cower before destiny as if it were a serpent ready for a final strike. But not you!' Khardeen's ego relaxed on the massage table.

'Go on . . .'

'*They* cling to the fragile crumbling apron-strings of the past while you forge ever on . . .' Bharkleed manipulated the knotted muscles around the ego's neck, chopping and slapping more oil on.

'You could say that . . .'

'*They* live in terror of the inevitable. But not you, Sire!'

Khardeen's chest swelled with pride as his ego was pressed into the massage table.

'You outclass those snivelling wimps. You shine like a star above their petty candles of honour. You are a *true* ruler!' Another slap of warmed oil.

streets. At the drop of a hat she selflessly set about a session of intense personal research to prove it.

Countless 'criminals' (chosen exclusively on the size and shape of certain physical attributes) were sentenced to hours of sensual harassment with sponges and baby oil, or long periods of carnal punishment in scented volcanic springs.

Having failed to convert Princess Copula to the Church of St Lucre, and barely escaped with his body intact, Bharkleed foolhardily approached Queen Fornicula with the same vial of scented body rub. He only escaped the dubious honour of becoming one of her many, many laboratory specimens by pointedly ignoring her questions, avoiding her lustful gaze and running away terribly fast. Fortunately for Bharkleed all of the guards were otherwise engaged in research.

It was following this narrow escape that Bharkleed decided to treat all royalty with the contempt that they deserved.

He also memorised a few other salutary lessons for the future.

1) Never set foot in the Palace of the Nhubyle Peoples of Southern Hedon without the precaution of wearing one fully armoured, cast-iron codpiece. Locked.

2) Never agree to go skinny dipping with any female member of the Royal Family of Southern Hedon. And,

3) Never enter a room in Southern Hedon with more than one female member of the Royal Family, especially if they have that certain look of 'research' about them.

Interestingly, following the introduction of carnal punishment to Southern Hedon the crime figure and number of young males arrested rocketed.

'Yes, well. Of course!' answered King Khardeen, polishing his nails on the ermine collar of his robe.

Reverend Unctuous squinted out from beneath a pew and stared at Bharkleed in utter shock. He had never heard anyone talk to the King with such sheer gall. Never in a million years would he have had the courage to do that himself.

'Have you ever considered *why* you have this power?' asked Bharkleed, confident that Khardeen's ego had been manipulated enough, certain that the King would be softly spreadable enough to ooze into the warm brown contours of the crumpet of belief.

'Because I'm the King!' snapped Khardeen, his egotistical shoulders tensing into immovable hawsers. 'Now, I really am very bus . . .'

'I'll tell you why you have this power!' blurted Bharkleed as the initiative slipped, cringing as the knife of persuasion buckled against the suddenly frozen yellow pat of the King's soul.

'*I* just told *you!*' growled the King moving rapidly towards the door. 'I'm the King. Now move!'

'It's because you believe in the afterlife!' shouted Bharkleed, instantly wishing he hadn't.

'Afterlife! *Afterlife!* Oh, that's a good one! You clergy are all the same. It's that incense, I'll bet. Cooks your brain from the inside!'

'But, your Highn . . .'

'The afterlife is a myth perpetrated by the likes of you lot to increase membership! It doesn't exist! And if I hear you mention it in my presence again I will personally see to it that you find out the truth sooner than you would have hoped. I am very handy with several methods of despatching, you know.'

Bharkleed held his neck and swallowed.

Khardeen turned and flustered out. 'C'mon, Khenyth. We've got a flogging in *this* life to attend! Afterlife,' he growled as he stomped away down the corridor, 'they'll

147

be telling me about angels and tooth-fairies and goblins next!'

'Well, I hope you're satisfied,' snapped Hirsuit as the chapel door slammed shut. 'Really convincing that was! Really captured a new believer there! You're slipping, Bharkleed. Losing your touch! Hey, are you listening to me?'

A voice from the recent past fluttered and echoed through the evil recesses of Bharkleed's mind . . . 'N . . . n . . . Now that I'm a believer . . . r . . . r,' it said, 'c . . . c . . . can I pray for something? . . . ing? . . . ing?'

'Y . . . y . . . Yes, yes. Anything at all . . . ll . . . ll' he heard his distorted voice answer in the Market Square.

'O . . . o . . . oh, goody! I've always wondered how to get rid of Turbot Gurnard! . . . ard! . . . ard!' echoed the memory of Surfeit the pastry cook.

'At least have the decency to listen to me when I'm insulting you?' snarled the real voice of Hirsuit in the very immediate present. 'I said you're losing it!'

'Oh, losing it, am I? Well, we'll soon see about that!' muttered Bharkleed, his eyes burning with the fires of determination. 'We'll see about that! Time to put part two into action! C'mon!'

Bharkleed breezed out of the chapel in a flurry of indigo and strode off towards the palace kitchens, two extremely baffled accomplices scurrying in his wake.

In the now once more deserted chapel of St Absent the Regularly Forgotten, the Reverend Unctuous III crawled out from beneath the pew, stared forlornly at the two gold coins in the palm of his hand, his forehead still smarting from where they had struck him, and shuffled up to a small wooden collection box nailed to the wall.

Sighing a long sigh, he dropped the two coins through the slot, blissfully unaware that three months ago that particular style of monetary token had been withdrawn from financial circulation. Khardeen insisted that it didn't show his best side.

And besides, it was a particularly good opportunity for reducing the size of the coins in circulation and hiving off the extra gold into the Personal Royal Packet.

As the saxaffron-robed wizard rustled melodiously and finished describing life beyond the Space-Tome Continuum as best he could to Three Horsemen of the Apocalypse, the Editor's face fell ashen. 'No, no,' he said dribbling with incomprehension. 'How do they stand it?' he asked. 'Are you telling me, Merlot, that there are *no* fairies in reality?'

'Well . . .'

'. . . that no one can fly?'

'In a few years they can. Aerop . . .'

'There's no dragons?'

Melot gave up trying to answer. He just nodded silently.

'No happy endings?' The Editor looked up from his hands, shaking. 'We can't let it happen here! It's hideous, people ruling their own lives! It's a total breakdown in discipline! You must do something about it!' War and Pestilence nodded.

'Me? Wh . . . wh. . . !' spluttered Merlot.

'Yes, you!'

'Why me? I'm just a poor little wiz . . .'

'You know more about reality than anyone else. That's why!' insisted the Editor, leaning forward in his sofa.

'I've always thought there was something weird about him!' growled War.

'No fairies at the bottom of the garden!' sobbed Death. 'How do they stand it!'

'I've told you all I know,' pleaded Merlot.

'Excuses! Look, you've been there. Go back and find out what's going on!'

'But, I . . . I . . .'

'That's an order!' shouted the Editor.

'I . . . er . . .'

'I'll have you serialised if you don't!' he threatened, 'Cliffhangers every week for the rest of your life!'

'Ah hah! Love to go . . . Ha, love to, what?' cringed Merlot as he turned on a heel and a key change and trudged out of the Editor's suite.

Serialised, indeed! he thought swallowing nervously as he contemplated the concept of being spread out over countless episodes of thirty minutes each.

It shouldn't be too bad going back to reality. It wasn't that unpleasant last time. Merlot looked back almost with fondness at the adventures in the past. That little bookworm! What was his name? Ch'tin, yes. Maybe he'd know what was going on.

Merlot sat down on one of the hundreds of benches that lined the yellow tarmac road away from the Editor's pad, closed his eyes and recalled the tiny green bookworm. He let his mind wander across the vast distances that separate reality from fantasy, trying to make contact.

Ch'tin was his best chance. If you viewed the world of reality through thaumal imaging spectacles Ch'tin would light up like a beacon of inherently magical worminess, a bright landing-light on the staircases into reality. It was this that Merlot searched for now, as he unhitched his mind from the drudgery of daily fantasy, unbuckling the harness and slapping it across the fetlocks in a final ecouragement. Go, he thought, find Ch'tin! Fetch!

Looking back only once his mind sprinted away, puffs of surreality springing from its heels as it dashed towards the great unknown, before turning into a tiny pin-prick of a spark and vanishing, searching for a sign to guide him and Arbutus across the trackless wastes of the Space-Tome Continuum.

A thought, like a vague intangible mollusc, crawled through the silt in the vast saurian brain of the huge gold dragon as it sat watching the fifteen gibbets burn.

Something was different. Very, very different.

A splintering crack sounded through the Hanging Court-yard of Rhyngill as one of the gibbets buckled, swayed and

150

collapsed in a crimson shower of sparks. With a three-foot curling claw, the dragon scratched the back of its enormous gleaming head as it watched the gallows being engulfed in flame, consumed by the insatiable hunger of fire.

Now *that* had never happened before, thought the dragon. Weird! Through all the centuries of blasting things with searing sheets of flame, that's the first time anything had actually burned.

It watched the yellow and gold flames dance skywards like the tumeric-dyed veils of deranged maidens at an evening orgy; thrilling as the heat and light glistened against its polished auric skin; roaring with draconian delight as pockets of resin boiled and exploded in ashy fountains.

Pretty! it thought.

Taking a deep gulp of oxygen, relighting its pilot gland and charging its heating coils, it belched, kicking in the vast organic afterburners. Wiping a nonchalant claw across its huge mouth it launched another searing sheet of flame at the banks of chairs. Dozens of small wooden stools, hundreds of seats and a significant section of the wooden banking ignited instantly, sending plumes of smoke into the still air. As fountains of black ash tickled its nostrils the dragon giggled. This, it thought, was very satisfying indeed.

For the first time in its life, the dragon felt the overwhelming smouldering passion of arson. Suddenly everything in sight was flame fodder – rows of seating turned into reams of ignitable blue touchpaper.

It had never been like this before. Literal fire in the Chapter Dimensions lacked that certain vital ingredient – destruction! All the adjectives in an over-stuffed thesaurus just couldn't hold a candle to the lashing tongues of flaming hydrocarbons! It didn't matter what they said – literal reality *wasn't* the real thing.

The dragon took in the entire sizzling spread, leapt from the stonework on to the thermals of its own creation and launched into an uncontrollable frenzy of combustible chaos, burning buildings, torching towers, flambe-ing flags.

151

With a sound more sinister than the surly smirk of an iguana, more alarming than a crocodile's humourless grin, the dragon threw back its head, blasted another sheet of flame skyward (toasting an entire wedge of geese, three sparrows and a very embarrassed owl) and, quite literally, roared with laughter.

Pyromania had struck.

The solid unmistakable slap of a wet fish struggling to snatch its last breaths from the stone slab echoed around the midnight-deserted expanse of the Cranachan Imperial Palace Kitchens. Sadly, the whiting's fin-flapping bid for freedom was about to end in another piscine tragedy.

Turbot Gurnard, Chief Royal Fish Cook, snatched at the gasping fish, grasping its tail firmly with his bulbous white fingers and, with a deft flick of the wrist, brought the whiting's head sharply down on the blood-stained slab. Slap. Slice. Gutted. Fillets!

All around him thousands of crustaceans, molluscs and fish bubbled sighs of relief from their tanks as they, once again, escaped the plate.

Gurnard wiped his hands and ran his finger down the list by his side. Half a dozen large lobsters. He turned to the huge tank behind him and grinned, 'Okay, lobbies, come to Uncle Turbot! Six volunteers, please, take one step forward!'

Crustacean alarm bells rang through the tank as the Cook stoked the fires beneath the boiling cooking cauldron, rolled his sleeves up, skirted the edge of the low-slung snail tank and moved towards them. Lobsters dashed for cover, clamouring to hide beneath one another as crabs, shrimps and snails in the other tanks lined up to watch the fun. He advanced, his ageing bulk undulating as he revelled in the sport of lobster baiting, plunging his hand into the tank and snatching at the terrified decapods springing backwards out of reach.

'Come 'ere, you little blighters! Don't you want a nice

warm bath, eh? You'll look lovely afterwards, all pink and delicious!'

A huge male snatched at the stubby fingers waggling before his claws, catching the bulbous pinky, cheered on by seething bubbles of crustacean support. Gurnard squealed wildly, tugging his hand from the tank, pulling the lobster topside. Releasing its claw-grip scant milliseconds before the Cook's hand caught it, the lobster dropped into the tank to the admiring snap of decapod applause and the coquettish waggling of numerous female eyestalks. He was an instant hero.

Gurnard, turning the exact shade of crimson a lobster would rather not, sucked his crushed finger pitifully.

'Turbot Gurnard?' asked a voice from the door in a firmly polite manner.

'Mmm. Waggyu wommm?' came the muffled reply around a throbbing little finger.

'My colleagues and I are from "Mollusc Breeders' Monthly",' lied a tall indigo-clad figure. 'I wonder if we could have a few words?'

'Mmmm. Bee bewhytd!'

'Er, without the finger, please?'

'Oh, sorry. Be delighted! One of the hazards of being the King's Chief lobster-handler, ha!' said Gurnard, forcing joviality and rubbing his finger and he stepped around the edge of the vast snail storage area. The tanks in this room were arranged in a series of steps down so that water would flow from one to the other, the last was seething with snails and set into the floor. 'What's that rattling noise?' asked Gurnard, accompanied by another avalanche of clattering from one of the other three reporter's knees.

'Oh, that! Ignore him, he's just recording all this on a state-of-the-art lap-top printing press. Now, what we'd like to do is discuss a day in the life of Turbot Gurnard with particular reference to the handling and storage of sea snails.'

'Fine, fine!'

'Good, now if I could conduct the interview with you standing over by that tank of snails then my illustrator here could be sketching while we talk.'

'Fine, where do you want me?'

'Back a bit,' said the purple-robed illustrator. 'Bit more,' he added as he set up his easel. 'No, sorry. I can't get you in. Back a bit more.'

'Er, I'm right on the edge of this tank now.'

'Yes, do be careful. Er, back just a wee bit. Nearly. Bit more.'

'I think I'm slipp . . .'

'Perfect!'

The bulk of Turbot Gurnard trembled on the edge of the disaster for what seemed to the three Mollusc Breeders' Monthly reporters a lifetime, his arms windmilled desperately as he clawed at the air, attempting to prevent the inevitable. But, with only the merest of prods from Bharkleed, he finally overstepped the see-saw of equilibrium and plunged backwards, vanishing below the seething mass of black shells in one agonising instant. His head broke surface only once before Bharkleed stepped forward to offer assistance to the pack of snails suddenly able to wreak revenge on the murderer of generations of their brothers, sisters and cousins, half-cousins . .

The sole of Bharkleed's boot rested for a few difficult moments atop the shiny dome of the soon-to-be-ex-Fish Cook of Cranachan, waiting for the bubbling to stop, certain that the snails had succeeded in their mass suffocation.

'Thought he'd never go,' grumbled Whedd, packing his easel away.

'I think there'll be a promotion soon,' said Bharkleed smugly as he pinned a small sheet of parchment to the lobster tank. 'Ha ha! Another miracle! Things do work out in mysterious ways!'

The three men slunk quietly out of the room, leaving one vital clue.

The parchment note read:

Did he fall?
Or was he pushed?

Love and kisses
The Appropriator

'But there aren't any dragons in Rhyngill!' panted Hogshead, still out of breath from the mad, Courgette-led dash through the forest to her favourite secret clearing.

'Well, what would you call that thing, then?' snapped Firkin pointing at the gold lizard soaring and searing in the plumes of smoke billowing from the courtyard of Castell Rhyngill. 'A pixie? or a mad fairy?'

'If I close my eyes will it go away?' pleaded Dawn from behind a large tree.

'But dragons don't exist!'

'No,' pondered Firkin ignoring Dawn, 'maybe it's an overgrown glow-worn . . . or an outsize basilisk!'

''Tis ye fire-worm,' insisted Courgette clutching Exbenedict. ''Tis big, flyeths and breatheth it fire! Dragon!'

'But, dragons don't exist!' repeated Hogshead, his head spinning, wondering what had changed with Courgette.

'Look, *I* know dragons don't exist and *you* know dragons don't exist, hold on while I go and ask the dragon it anyone's told it!' scorned Firkin.

'Don't be stupid!' snapped Hogshead.

'Face it!' ranted Firkin. 'Do you think that all that smoke and flames and stuff's just a bad chip-pan fire? A dragon did it. D-r-a-g- . . .'

'But where from?' pleaded Hogshead.

'Well, you get a mummy dragon and a daddy dragon and . . .' mocked Firkin.

'Yffe thou canst not utter sense, shuttest ye up!' snapped Courgette.

'None of this makes sense! You're talking nonsense. Were you hit on the head?' whined Firkin, glaring at the fiery sword-toting redhead.

155

''Tis thou that speakest nonsense!' glowered Courgette, images of chains and railings and a gagged Firkin rising in her seething mind. 'Thy time in prison hath affected thee.'

'Rubbish!' protested Firkin.

There was a brief feral snarl, a flurry of wild swirling blade and Firkin was flat on his back squinting up at the rock-steady point of Exbenedict, hovering a quarter of an inch from his head. 'What wast thou saying?' asked Courgette nonchalantly, triceps bulging.

'Ah . . . aha, er, Rubbish . . . there was rubbish everywhere in the prison. Needs a good clean,' whimpered Firkin, swallowing extremely cautiously.

'Hast thou ought else upon thy mind?' queried Courgette, green eyes flashing.

'Nooooo . . . noooo. Everything's fine,' grovelled Firkin. 'You just carry on and talk any way you feel like. Don't mind me.'

With a curl of her lip Courgette stepped off Firkin's chest.

'But, if they don't exist, where did it come from?' asked Dawn, pointing at the hundred-foot gold dragon soaring over Rhyngill.

Firkin tutted, brushing a pair of muddy marks off his chest. 'Why are we wasting time wondering where dragons come from when we should be off talking to Klayth about burning down Middin!' he insisted. 'Remember!'

'Maybe a dragon did that,' grumbled Hogshead unhelpfully.

Unseen to anyone a tiny, microscopic twinkle of light flashed into existence fifteen feet above Hogshead's head. It bobbed about, orienting itself to the strange new surroundings and wrestling with the tug of gravity.

'You mean you want to go back in there?' shuddered Dawn, registering Firkin's words, stroking her neck nervously. 'If the dragon doesn't get you, Swingler will!'

'Klayth isn't in there,' answered Firkin smugly.

'Good job, too. He'd be a bit sizzled if he was,' said Dawn.

'Dragons are fictitious!' said Hogshead almost to himself,

156

clawing at something at the back of his mind. The tiny spark of light swooped down towards Hogshead's pocket, flashed into the dark and squirmed its illuminant way into the dark inside of the book it found there.

'We've got to go to see Klayth!' ranted Firkin. 'I want answers!'

'Dragons *are* fictitious!' repeated Hogshead, trying to confirm the fact to himself as he stared fixedly at the hundred-foot pyromaniac, torching everything in sight.

Lighting the hollowed book like a dust-caked archaeologist invading an Egyptian burial tomb, the pin-prick caught its breath as it stared at what it expected to be Ch'tin. The spark of light screamed a fraction of a decibel scream as it took in the hideous sight. It remembered that Ch'tin was ugly but he was never *this* bad. Clutching at what passed for its tiny massless stomach, it fled in sparkling terror.

'He's got some explaining to do about Middin!' continued Firkin.

Courgette scowled, her hands crossed over the hilt of the sword.

The sparkly centre of Merlot's consciousness tore up the side of the giant Hogshead and pounded at the door to his brain. Screaming and hammering with mounting alarm, microscopic flares launching from its surface, it failed utterly to make its presence felt. Stepping back from the nape of Hogshead's neck and flashing a few involuntary prominences it raced forward in the starry pin-prick's equivalent of a full shoulder charge.

'Dragons are *fictitious*!' shouted Hogshead slapping the nape of his neck. 'Uh-oh!' in the back of his mind a connection was made. A connection he would rather not have thought of.

'Yes, yes! We cleared that up ages ago!' grumbled Firkin irritably. 'We're on to Middin and ashes and where to find Klayth, remember?'

Hogshead wrenched his attention away from the dragon and stared at Courgette. 'Where did you get that sword?' he snapped suddenly.

'Yonder,' she pointed meaningfully away through the trees.

'Don't any of you want to know where Klayth is!' complained Firkin to the three pairs of deaf ears.

'And it was just lying there, waiting for you?' continued Hogshead, seeing things in a strangely different light. The cold light of the dawning of a new idea.

'Nay! 'Twas mayhap good fortune spared me being cleaved in twain! It tumbled upon me!'

'Out of a tree?' asked Hogshead.

'A swordtree?' began Firkin. 'I've heard of a swordsman, and a swordfish but I've never heard of a swordtree! What about Klayth!'

'Nay,' answered Courgette, ignoring Firkin's comment, 'Tumbled from ye sky!'

'Are you honestly trying to tell me that sword just fell out of the sky?' asked Hogshead incredulously. The idea's corona shining yellow as it clawed its way over his mental horizon, beams of inspiration lighting the dark terrain of the mysterious unknown.

Courgette nodded and patted the leather of the handle almost affectionately.

'And you expect us to believe that?'

Courgette nodded again. 'Yeah, verily. 'Tis troth!'

'But doesn't it have a name tag on it?' queried Firkin. 'Somebody must have lost it! I've heard of huge hailstones falling out of the sky, and even fish, but never four-foot, jewel-pommelled broadswords! We're wasting time. Klayth . . .'

''Tis a sign!' insisted Courgette for probably the hundredth time. 'Destiny leadeth and I followeth!'

'Don't talk rubbish!' snapped Firkin. 'You pick up a sword in the middle of the forest and suddenly, Flash! – you think you're the saviour of the universe!'

'Fell from above!'

'Probably hit you on the head,' grumbled Firkin.

'Yt didst not!'

'Did!'

'Didst not!'

'Did, did, did, d . . .'

'Shutup!' shouted Hogshead.

'Didst not,' whispered Courgette.

'Both of you!' growled Hogshead, scowling at them. 'Let me have a look at it!'

'You can do that later,' snapped Firkin. 'We're wasting time, we need to see Klayth!'

Hogshead turned, fixing Firkin with the type of very hard stare which would one day make a small bear famous. 'If my suspicions are correct, there may not be a later!' Firkin, despite his better judgement, turned pale and shut up. Something was going wrong here; *they* were telling *him* what to do!

Hogshead's gaze slid up and down the weapon, staring at the hilt, looking at the handle's inscriptions without any clue to their meaning, admiring the workmanship and feeling, somehow, that the sword was familiar. He rubbed his hand down the length of the blade and suddenly let out a scream.

Courgette stared at his hand in fear.

'Here it is! Look, look!!' cried Hogshead.

Firkin peered over his shoulder. 'What? I can't see anything.'

'There! It's just as I thought.'

'All I can see are little bits of stone,' grumbled Firkin. 'Come on, let's go.'

'Where do little bits of stone come from?' asked Hogshead. 'Bigger bits of stone!' he answered, not pausing for Firkin's expected comment about mummy stones and daddy stones, his mind racing now that he had some tangible evidence. Merlot's exploratory consciousness panted with the effort and tried to remind Hogshead of the bookworm in his pocket.

'So what?' moaned Firkin, very miffed at being ignored.

'So! This sword has been embedded in stone. And, if I'm not mistaken, an anvil!' finished Hogshead.

"Tis falsehood you speak,' defended Courgette. 'Rope and wood only have I cleaved!'

'No, no! I mean, in the time and place *before* you found it,' said Hogshead, eagerly, the truth bubbling inside him, ready to explode.

'The glade of meeting was bare,' said Courgette.

'Hogshead, you're wrong!' snapped Firkin, his temper snapping. 'We need to talk to Klayth, not be examining each other's weapons. Let's go to Cr . . .'

'I don't understand,' confessed Dawn beginning to feel that something wasn't entirely right.

'I do!' said Firkin. 'He's flipped. Gone barmy!'

'Look, do I have to spell it out!' Hogshead insisted, the nooks and crannies of mystery bathed in inspirational light.

'Yes!'

'This sword has been in a stone and anvil! Sound familiar?'

'Dost thou meaneth tis *Ye* Sword in the . . .' began Courgette, awestruck.

'Yes! That sword in your hand is Exbenedict!'

'Oh, come on! That only exists in stories,' said Firkin.

'Exactly!' proclaimed Hogshead. 'And where *do* dragons come from?'

'Ah! Oh . . .'

'What deviltry occurs?' asked Courgette, suddenly worried, staring at the weapon in an entirely different light.

'I really don't know,' confessed Hogshead, shaking his head as if something deep inside was itchy, 'but . . . but . . .' he faltered, closing his eyes to concentrate. Merlot's sparkly consciousness flared and pounded and cursed the sluggishness of Hogshead's neurons. 'But I know a bookworm who might!' he finally finished.

'Of course!' whispered Dawn.

Carefully, almost dreamily, Hogshead pulled the battered copy of 'Lady Challerty's Loofah' out of his pocket and opened it. 'Ch'tin. Ch'tin,' he called gently, well aware of the temper the three-quarter-inch bookworm could have if awoken on the wrong side of the page. 'Ch'tin!' he squealed, staring open-mouthed into the book. Instead of the familiar tender green body with the large eyes, squirming and looking up at him, he stared at the type of hideous brown object a constipated Ammorettan Death Lizard would struggle long and hard to pass. It squatted in the corner of the book glistening as it hardened.

'Now can we go to Cranachan?' asked Firkin, heartlessly.

'Shutup!' snapped Hogshead, Courgette and Dawn simultaneously.

Unseen by anyone a tiny white pin-prick of Merlot's consciousness shot out of Hogshead left nostril, swooped upwards and vanished.

It was no good. He would have to get his hands dirty in reality.

Scattered footprints sprinted across the black desert of the Hanging Courtyard of Rhyngill where twelve unbelieving convicted criminals had grinned collectively at Freedom, hugged their faces to her matronly apron, turned and dashed in every conceivable direction, fleeing before heavily gauntleted Black Guards had a chance to stop them.

The sobbing bulk of 'Long-drop' Swingler tore imaginary hair from his leather Balaclava as he screamed at the carbonised wasteland. He had intended to bring the house down, but to be upstaged by a dragon!

Suddenly, like a killer whale erupting from a black sea, Vhintz exploded from beneath a heap of soot, inchoate clouds fighting with blue curses. Around him were shards of glass and fulminating pools of overheated potions, the sole remains of his entire stock of wart remover.

With a shriek of terror he suddenly realised that his wand had gone. So had his book, the enormous leather-bound tome given to him by his grandfather, 'Ye Aynshent Almanacke of Conjoorynge, Magycke and Such'.

Panic surged inside Vhintz and in a flash, where there was once a tall, scorched man there appeared a wild whirlwind of flying shards of torched wood, clouds of sooty black and volumes of curses as he broke fingernails and pulled muscles in his frenzied search through the wreckage. Fountains of black skeletal beams flew over his head as he burrowed through the destruction like a frantic beaver with a deadline to meet, tossing supports and joints through the plumes of soot.

Then without warning, he stopped. There before him, unearthed like an ancient tooth from a long extinct fossil, lay the book. Fountains of relief doused the fires of panic as he saw that it was still intact, its ancient leather bindings unharmed except for a slight scorch mark on the spine and a pile of soot rubbed into the gold lettering.

He reached out. And screamed.

Before his hand could contact the tome it exploded into a blazing conflagration, flames leaping skyward, snatching at Vhintz's beard.

'My book!' he screamed, starring wild-eyed at the tiny inferno, tugging off his cloak to smother the flames. As he leapt foward, a stygian toreador in for the kill, a wild squawking sprang from the flames, a beak stabbed out, golden wings flapped and a sweating bird shot from the thermal uprush. With a 'phut' the flames died, leaving a small heap of herbs and spices.

The phoenix stretched its reincarnated wings, smacked its beak and yawned, scratching its belly with its left index claw. Vhintz stood motionless, unable to believe what his eyes were fervently insisting was true. He was staring at a phoenix. A real, live, honest-to-goodness, oven-ready phoenix. Shelf-life five hundred years, guaranteed to self-destruct on its own personal funeral pyre accompanying itself with a melodious dirge. Clean, loving and thoroughly temple-trained, yours for only . . .

Vhintz bent and snatched his book from beneath the yawning bird as it examined its newly reincarnated body, thrusting out its chest and striking poses like some freshly greased body-builder revelling in a narcissistic ego trip. The phoenix shrieked with irritation at the disturbance and took to the wing. Vhintz cradled 'Ye Aynshent Almanacke of Conjoorynge, Magycke and Such', stroking it and cooing as if it were some small furry animal he had just saved from a weighted sack in a surging river.

He couldn't comprehend it. The book was still intact and as usable as ever before.

The phoenix flapped away, caught a thermal under each wing and soared off to bother a few pigeons.

In a clearing in Rhyngill Forest, in a tunic pocket, residing in a book (chapter 5 to 76 inclusive) a small brown chrysalis squirmed as it recovered from a very hot flush.

It's all right, Ch'tin told himself, nothing to worry about. Hot flushes are very common at the time of the change.

Eighty-five feet below the crumbling peak of Martelloh Tower two figures were deeply engrossed in their covert operations. Nobody knew they were there. In fact, since the introduction of Imperial Directive 538 banning the populace of Cranachan from staring at anything above the height of the King's visage, nobody knew that the tower was there. Except for the resident clump of owls.

'I *really* think datt you should look at disssss!' said Vlad for the third time that evening as he pointed beyond the eyepiece of the telescope and over the top of the Talpa Mountains.

'What's more important than this!' shrieked Fisk, slamming the back of his gauntlet against the freshly stolen copy of the *Triumphant Herald* (Evening Edition).

'Datt isss vhat I'm tryink to tell . . .'

'Someone's using my name! How dare they!'

'I think dat you vill find disss more usssssefull dan ein murder!' hissed Vlad as he returned his watery eye to the telescope and peered from the top of their watch tower.

'I was nowhere near the fish-cook. I had nothing to do with it,' shrieked Fisk, bewildered at the unique feeling of protesting his innocence for a crime that he hadn't committed.

163

'Der atmosssssphere isss really hottink up over dere now!' hissed Vlad focusing in on a sheet of flame as it erupted skywards.

'Someone's trying to frame me?' snarled Fisk wringing the newsparchment between his creaking gauntlets. 'Who?' What do they stand to gain? Apart from *death*!' He screamed, pounding his fist on the arm of his chair, the sound resonating in the bare circular observation chamber. Fisk's frustration reared its volatile head in its usual manner – fuming anger. It was easy to tell that Fisk was not his usual coldly calculating, murderous self just by listening. The sudden increase of creaking leather gauntlets, the doubling tempo of percussive steel toecapped taps and the sharper panting breaths issuing between gnashing molars and wickedly sneering lips were something of a give away.

'What's going on out there?' he bellowed rhetorically, the years of relying on stolen newsparchments, snatched snippets of conversation and glimpses of events through holes in pictures or one-way mirror glass finally letting him down badly. Things were happening that he knew nothing of, except for infuriating rumours and half-heard whispers. His grip on the people of Cranachan was slipping, he could feel it, they were no longer as terrified of him. They no longer gave him the respect he deserved, and now, using *his* name for a murder! It was the ultimate insult!

'What's happening?' he snarled through grinding teeth. It was a wonder that there was any enamel left on them.

'Ssssheetsss of flamesssss!' sussurated Vlad through his two front teeth.

'What do you mean, "flames"?' snapped Fisk suddenly hearing the vampire's words.

'Hot thingssss, burny, burny . . .'

'What! Where? Give it here!' shouted Fisk flinging the now shredded *Triumphant Herald* across the room and snatching the telescope from Vlad's pale, cold hands.

'I see no inferno!' he complained, peering hard through the tiny eyepiece.

'Er, vhatt about der eyepatch?' reminded Vlad.

'Damnation! Don't be so picky,' he shrieked, changing eyes and blinking in disbelief. Far over the Talpa Mountains, several hundred feet above precisely the spot where Castell Rhyngill should be, hung a pall of rapidly expanding dense black smoke.

'I don't believe it! What's going on?' Fisk barked the question with his eye jammed to the eyepiece. 'What's happening?'

'Der annual barbeque perhapssss?' suggested Vlad helpfully.

'No . . . more like a riot . . . or a siege . . . or . . .' Fisk pulled himself suddenly away from the telescope, blinking, rubbed his eye and stared again, shaking his head in complete disbelief.

'I could have sworn I just saw a . . . No! It can't be!' he cried. 'One of the flames. Must have been!'

'Vhatt, vhatt!'

'No! I've been working too hard . . . yes, that's it!'

'Vhatt'ssss it?'

Shaking his head and looking paler than he normally did, Fisk grabbed Vlad's head, shoving him towards the telescope. 'What do you see? Tell me everything you see?' The excitable urgency in his voice made Vlad comply; he had never heard that tone before.

'Columnsss of flamessss sssshootink into der sssky . . . und sssmoke . . . und, er . . .'

'Yes? yes?'

'. . . er, lotsss of mountainsssss . . .'

'Nothing else? Nothing in the air?' pleaded Fisk.

'. . . er, nein, aber . . . oh! . . .'

'Do you see it? Do you?'

Vlad looked away from the scene of flaming destruction.

'Itssss . . . itsssss,' he struggled, 'it'sss a drakon!'

'But there aren't any dragons in Rhyngill!'

'Doessssn't look like there'sss much left off Rhyngill to not haff drakonssss in!'

165

'What's it *doing* there!' shrieked Fisk, ignoring Vlad.

'B . . . b . . . burnink thinkssss!' hissed Vlad enthusiastically, staring at the conflagration through the telescope. 'Torchink Casssstell Rhyngill . . .'

'All right, all right!'

'Dessstroyink everythink . . . ssssearink the land . . . creatink haffoc . . .'

Fisk's gaze turned cold and hard as he listened to Vlad and thought of the future. Suddenly he could see it, here was an exit from this shady underworld existence. In an instant he saw a way forward, the dragon offered a path to a new and utterly wonderful future, one where fear of King Khardeen would be a thing of the dim and distant past and people would give *him* a bit more of the respect he so richly deserved – or they'd die!

'This is it!' growled Fisk, wringing his hands together in a symphony of squealing leather, his face blossoming into the evil sneer to which it had become unaccustomed over the last few months of frustration. 'This. Is. *It*!'

'Vhat?' croaked Vlad, utterly baffled.

'My chance! My opportunity. It's perfect. Perfect! Time to move!' He dashed out of the watch tower and flew down the spiral staircase towards his subterranean throne room for what he suddenly felt might be the last time. He paused only to grab a large pottery gourd, a massive wicker basket and a tin of whitewash from a small storeroom.

On a small bench, one of hundreds along the length of a yellow tarmac road, a sleeping figure in saxaffron robe and matching pointy hat suddenly sat bolt upright, stood and sprinted off to his hut. The tawny owl watching from a nearby tree squawked in undignified surprise, bolted the remains of a recently captured vole and flapped off after the rapidly receding wizard.

'I'm hungry,' complained Dawn for probably the fiftieth time in as many minutes.

'Shutup and follow me!' snapped Firkin glaring at his little sister as they crept through the forest around the flaming bulk of Castell Rhyngill.

Glimpsed silhouettes of people were seen sprinting in a million different directions, hurling buckets of moat water over the wall in a feeble attempt at controlling the flames. Carts, sheep, horses and all manner of panic-stricken Rhyngillians poured out of the main gate and across the drawbridge. And all the while the pyromaniac dragon roared with laugher, swooping and incinerating everything even remotely inflammable.

'Are you sure Cranachan's the place to go?' asked Hogshead nervously.

'Yes, didn't you hear Swingler, Klayth is in Cranachan,' insisted Firkin fidgeting to move. 'That's why he wasn't at the hanging!'

'But it's miles!' whined Dawn. 'And I'm hungry!'

Trying to ignore Dawn, Firkin turned and headed off toward the rapidly approaching evening sky and the darkening bulk of the Talpa Mountains.

Over the constant whooshing of the fires, the incessant seething of boiling pools of water, the splattering sizzle of roasting carcasses, three figures strode unheard and ignored.

The staff of the Cranachan Imperial Palace Kitchens were far too busy with frantic preparations to pay even the slightest attention to three visitors. Even if these visitors *were* all dressed in bright acres of indigo robes and had a vaguely religious look about them.

The three High Priest of the Elevated Church of St Lucre the Unwashed strode through the sweat-laden culinary sauna, on a bee-line for the one man and several dozen eel-like fish that would hold the key to their successful fleecing of the entirety of Cranachan.

Surfeit, the newly promoted Royal Fish Cook, rinsed his gutting knife and attacked the first skein of lampreys for the Royal platter. He was an intensely happy man, overwhelmed by the sudden, and entirely unexpected change in his fortune, overjoyed to be in the position he had always wanted. It had only taken one little prayer! It *was* a shame about Turbot Gurnard though. Really sad.

Quite what he had done to bring the wrath of the Appropriator upon himself no one knew. The *Triumphant Herald* had speculated, the public had guessed, but nobody really had a clue. Nobody, that is, except Bharkleed, Hirsuit and Whedd. And Gurnard himself but he was unavailable for comment.

'Bless you, disciple Surfeit,' said His Eminence, Bharkleed the Fervently Exalted, striding up toward the feverishly gutting fish-cook, 'and I believe congratulations are in order!'

'Your Eminence!' gasped Surfeit in surprise, 'er, er, forgive me not tugging my forelock, but I . . .' he nodded to his blood-stained hands which were currently disembowelling a not-long-dead lamprey.

'Quite all right. I do understand,' grinned Bharkleed dismissively. 'Settling into your new position?'

'Yes, yes! I couldn't believe it when I heard about old Gurnard,' said Surfeit, excitedly eviscerating another fish.

'Doubt not the forces of destiny,' said Bharkleed raising his eyes to the ceiling. 'Sometimes they can work in *weird* ways!'

'Well, when I says "I couldn't believe it" I meant that I was dead surprised . . .'

'Not as dead, or surprised, as Gurnard, I'll warrant,' chuckled Whedd nudging Hirsuit in the ribs.

'You should guard what you say,' scowled Bharkleed looking at Surfeit and delivering a swift and accurate back kick to Whedd's left shin.

'Yes, yes,' stutterd Surfeit, 'I'll be more careful from now on.'

'Arrogant toe-rag!' muttered Whedd glaring at the nape of Bharkleed's neck with the vehemence of a very narked Jack Russell and rubbing his left leg up the back of his right.

'As I'm sure you will see from Gurnard's unfortunate

departure from this world, it really pays to have your afterlife sorted out!' smarmed Bharkleed.

'Oh, yes. I do agree. In fact, I was only telling Turbot about you lot on the afternoon before he, er . . . you know.'

'And was he interested?'

'Nah! Called you a bunch of bare-faced con-men who'd rip you off in an instant! "You watch them", he said, "You be careful or they'll have you for every penny you haven't even earned yet!" '

Bharkleed turned very pale. 'Ah! A-ha-ha. I, er, wonder where he got such a *ridiculous* idea?'

'Not a clue, Your Eminence,' said Surfeit casually slicing into another lamprey's tender underbelly with a deft flick of his glistening knife. 'Not a clue. But he was mad, you know.'

'Er, really?'

'Ooh yeah! Everybody knew about it. Totally loopy. Used to talk to the snails.'

'Really? Well, I never did!'

Surfeit polished off another lamprey, then turned and looked at Bharkleed, his hands dripping. 'Well now. It's really nice to see you an' all, Your Eminence, but as you can see I've got a bit of work to do,' his hand swept over the glistening morass of aquatic produce. 'Is there anything I can help you with?'

The next few days would have been *so* much simpler if he could have smiled sweetly, taken Surfeit by the shoulder and said, 'Actually, *we* made sure you got this job; *we* nobbled Turbot Gurnard and *we* ensured that nobody saw the advertisement in the *Triumphant Herald* because *we* bribed the postie not to deliver it! Don't you think it's time, bearing all that lot in mind, that you, as it were, returned the favour?'

Then Surfeit would surely have replied, 'You did all that for me? Oh, I'm flattered. Please, tell me what I can do.'

Then Bharkleed would have smiled a favourite-uncle sort of smile, pulled a small bottle of interesting looking white powder out of his pocket,* and handed it to Surfeit saying,

---

* Interesting mainly because it was decorated with a very tasteful picture of a black skull with two crossed thigh bones, a gravestone, a coffin beneath and the words POISON – YUK, NOT NICE.

'Make sure that two teaspoons of this stuff find their way into the King's food every day.'

Unfortunately, the conversation *actually* went:

'Ooh no, no! I, er, that is we, just popped in to say "Well done" and to see how you were settling in. We always like to hear of our disciples doing well in this world. Don't we, chaps?'

Hirsuit and Whedd grunted in overwhelming interest.

'Well, thanks, but . . .'

'Are those for the King?' blurted Bharkleed pointing at the lampreys.

'Yes, everything I do is for him. That's what being Royal Fish Cook, by appointment to His Majesty King Khardeen, Ruler of the Kingdoms of Rhyngill and Cranachan, Chief of the United Clans of the Foothills, Holder of the Most Spiky Glove of Tax Extraction and the Torch of Smouldering Retribution means.'

'Fascinating!' whispered Bharkleed in a very good impersonation of awe-struck interest. 'And what else does the role of Royal Fish Cook entail?'

'My favourite bits so far have been the time when a whole sturgeon came in and I had to . . .'

While Bharkleed supplied the perfect audience, intelligent, witty and enquiring, Hirsuit edged carefully toward the gutted skein of lampreys, their jawless rings of teeth gaping in silent fishy mockeries of the crowned head to which they would so shortly be served. Unseen, he removed a small interestingly (see page 169) decorated bottle from a perfectly hidden inside pocket and nonchalantly dropped the contents over the unknowing fishy accomplices.

Merlot stood up, rubbed his aching spine and stepped back to admire his handywork. A complex series of lines, circles, curves and blobs of chalky colour were scrawled on the floor of his hut. Then he looked at the book in his hand and grunted.

'Near enough, near enough!' he mumbled, tugging

nervously at his off-white beard and returning the chalk to one of the hundreds of pockets that lurked within his cloak. 'Bit shaky round the far pentacle and some of those lines are a bit wiggly but it'll do! I hope.'

'Me toooo!' agreed Arbutus, licking the post-pradial remnants of the vole from his beak and fluffing up his chest feathers.

Merlot snatched a large bottle from a shelf, hurled handfuls of pink powder over the pictogram and began to spin and shriek wildly like a dervish with St Vitus's dance.

Arbutus fidgeted restlessly. He'd seen Merlot do this sort of thing hundreds of times before. Often after consuming far too much red wine.

Before long the feathers around Arbutus's ankles began to itch as Merlot's whirling incantations grew louder and a cold, clammy wind ruffled his flight feathers. The owl stared intently at the centre of the pentacle. If anything was going to happen it would be there.

The bare wooden floor shimmered once or twice. Then without warning it turned utterly black and Merlot stepped forward and vanished. Arbutus squawked, took to the air in a flurry of angry tawny feathers, raced towards the centre of the floor, closing his eyes, bracing himself for a sudden collision with several solid floorboards. There was a noise like a goldfish exploding in a microwave as first Arbutus and then the black hole in the floor vanished.

'But it's true, Father! I *did* see a borogrove!' protested Klayth, expounding his adventure in the forest on his weekly meeting with King Khardeen.

'Mmmm, well as long as you enjoyed yourself,' the King mumbled, his mind on the name for a suitable tax to pay for the damage wreaked by the two-stone trolls. The Market Reinforcement Tax? nah! boring.

'. . . and there *were* four raths, Father! Just ask my teacher!'

171

'Yeah, yeah . . .' The Post-Troll Market Square Reconstruction Tax . . . hmmm.

'We had to run!'

'Good, good. Healthy mind *and* a healthy body, good . . .' Troll Tax . . . rubbish! Aah! Hang the name. What about how *much* it should be? Another five groats . . . ?

'I've never seen a rath before.'

Fifteen groats . . . ? Each?

Suddenly the door burst open and Commander 'Black' Archonite flew in, sweating and panting like someone who has just run up fourteen flights of spiral stairs, sprinted along three-quarters of a mile of corridor, dashed down eight leagues of battlements and attempted to screech to a halt on the slippery stone flags of the corridor to bring the King urgent bad news. He had.

'S-hire, I . . . I . . . brrr . . .' panted Achonite, gasping for breath, his arms waving in panic.

'What is it, man? Don't you knock?' roared the King, pulling himself from thoughts of more taxation.

'Ooh, Daddy. Is it a game?' asked Klayth.

King Khardeen turned to his son. ' "Sire", or "Your Highness", please!' he snarled. 'We have company!' He turned back to the panting Achonite. 'C'mon. Spit it out, man!'

'Fhhhh . . . fhhh . . .' choked Achonite.

'Has it got an "l" in it?' asked Klayth. 'Or a "q"?'

'Fhhhhh . . .' continued the red-faced Achonite, wriggling his fingers and pointing far over the Talpa Mountains towards Rhyngill.

'A "p"?' pressed Klayth.

'Quiet! This is important!' growled Khardeen trying to fathom the nature of Achonite's hoarsely wheezed message.

The Commander giving up with speech pointed frantically out of the window.

'What the . . . !' cried Khardeen as he saw the smoke in the distance. 'Are we under attack?' he barked at Achonite.

172

'Hhhhh . . .'

'Call out the guards, raise the Armies! Set to repel the . . . Eh?'

Achonite was shaking his head.

'No armies? . . . So we're not under attack then?'

Achonite nodded as he choked.

'Well, then. Battle stations, sound the alarm . . . ! Look, are we under attack or not?' snapped the King as he saw Achonite's wildly shaking head. 'We are? Then why no armies?'

By way of an answer Achonite's arm pointed suddenly out of the window again, flapping his arms, rolling his eyes and flaring his nostrils.

'Yes. Fire. I know . . .'

Achonite made gushing gestures from his mouth.

'You're feeling sick? Vomiting? Plague?'

Suddenly Klayth shrieked with amazement as he followed Achonite's gestures. 'A dragon, look. It's a dragon!'

'Don't interrupt! This is royal business!' snapped Khardeen.

'But, I *am* the Prince!' answered Klayth.

Achonite's head was nodding wildly behind the King.

'Oh, mmmmm. Well, this is grown-up royal business . . . What did you say? A drag . . .' He nearly ripped the window off its frame as he stuck his head out of it, staring horror-stricken across the mountains. 'It's a d . . .d . . . .'

Achonite nodded, shrugged and sprinted out of the room hot on Khardeen's heels, while the dragon roared and soared and seared over Rhyngill.

A small brown sparrow hopped stealthily across the criss-cross of dead leaves in the clearing of Rhyngill Forest, a snack in sight. His diet that day, it has to be said, hadn't been the best ever, the bottom-half of a week-dead centipede and a clawful of last year's seeds. He took a slow breath, licking his beak as he relished the worm ahead, readying himself for the final dash . . . After three . . . He expanded his tiny chest for the coming struggle . . . two . . . One final check for any obstacles . . . one . . . It was in his sights . . . Go . . . He hopped forward in a surge of speed belying his small stature, racing the last few inches. And crashed into a wall of solid blue canvas . . .

'Damndamndamndamndamn!' squawked the small brown bird furiously, lying spread-sparrowed across the enormous canvas object, watching the worm slink below the leaves. 'Come back! You're supposed to be my dinner!'

Above his head, something was ringing. A gentle tinkling on the toe of an enormous canvas shoe. The sparrow squeaked with surprise, hopped backwards and looked up. There, where a second previously had been nothing, was a pair of pink and white striped woollen legs extending forever vertically, vanishing into the infinite expanse of a vast saxaffron robe.

'It's all right!' boomed the voice above the sparrow's head. 'Don't panic I'm here to . . . oh, bum! Too late!'

Suddenly twigs and leaves spewed everywhere as an extremely miffed tawny owl hurtled out of the undergrowth and cannoned towards the wizard towering above the tiny terrified sparrow.

'So, planning to leave me there, were you!' shrieked Arbutus as he spun around Merlot's peaked hat. 'Don't want me here, eh? I thought you were my friend! It'll take a lot of mice to make up for this one I can tell you. A personal snub, it is!'

Merlot was becoming dizzy trying to keep up with the whirlwind of chattered comments as Arbutus spun around his head.

'Okay! So why are we here?' croaked the owl as it flicked a few nonchalant flight feathers, trimmed a casual aerofoil surface and swung in to execute a perfect landing on the baffled-looking wizard.

'Eh!' he grunted in response as he fiddled with his fingers deep in thought.

'What are we doing here?' repeated Arbutus irritably.

'Bah! Fiddlesticks!' grumbled Merlot.

'I only asked,' complained the owl preparing to sulk if he didn't receive any answers soon.

'Too late!' mumbled Merlot, picking up a dry beech leaf and grinning at the bewildered sparrow at his feet. He sniffed the leaf, threw it into the air watching which way it fell, pointed left and reached a decision.

'That way!' he declared, plunging through the undergrowth to the right.

The sparrow collapsed on to the forest floor, trilled a bewildered sob and folded its head into its wings.

Owls, wizards *and* swords? he pleaded. I'm working too hard! Time for that holiday. Now, which way's south?

Having saved as much of the stock from the flames of Rhyngill as possible, loaded it on to his fleet of seven wagons, coupled them all together, Magnus the Carter had set off on his regular weekly trip to Cranachan. With a well-practised flick of the wrist his whip had cracked over the back of six hulking beasts of burden. Slowly they'd taken the strain, the leather harnesses creaking against their massive flanks, and the wagon train had rumbled forward on its regular non-stop overnight Trans-Talpine journey.

All that had been hours ago and the steady regular rhythm of the wagon train had lulled Magnus into a deep torpor as the animals headed up the long drag of the Foh Pass. Suddenly the front cart jolted over a large stone, shocking Magnus into sudden abrupt wakefulness. With his pulse racing and reflexively unsheathing a short dagger in a flash, he stared around, checking for bandits. Sharply the cart bucked again as the rear wheel hit the stone. A brief wave of acute embarrassment raced through Magnus's mind. Swiftly resheathing his blade, he cracked his whip across the backs of the team just to let them know he was there, 'Ha! Donner. Giddyap, Blitzen!' he shouted and was almost totally ignored by the slowly plodding sextet of vast rhinoceroses.

Blitzen curled her black lip, tossed her horn, snorted in mild pachyderm irritation and trudged on up the long curling incline.

Several hundred ells ahead of him, just round a sharp corner, a group of four youngsters trudged wearily up the same bleak slope.

'Are we there yet?' complained Dawn yet again.

'Have a wild guess!' moaned Firkin. 'Take a look around you and tell me, honestly what you think!'

Dawn stared at the huge mountains rising either side of the steep path, scowled at the setting sun as it made its eager way towards the horizon, grumbled and spat as she kicked out at one of the stones lying in the uneven path. It is amazing how the influence of a big brother manifests itself.

'Well?' asked Firkin.

'Humph!' grunted Dawn.

'It is not meet to remain in this valley long,' said Courgette peering ahead and fondling the grip of Exbenedict. 'It offereth no cover.'

'We don't need cover,' said Hogshead wearily. 'I don't think it's going to rain.'

'Nay. Thou wert misprised of my meaning. If strangers follow in our footsteps,' she snapped, tutting. 'In case of ambush . . .'

'Oh, so we can hide?' said Hogshead.

'Nay, nay!' complained Courgette. 'We canst ambush them!' she added, patting Exbenedict.

'Ha! Of course, silly me,' said Hogshead shrugging his shoulders. 'But, it doesn't matter,' he continued, 'because we're all alone here in the mountains. There's no one coming . . .'

''Tis risible thou shouldst say that . . .' said Courgette grinning. 'Hark!'

It had been too quiet to hear but now that Courgette had mentioned it Hogshead was unnervingly aware of a low rumbling coming from around the corner below them, out of Rhyngill. A sharp crack sounded and a distant yell followed.

'What is it!' he whispered nervously.

'Big,' answered Courgette. 'And it approacheth.'

'Oh no. We're not going to have to run away *again*, are we?' moaned Dawn, pouting miserably. 'My feet are killing me!'

'Nay. We stand and fight,' said Courgette grinning with anticipation. 'Fights for women.' Something defiant began to grow within her heart. She wanted to fight. And if she couldn't, well she'd just jolly well chain herself to a railing until she could. It just wasn't right that men could . . .

'Courgette!' shouted Hogshead shaking her by the shoulders. 'Courgette! Put your sword away!'

'Thou art a wimp!' she grunted and struggled.

'We don't know what it is!' insited Hogshead.

'Or how many of them there are,' added Firkin.

'I think I'd rather run away!' moaned Dawn even more feebly.

'Thou art cowards!' growled Courgette.

'Let's find cover, assess their strength and then decide whether to kick them in, eh?' pleaded Hogshead as the rumbling grew louder, enhanced by the echoes from the pass walls.

'Running away!' snarled Courgette. ''Tis pathetic.' Her hands wrung the hilt of Exbenedict.

'Look, it's safer! It's called a tactical withdrawal,' said Hogshead half hoping that Courgette would go wild and attack whatever it was that was approaching. The thought of the sight of her in full battle-frenzied mood once more made him weak at the knees. He hadn't quite recovered from the rescue in Rhyngill. With an acutely embarrassed shock he realised that he was dribbling. Again.

Suddenly from around the corner a large grey snout appeared, followed swiftly by another and a pair of large curving horns as the first two rhinos appeared.

Courgette's jaw dropped momentarily. Vast approaching armies of men were one thing to raise arms against, injustices to human rights were another, but rhinos . . . ?

Dawn stifled a squeak of alarm. 'Run?' she asked.

Firkin and Hogshead were already scrambling up the valley walls frantically trying to stretch a small shrub to hide them both.

Another pair of rhinos lumbered around the corner, filling the pass with several tons of pachyderm pulling power.

Courgette stepped backwards, turned and scrambled up the bank, after a frantically panting Dawn.

'You ran away!' squeaked Dawn diving behind a tiny clump of grass.

'Methought mayhap twas meet to assess the benefits of a tactical whatsit!' snapped Courgette embarassedly.

'See? You ran away!' jibed Dawn.

Below them, captained by the now slumbering figure of Magnus the Carter, seven carts passed by hauled by the sweating bulk of six rhinos.

Suddenly Courgette had an idea. 'Come,' she urged above the rumbling wagon train. 'Heed my footsteps and comply!'

'But I don't want to ambush it!' complained Hogshead.

'Come!' repeated Courgette as she sprinted down the bank, turned and ran after the seventh cart. In a few moments she had caught the ropes holding the covers in place, working them loose as she ran behind. 'Swift, be fleet of foot!'

Three steps, a leap and suddenly Courgette was in the cart, her arms waving in frantic gestures of encouragement. Dawn clicked instantly and flew down the slope, squeaking, 'Free ride, free ride!'

Firkin sprinted, outpacing Dawn and leapt into the cart, followed by a profusely panting Hogshead who rolled in on top of the sacks.

Dawn struggled on, encouraged by Courgette's waving arms. She half ran, half fell towards the cart, gaining ground painfully slowly, feeling as if she was running through syrup.

'Slow down!' she croaked. 'Come back!'

Almost as one the three new passengers in the cart realised that she wasn't going to make it.

Unless . . .

Hogshead spotted a lever above the wheel. All the carts had them. In a flash he realised what it was, he stood and pulled hard on it. At the front of the wagon train the load on the rhinos increased. Blitzen snorted and leant into her harness harder. Hogshead tugged on the brake lever, splinters of wood and metal flying in showers as he strained against the sextet of rhinos. The cart slowed, creaking its angry protest.

Dawn struggled on, gaining a few feet.

Firkin tugged on another lever. Donner snorted. Magnus snored, oblivious of the desperate tug of war being waged around him.

Hogshead's arms screamed in anaerobic agony, suddenly clenching in lactic acid cramp. The brake pads, designed only to slow the carts during the long descent on the other side, smouldered and wore out rapidly.

So did Dawn. She staggered now, energy flagging, on her last legs.

Suddenly, one of the wheels locked, dirt and rocks piling up before it as a rut formed. Dawn surged forward wildly and was snatched inside by Courgette's flailing arms.

The boys released their levers, arms screaming and the whole train surged foward.

At the front Magnus jolted awake again, cracked his whip across the back of Prancer, shouted a hail of sleepy abuse at Dancer and dozed off once more, blissfully unaware of the four stowaways he had just acquired.

The ant's antennae waved as they picked up the unmistakeable scent of a female of the species. Her pheremones floated on the gentle evening breeze like hundreds of aromatic dinner invitations. In a moment, his mind captivated totally with sweetly-scented messages of nasal seduction, the ant had forgotten things like danger, physical hardship or work as the wafts of chemical femininity drove him wild with insectile desire. One word filled its mind. Lust.

In a flash he dropped the piece of leaf he had been wrestling with, turned on all six heels and skittered away, thoughts of wanton carnality uppermost in his mind. With an act of unrivalled determination he forded a ferociously babbling mountain stream, scrambled up a precipice and hauled himself, dripping, on to the edge of the path spurred on by the overwhelming powers of rampant lechery.

Suddenly he saw her standing on the far edge of the path. His mind filled with hundreds of compound images of her shapely black beauty shining in the setting sun. Wow! Now that's what I call a thorax! And what an abdomen . . . enough to drive a nest of ants wild! She turned gracefully on six stilleto heels and wiggled her mouthparts seductively.

He wanted her. She pouted at him. Nothing could stop him now . . .

However.

There are times when Coincidence, being the interfering, maliciously sadistic imp that it is, has other plans. Unfortunately this brave anty gigolo had been antennae-marked to provide a tiny fragment of Coincidence's heartless fiasco of fun for this evening.

Suddenly, above the insect's head, a pair of blue canvas shoes appeared, hovered for a split second, tinkled, then dropped a few inches to land solidly on the dry mountain earth.

'It's all right!' boomed the voice that belonged to the pair of feet and all points north. 'Don't panic I'm here to . . . oh bum! Not again!'

Merlot stood in the Foh Pass and looked around him, frowning.

A dark, angry shape soared out of the fiery ball of the sun and flapped straight at him. The sky was wings, squawking and talons as Arbutus landed in a flurry of feathers and chastisements.

'I dooo wish you'd have the decency to *tell* me when you're going to just vanish!' he snapped, tapping a claw irritably on Merlot's saxaffron shoulder. 'It really is *most* disconcerting!'

Merlot looked up from the tell-tale dash of footprints and a gouge from a locked wheel and stared at Arbutus. 'They went thataway! Cranachan, what!' he said, held his right hand out, counted three and vanished, saving the puff of blue smoke for another occasion. Arbutus squawked a host of irritable curses in a manner very likely to bring owl-kind a bad name, spat and flapped angrily off towards the setting sun and Cranachan.

As a tiny lust-crazed ant hauled itself out of a foot-shaped indentation, shook its head and headed off for the object of its pheremone-addled insect desire, Coincidence put his hands on his hips and laughed long and loud. Then he too vanished. Disappearing to check on the results of a little experiment he had set up earlier involving a large bale of straw, several cans of paraffin and a fire-lizard with a bad case of hayfever.

Riddles in the Dark

Instead of the gentle tinkling which the King's Bell normally made when he rang to order food, it growled, snarled and spat clangorously in the kitchen, eloquently telegraphing the anger and manic fury with which it had been pulled.

At the far end of the bell-cord King Khardeen sat in his private quarters, swearing and cursing angrily, reviewing the day. It was late, he was tired and he wanted his supper – now! Somehow he had managed to convey all of these things in the way he had set the bell clanging far below. The red bell-cord now lay amongst a heap of plaster dust, stone fragments, shattered pulleys and twisted broken brackets. Just another irritation to add to dragons, trolls and fire and . . . !

There was the patter of feet outside, sprinting down the corridor with the haste of imminent decapitation, a screech of heels and a timid but urgent knock and the door eased open.

'Your supper, Your Highness,' whispered Surfeit, placing the platter of fried lampreys* on to the bedside table, turned on his heel and made a swift, but not too hasty exit.

King Khardeen unfolded himself from beneath the cloud of anger-filled gloom and stalked towards his supper.

* Prior to the investiture of King Khardeen upon the throne of Cranachan, lampreys were eaten with a side dish of utter revulsion and hysterical nausea. And then only by hapless foreigners who knew no better. Common folklore insisted that the eel-like fish issued directly from the intestines of the devil himself and if consumed would recongeal and devour the victim from the inside out. This was probably something to do with their unfortunate habit of causing acute, explosive and often fatal gut-rotting flatulence.

Ostensibly to carry favour with the new King on his first night (but in reality to give him the greatest dose of terminal botulism ever) Khardeen was wined and dined on lamprey by a Cranachan spy. However, having been weaned on stir-fried Ammorettan Death Lizard, the botulism lost.

Later, Khardeen went on to experiment with herbs and spices, finding that deep-fried lamprey bisque with garlic mornay was his favourite.

The day had started badly enough, having to visit the Chapel of St Absent the Regularly Forgotten and meet those priests! 'Don't they know the afterlife doesn't exist!' he snarled as he chewed on a lamprey. 'Should have had them executed for blasphemy!'

'Should have everyone executed!' he shouted smashing his fist on to the table. 'Useless, they're all useless! Ask them a simple question and they shrug pathetically!

His seething mind flew to the hastily convened meeting at which the recent happenings were discussed with a view to getting some answers.

'Might as well have been talking to parrots,' he seethed, his voice mocking as he cried, 'Where did the dragon come from? "Don't know, sire." Who sent it? "Don't know, sire." Why is it here? "Don't know, sire." How can we get rid of it? "Don't know, sire." '

The only answer he had received from the combined intelligence of Commander Achonite, General Bateleur, Colonel Rachnid and Commander-in-Chief Lappet was to the question 'What were those things that smashed the market Square?' They had all seemed so smug when they had chorused 'Trolls, sire!'

'Intelligence, indeed!' Another of Surfeit's lampreys was gulped down. 'Idiots!' he growled.

A few moments later, the plate cleared, he settled down to a very fitful night's sleep.

'But vhatt are you goink to do mit dem?' hissed Vlad, hurrying in the wake of Fisk through passageway after storm-drain, heading to the far eastern end of the Imperial Palace Fortress of Cranachan.

'Wait and see!' gloated Fisk, struggling with the freshly whitewashed pottery gourd nestling in a massive whicker basket surrounded by about a bale of straw. 'We're nearly there.'

'Vhere!' asked the vampire, staring about him and trying to pinpoint their current location.

'Second stairs on the right, straight on to Khardeen!' Fisk shook as he tried to contain the excitement within. It was three in the morning and if everything went as Fisk planned, tomorrow would dawn with him in charge, freed from this undercover world of secrecy and shadows – a free man, with all the power he wanted. Soon he would have Cranachan and Rhyngill. Soon he would be in control!

He counted off the secret doors on the left.

One – the King's sitting-room.

Two – the King's ablutions.

Three – straight ahead – the King's bedchamber. This is it! With only the slightest popping sound a small plug of canvas was removed from the left eye of the portrait of King Stigg. Fisk pressed the side of his nose against the back of the painting, sneering at the sleeping monarch's rapidly twitching eyes. He was dreaming! At his most vulnerable to suggestion. Absolutely perfect!

In a flash Fisk had unlatched a tiny secret door and vanished into the King's bedchamber, tugging the white-washed gourd in a basket behind him.

King Khardeen groaned in his sleep, rolling over, his sweating brow furrowing as if his thoughts were boiling in angry confusion and seething nightmare bafflement. They were.

All the recent events danced and cavorted, twisting death-mask faces in wild cackling mockery: trolls destroyed the Market Square with vast seismic strides, smashing the Palace with the manic relish of battle-crazed mongol hordes; dragons soared and swooped, torching Castell Rhyngill, charring walls in enormous, engulfing waves of fire, roasting and toasting everything in rising tides of unstoppable destruction. All of his empire flashed and screamed, burned and collapsed before his very eyes in extended wide-screen colour and full-volume surround sound – the director's cut of the end of Khardeen's world. And there wasn't a break for popcorn and ice-cream.

Fisk placed the basket and gourd at the foot of the bed and

leant over the thrashing nightmare-gripped monarch, sneering a grin of evil calculating intent.

Vlad peered through King Stigg's left eye socket as Fisk leaned closer, whispering in Khardeen's ear.

Through the smoke and flames of the blackened Rhyngill, over the nightmare clouds of Cranachan's dust, a giant dark face floated ominously, turned and glared at Khardeen. A black leather eyepatch covered one eye, plumes of charcoal hair faded into the billows of inchoate smoke, the light from leaping crimson flames shone on the scythe-like curve of the nose and the glistening arch of the evilly sneering upper lip. The vast mouth opened, inhaled, then spat words at him.

'Tut, tut! Whose been a naughty King then!'

In his nightmare world Khardeen screamed, his crown and cloak blown off him in the breath of the demonic face.

'All you've seen so far is just a taster,' roared the face again. '*I* control the dragons, they'll do anything *I* tell them to.'

Khardeen shuddered, sweat beads gleaming on his forehead as he thrashed fitfully.

'Do *exactly* as I say and you can keep what's left of your precious empire. Fail, and the ever-so-possessive mother of the egg at the foot of your bed will be told who stole it, where it is and how to get there. Got that?'

With another shudder Khardeen nodded.

'Now, here's what I want . . .'

Vlad watched in utter amazement as Fisk listed his demands into the ear of the nightmare-gripped King, ending with a dire warning.

'Don't even think about moving or even touching that egg. The smell of humans lingers long and dragons have *extremely* sensitive noses and very, *very* long memories! Especially for revenge!'

Silently, mentally rubbing his hands together in the evil victory of corruption, Fisk vanished from the terrified King's side, barely containing a shriek of excitement.

It would be all over soon. Just a matter of time . . .

Creeping stealthily through the moonlit terraces and alleys of the Imperial Palace Fortress, Hirsuit was bursting with questions. 'Bharkleed!' he whispered as he stumbled over the wing of the six-foot parchment cherub he was carrying. 'What the hell are we doing?'

'Patience, Brother Hirsuit. All will become clear,' answered Bharkleed, manoeuvring a similar sized angel past a large dark green bush.

'I'm *sick* of being patient! I want to know what I'm doing with this cherub!'

'It's for the King if you must know,' snapped Bharkleed.

'Oh, great! Have you gone out of your tiny mind!' growled Hirsuit. 'I did *not* come here to perform nativity plays!'

'Neither did I,' agreed Bharkleed and snuck through a tiny doorway to the left, tutting irritably as he creased the angel's wing and put a grubby mark on her halo. Whedd grumbled as he negotiated the door with his angel.

'What d'you mean?' questioned Hirsuit a minute later when he had struggled through with his home-made cherub.

'These *aren't* for nativity plays,' answered Bharkleed. 'Wrong time of the year anyway. You told me you'd revised "Religious Festivals".'

'Yes . . . well, I did a bit,' flustered Hirsuit. 'But, that's got nothing to do with this lot!' he added, shaking his cherub.

'True,' murmured Bharkleed, turning a sharp left. Putting an urgent finger on his lips he stopped, looked up and whispered. 'Here we are!'

'What?' gasped a shocked Hirsuit looking around the tiny deserted courtyard below a steep bare wall containing one solitary window.

'Should be the perfect time,' whispered Bharkleed consulting his nice new 'Nocturne' sundial, which he had casually pocketed in Shirm. 'He should be ready!'

'Who? Ready for what?' Hirsuit was getting desperate. 'C'mon. Explain!'

186

'The King!' grumbled Bharkleed. 'Haven't you been listening?'

'Yes, but I still don't . . .'

'All right, all right,' conceded Bharkleed. 'We haven't got long. It'll have to be quick. Now what don't you understand?' he asked, rummaging in the bushes at the base of the wall.

'Everything!' moaned Hirsuit.

'Oh, is that all!' answered Bharkleed, withdrawing several long stretches of branch and a small ball of string. 'Tie these together whilst I explain,' he said and sat down cross-legged on the ground, sticks in one hand string in the other. Whedd looked at Hirsuit in utter bafflement and did likewise.

'Up there,' whispered Bharkleed pointing to the window, 'is the King. And right about now, just after three in the morning, he should be at his most vulnerable.' He expertly joined two sticks, one extending the other.

'So we're going to attack him, are we?' croaked Whedd enthusiastically. 'How do we get up to him?'

'That's what these sticks are for, idiot!' snapped Hirsuit, the knot he was attempting to form unravelling before his eyes.

'But it's miles up there . . .' began Whedd's protest. 'These sticks won't hold me!'

'No, no! Shutup and listen!' growled Bharkleed. '*We* won't be climbing up there. We'll be sending winged messengers!'

'Eh? You mean pigeons?'

'No! *These*!' he growled shaking his angel forcibly.

Whedd, tongue still hanging from the corner of his mouth in concentration stared at Bharkleed with even greater lack of comprehension than before the explanation had begun.

'Look,' said Bharkleed wearily. 'Five hours ago, if Surfeit was on time, the dear King up there will have finished his supper and gone to sleep.'

'That's where I should be,' grumbled Hirsuit.

'So what?' asked Whedd, scowling at a very floppy knotted joint.

187

'So, the supper was lampreys,' said Bharkleed, his whisper dripping with significance.

'And?' pressed Hirsuit still as lost as Whedd.

'Lampreys,' insisted Bharkleed, '*The* lampreys. The ones we doctored before, remember?'

'Oh yeah. What was that stuff I put on them?' asked Hirsuit. 'I've been meaning to ask, only what with all these cherubs and the like I never got the chance!' he grinned sheepishly in the moonlight.

'Ellis Dee's* Celebrated Undetectable Odourless Hallucinogen Powder,' answered Bharkleed proudly.

'You fed him Ellis Dee's?' spluttered Hirsuit his knot unravelling with his shock.

'No. *You* did!'

'Why?' chorused Whedd and Hirsuit.

'Encouragement. To make his mind malleable to the concept of belief in the afterlife.'

'Eh?'

'Look, the King of this place is the most devoted materialist I have ever seen,' explained Bharkleed tying another stick on to the end of an ever-growing pole. 'He has *no* idea of the power of the afterlife, no inkling of heaven, no

---

* Ellis Dee, alias 'Hiyzah Kyte', alias 'Ohpyum Pappy', alias almost as many other aliases as kingdoms in which he was wanted (both by the 'law' and by hundreds of eager customers ready for another sniff, swig or gurgle of his preparations, tinctures and powders), was an infamous alchemist.

Having realised that the profit margins from turning lead into gold were far, far less than those to be had from turning plants into dope he cancelled his standing order of five tons of lead ore a month from the Cerussite Mining Co. Ltd, sold his philosopher's stone, and set off to find the mythical Auric Triangle (an area of the Culmen Mountains famed for the unexplained disappearance of thousands of drug-crazed Nugh-Age Travellers, hundreds of believers in 'free love for all' and several dozen members of kingdom's various vice-squads).

Ellis Dee spent years in the Auric Triangle harvesting, distilling, extracting and processing as many different botanical specimens as he could lay his alchemical hands on, and trying the resultant powders, tinctures and balms out on a plethora of willing volunteers.

In a very short time there was almost nothing that he didn't know about certain poppies, turnip-shaped cacti and extracts from hundreds of berries. His most famous preparation was his 'Celebrated Undetectable Odourless Hallucinogen Powder', known simply as 'Ellis Dee's' for short.

188

ken of the chthonic terrors of hell. Once he's shown that they *do* exist . . .'

'But we made all that nonsense up!' protested Hirsuit.

'I know that, *you* know that. I don't see why we have to be *entirely* honest with all our devotees,' answered Bharkleed smoothly. Whedd chuckled conspirationally.

Bharkleed continued, 'Once Kingy up there is convinced that the predictable materialism of *this* world is lost in the transition to the next, and pain, suffering . . .'

'Ooooh *lots* of suffering,' chorused Whedd.

'. . . and *stacks* of anguish awaits those who have no faith, then he'll be desperate to believe! Simple!' grinned Bharkleed. 'It might take a steady dose of Ellis Dee's and constant pressure over a few nights from our winged friends here, but he'll crack. And when he does we'll be there ready for his donations!'

Bharkleed, a fire burning in his eyes almost as brightly as that still raging in Rhyngill, finished tying his angel to his stick, frowned at the other's progress, or lack of it, and began to raise his winged messenger to the window.

High above, in the boiling turmoil of Khardeen's nightmare mind, the sheets of flame that were Rhyngill screamed skywards, stoked by the incessantly circling golden dragon. In his inter-cranial world the trolls revelled in the destruction of Cranachan and the eye-patched face from Hell berated him with ever increasing ferocity, tearing off larger and larger strips of his pride and pointing ever growing fingers of scorn and derision.

It was probably the most unpleasant night of his life.

It was about to get worse.

Outside the window, bobbing and fluttering like lumen-starved moths snatching photons from a spluttering candle, two angels and a cherub appeared.

King Khardeen's somnolent eye flicked open for a moment, subconsciously registering the heavenly glass-tapping visitors whilst the rest of his mind seethed on, gripped in fascination at the nightmare images flashing and dancing before him.

Suddenly, out from the imagined flames of Rhyngill three tiny white shapes flew. They soared towards the ranting eye-patched face in tight battle formation despite the myriad thermals popping from below.

The two cut-out angels and the parchment cherub continued to bombard the window whilst their imaginary counterparts soared onwards in a tight seraphimic triangle.

'How much longer do we need to keep this up?' moaned Hirsuit crashing his cherub against the window. 'My arms are killing me!'

'Long as it takes,' grunted Bharkleed, wishing privately that he had made his angel smaller. 'We'll know when it starts to happen.'

'When what starts?'

'The Royal Conversion,' grunted Bharkleed, cursing as a light snatch of breeze smashed his angel against the stone work, finally dislodging its halo.

Khardeen tossed fitfully, whimpered, shook, then awoke suddenly in jolting sweat-soaked alarm, thumb jammed firmly in his mouth. Snatching at his pillow he squirmed towards the headboard, curling foetally as the ghostly figures whirled at the window. Bharkleed's angel tapped again. Khardeen screamed and dived beneath the bedclothes.

'Bingo!' whispered Bharkleed, snatching his angel earthwards.

Khardeen's mind spun with terrified confusion as the effects of the Ellis Dee's blurred the lines between nightmare and reality; the alkaloidal boot kicking chemical dirt over the vague chalk mark between actuality and imagination. He had seen angels! They were there at the window. Dare he look again? Should he peek beyond the security of his blankets?

Dread trickled down his sweating back as images of terror lurked menacingly with claws unsheathed, teeth glinting unlipped in the moonlight. He held his breath in a double nelson and eased back the covers.

The vast sneering face, scowling and spitting threats against

190

a background of devastation glared back at him no more. His breath choked and struggled frantically. He stared at the windows fearful of armies of angels pounding for entry. Nothing. Not even an itinerant cherub. Poking a timorous foot out of bed he crawled to the window, shakily looking out at the now empty couryard below. He was safe. It was all over. Just a normal everyday nightmare.

Suddenly, in a heart stopping moment, he saw the vast dragon's egg at the end of his bed. His breath broke the double nelson and surged out of his lungs, racing through his terror-stricken trachea, fleeing his quaking body in a fear-laden scream only marginally faster than he fled the room.

Hogshead noticed it first.

Distant voices filtered beneath the tarpaulin and into the ears of the youngsters, joining the creaking rumble of the wagon train.

Peering out from under the covers he could see nothing unusual – the end of the Foh Pass, the Talpa Mountains receding, a trail of haulage-rhino prints – but suddenly the view was blocked by the vast unbroken expanse of the Cranachan outer wall. Well, it would have been unbroken were it not for the recent interference of two very large stone trolls. Hogshead gasped as the scene of trolloid destruction unfolded before his eyes. In a flash he was joined by the other three, their heads turning and nodding at the rear of the cart like cheap imitation canine decorations.

'Cranachan didn't look this bad, did it?' murmured Hogshead as the flattened fragments of ex-market-stall upon ex-market-stall drifted past their field of view. The cart bounced roughly as it was hauled through a vast stone footprint. Blitzen snorted complaint as Magnus the Carter's whip lashed over her thick-skinned back.

''Tis ye battlefield!' said Courgette, staring at the wreck-age, feeling war-like emotions stirring within.

'I don't think it's as simple as that . . .' said Hogshead mytseriously, his mind desperately trying to piece together a multi-million piece jigsaw of conflicting information. It was like trying to herd a flock stubborn amoebas.

Suddenly the cart jolted to a halt and a flurry of shouts wriggled into earshot. Dawn flashed an alarmed look of query at Courgette as a muffled conversation stole into the cart.

'All right, Magnus? Good journey?' asked Jhymmy the Carter, the thirty-ninth ex-president of COSHH* and infamous peanut grower, strolling up, clipboard in hand.

'Not so bad,' grunted Magnus, stretching and climbing off his cart. He unclipped the pachygraphs† from the rhino's feet and handed them to Jhymmy, stifling a yawn.

'These say you've been driving all night!' snapped Jhymmy scowling at the parchment read-out and tutting. Magnus grinned slyly, rustled in his tunic pocket and handed a few gleaming gold tokens to the man with the clip-board. 'They must be playing up again,' complained Jhymmy noting a rest stop of two hours on the timesheet. 'Technology!' he tutted, scrunching up the parchment traces and hurling them into the blazing brazier by his hut. He turned and shouted to a large figure in a yellow cloak, 'Jaycee, be a good lad and unload this lot will you?'

---

* COSHH – the Cranchanian Overmountain Society of Hireable Hauliers, set up to investigate the numerous dubious working practices, frauds and scams perpetrated by the Trans-Talpine Hauliers. It took two years of demanding undercover graft, months of communal head scratching and a very hefty legal consultation fee, but eventually the COSHH Regulations were drawn up.

Overnight the volume of parchment-work required to be filled out prior to loading increased a hundred-fold. Information had to be supplied and recorded in triplicate regarding toxicity, flammability, explosivity and addictivity. And everything had to be cross-referenced to all the other items being transported on any specific load.

And beneath the smokescreen of increased parchment-work, a unified masterstroke of financial prestidigitation began – whilst the customers' attention was held by the flurry of scribbling quills, their pockets and purses miraculously emptied up the hauliers' sleeves.

† A device designed to prevent 'clipping' – the virtually undetectable toe-nail extension perpetrated by the more unscrupulous dealers in order to increase resale value of high-mileage pachyderms.

Panic rustled through the seventh cart as they heard this last phrase.

'They're unloading! We'll be found!'

Courgette eased herself into the shadow of the wheel, staring around at the stacks of boxes and piles of sacks strewn everywhere. The vast man busied himself unloading the cart whilst Magnus and Jhymmy walked the rhinos off to the stables for a well-earned mud-bath. In a flash Courgette dashed unseen behind a wall of sacks waving at the others to follow.

'I should be doing that,' grumbled Firkin. 'I'm the hero!'

Dawn stifled a giggle and followed Courgette's lead vanishing behind the wall of flour.

'Ok, now what?' asked Firkin petulantly a few moments later as the foursome squatted uncomfortably in the dark behind the sacks.

Before Courgette could answer an officious sounding voice bellowed out across the loading area. 'Right lads, start with that pile over there and hurry up about it. This lot should have left last night!' The youngsters looked about in panic as they heard two heavy boots stomping towards them and a sack was grabbed and manhandled into a waiting cart, Dawn snatched her breath in frightened alarm.

'Well done,' complained Firkin scowling at Courgette. 'Out of the frying pan into the flour! We can't stay here!'

'But . . . where can we go!' whimpered Hogshead, pausing as another sack was removed.

'Easy,' whispered Firkin confidently. 'When their backs are turned . . .' Another sack. '. . . we make a run for it . . .' A grunt and a sack vanished. '. . . across to that other pile over there!' he pointed.

'C'mon, hurry it up!' yelled the officious voice as another sack was removed.

'But we'll be seen!' protested Hogshead.

'Not if . . .' Sack. '. . . we're quick! It's all down to . . .' Sack.

'. . . timing!' He turned and surveyed the terrain through a

193

small gap in the flour wall as it was disassembled brick by hessian brick. Straight to the onions, round the turnips, over that pile of boxes and we're free. Easy!

'Ok, when you're ready!' whispered Firkin around another vanishing sack. 'I've got it!' He turned to see a frantically waving Hogshead disappearing down a hole in the ground barely wide enough for him.

'C'mon!' mouthed Hogshead.

'But what about my way?'

'Too risky!' answered the head and shoulders of Hogshead. 'Courgette said so!'

Firkin fumed as a fountain of flour from a splitting sack rained down from above.

He scurried forward and followed Hogshead down the hole.

'Courgette says "Forget ye not to replaceth ye grate!" ' whispered Hogshead from the inside of the drain.

Nag, nag, nag! thought Firkin. Who does she think she is!

Just as the last few sacks of flour were loaded on to the waiting cart a metal grate silently eased its way back into the drain where it belonged.

King Khardeen burst into 'Black' Achonite's bedchamber in a panicking flurry of limbs and nightshirt. He surged across the room grabbing his Commander by the shoulders, rattling him awake.

Khardeen's brow dripped with the sweat of fear as he stared wildly into the pair of still sleep-ridden eyes.

'Dragons . . . here!' he cried.

'What time is it?' muttered Achonite through a dense curtain of thick weariness.

'Eggs . . . my bed!' squealed the King shaking Achonite wildly.

'Eh? Oooh, not so rough, my head . . .'

'. . . and angels . . .'

'Any pink elephants?' muttered Achonite scratching his head.

'. . . cherubs . . . devils . . . dragons!'

'Stop shaking me! I can't think if I'm being shaken!' moaned Achonite as the possessed King flung him about.

Suddenly Khardeen stopped and stared wildly around him. 'They're here! Can't you hear them?'

'No, I . . .'

Khardeen turned and tore open Achonite's wardrobe, searching for something.

'There's dragons here, I know they're here, they're everywhere. I didn't touch your egg, it wasn't me . . .' he shouted, looking apprehensively at the ceiling, feeling hunted.

'What's wrong? What's going on?' asked Achonite in utter bewilderment, still trying to reluctantly haul himself out of the particularly pleasant, and ever-so lust-ridden, dream he had been so rudely distracted from. He hoped he could pick it up later. He desperately wanted to know what the panting maiden was going to do with that length of silk rope and that lemming skin glove . . .

'Dragons . . . dragons!!' yelled King Khardeen clutching his head as if it were about to explode, turning and fleeing Achonite's bedchambers, his bare feet and screams slapping and echoing down the bare Palace corridors.

Achonite followed, skipping across the floor as he tried to haul on his other slipper and wrestling with his high-security leather dressing-gown (replete with dagger in the pocket). He sprinted after the Regal Shrieks, skittering round the corner into his quarters just as the terror-filled wailing stopped.

Fearing the worst, Achonite edged into the monarch's bedchamber and stared at the scene before him.

It was as if a wild demon had erupted from the centre of the royal berth. The sheets and blankets were strewn in a trail from the bed to the open window and out of the door, the pillows tossed randomly everywhere. Achonite smirked as he glimpsed the tiny brown paw of a small bear poking out from beneath a scattered pillow. Well I never . . . he thought.

'No! No, No!' screamed Khardeen suddenly shaking with confused terror. 'It's gone!' he cried wildly, leaping into the pile of blankets and searching frantically for the dragon's egg. 'How did she know it was here!'

'What's gone, Sire? asked Achonite.

'She's taken it . . .' he sobbed.

'Er, is this any help?' asked Achonite handing the King a piece of parchment which he had just found on the floor.

'It's not here . . .' answered the King taking the parchment absently, blowing his nose noisily and returning it to his Commander.

Achonite wrinkled his nose in distaste and handed it back. 'I think you're supposed to read it. It's addressed to you, Sire,' he answered, surreptitiously wiping his finger and thumb on one of the royal sheets.

King Khardeen's face suddenly changed from the skimmed milk of abject fear to the fuming nitric acid of vehement anger. 'What's this!' he hyperventilated. '*What's this*?' Achonite squinted over the King's night-shirted shoulder. All he saw made him even more confused. Just before Khardeen screwed the parchment up in an impotent surge of molar-crushing rage that cleared the last milligrams of Ellis Dee's Celebrated Undetectable Odourless Hallucinogen Powder from his anger-ridden body, Achonite glimpsed the words.

. . . and if you *don't* comply, then I tell Mummy where her egg is!
   Sweet dreams,
   The Appropriator.

Barely managing to stifle the evil peal of wicked laughter welling up inside him Fisk sneered happily and turned away from the back of King Stigg's portrait. Negotiating the large whitewashed gourd 'egg' he headed off down the passageway, his body seething with self-satisfied evil thoughts.

Perfect, he sneered, perrrfect!!!

'Now what are we supposed to do?' grumbled Firkin, his voice strangely muffled by the moss on the walls of the drain. 'I don't actually think that we're going to bump into Klayth down here! Not exactly regal enough, is it?' His voice dripped with almost as much sarcasm as the walls did water.

Courgette scowled in the gloom.

'Look ye, 'tis time to straighteneth yon matter out,' she said, green eyes smouldering angrily. 'Dost we or dost we not pledge allegiance to a leader? Dost thou command us?' she added scowling at Firkin.

Mutely shaken heads answered.

'Verily. 'Tis a democracy,' she concluded.

'Suppose so,' conceded Firkin.

'As I thought,' said Courgette. 'A relief 'tis clarified. Now hark, and hark well, here's what we shallest do!' She cocked her head to one side and listened carefully. ''Tis clear outside, we canst head off to find Klayth. After you, Firkin.' She pointed to the grating above his head.

Firkin, grumbling under his breath and trying to work out quite how she had managed to tell him what to do, *again*, stood and pushed at the grate.

Then he pushed again harder.

It stubbornly refused to move.

Had arc-welding been invented, and had Firkin known anything at all about the use of high-energy electricity to permanently fuse sections of metal in a bond of quite outstanding strength, he would quite categorically have sworn that the grate had been arcwelded shut!

'Dont be stupid!' chastised Dawn. 'That's the way we came in!'

'I *know* that,' grunted Firkin, jamming his shoulder against the grate once more and turning red with the strain of not moving it.

'But it won't open now! It's stuck!'

'Come, jest ye not . . .' began Courgette.

'It's stuck. S-T-UCK. Stuck!'

'Er, I hate to say this,' began Hogshead. 'But if that's stuck, then so are we!'

'Great!' grumbled Firkin rubbing his shoulder and slouching against the mossy wall. 'Should've gone my way, out behind the onions . . . easy!'

'We shouldst have been seen!' countered Courgette.

'You can run, can't you?'

'Yea, verily.'

'Well, then . . .'

'Shutup!' snapped Hogshead, alarm glistening at the edge of his words. 'Listen, I can hear voices!' he whispered.

'Yeah, it's the hauliers up above . . .' began Firkin before he was cut off by Hogshead's very hard stare.

'No,' he mouthed nervously. 'Down *there!*' he pointed into the inky blackness of the drain where it emptied into a larger passage running left to right. Slowly the others became painfully aware of the sharp click of pointy steel-toe-capped boots and the smug arrogance of a sneering voice echoing off mossy walls.

'. . . easy, so perfect! Fell for it completely. I'll have him in the palm of my gauntlet soon and *then* who'll rule Cranachan, eh?'

Hogshead froze as he listened.

'Verry ssshrewd, dat vhasss ein cunninck plan! Ssss sss ssss!' sniggered the second voice evilly, its vampire sibilance slicing into the very marrow of Firkin's soul.

The pair's approaching light from the side passage lit the circular mouth of the minor drain, glistening intermittently off the lining of moss and lichen.

'Soon I'll be free from this sewer. Soon I will stand tall and be worshipped!' cackled the first voice.

'Sss sss sss!' answered the second.

'No more skulking like worthless sewer rats, no more hide and sneak . . .' sneered the voice as a single candle flashed down the drain, illuminating the youngers like a group of escapees in an eighty-thousand lumen spotlight, countless gunbarrels levelled unseen at their hearts, cocked and ready,

safety-catches filed off long ago, one false move and . . .
and . . .

The candle passed into the gloom casting a shadowy arc
behind it the ranting pair too engrossed to see the cowering
foursome.

'. . . and power so very soon!' spouted the first voice, 'I
will herald the dawning of a new age!'

'Ssss sss sss!'

'The age of the obsequious. An age of slavery and
servility . . .'

'Ssssubsserviensse and grrrovelinck . . . !'

'. . . crawling and fawning . . .'

'. . . sssycophantic ssssubmissssivenessssss!'

'. . . my boots will be polished by the tongues of
Cranachan slaves!'

Unheard by anyone in the drain Blitzen removed her front
hoof from the cover and strolled off for her turn in the
mudbath.

'Look to the East, good people!' cried Bharkleed, his indigo
robes billowing as he ranted fanatically at the early-morning
throng humming and crowding into the remains of the
Cranachan Market Square. 'The rubble you see around you
is a warning – a trial size portion of Armageddon. The End is
Nigh! Are *you* ready to face it?' He pointed accusingly at the
closed scurrying faces of the people from atop his rickety box
and yelled hoarsely. 'The End of the World is Approaching!
What are you going to do about it?'

'Hear that, Mayvhis? Better get extra turnips this week,'
shrieked a bustling hutwife as she battered her way through
to the few remaining stalls.

'The fires of destruction are being stoked . . .' bawled
Bharkleed.

'Think I'll get some boar, too. I like a good barbecue,
don't you, Mayvhis? Be a shame to waste those fires, eh?'

'Join us in the Elevated Church of St Lucre the Unwashed
and *you* will have a glorious afterlife!' screamed His

199

Eminence above the tide of ignorance sweeping into the market.

'Not doing so well this morning,' muttered Hirsuit, waving a placard advertising Apartments in Hell.

'No. He looks tired,' agreed Whedd folding his arms and leaning nonchalantly on a chart indicating the Hadean exchange rate benefits to members of St Lucre's over the non-affiliated deceased.

Suddenly, Bharkleed leapt off his box and stormed out of the Market Square, his face crimson with rage. Hirsuit and Whedd stared at each other, then sprinted after him.

'Such ignorance!' raged Bharkleed. 'They show more interest in their turnips than they do in their souls! Just you watch, you'll see! When the King's on our side they'll be flocking to join us. Flocking!'

'Are you *sure* this is a good idea?' whispered Hogshead stepping ankle-deep into a puddle of less than savoury quality.

'Nay,' whispered Courgette peering around a sharp corner and clutching Exbenedict. 'Hast thou a better idea?'

'No.'

'Well, follow or so shallst we lose them!'

'I'd rather not be anywhere *near* them,' whimpered Hogshead shaking his dripping foot as Fisk and Vlad rattled and hissed through the echoing underworld.

Courgette turned on him sharply. 'If thou willst retreat, be swift.'

Hogshead looked plaintively at Firkin and Dawn, shrugged and followed Courgette round the corner.

Ahead of them, still ranting furiously about someone called 'The Appropriator' and what he, or it, would do to Cranachan in the very near future, Fisk stomped ever onwards, his boots clicking on the slimy surface, his ravings punctuated by the cold humourless hissing of Vlad's appreciative laughter. Hogshead detested the way they both seemed to know where all the puddles were, and cursed silently as his foot found another one.

Abruptly, as Fisk turned another corner, his voice altered tone, the percussive consonants reverberating in evil relish, the high sibilants shimmering with sinister sharpness. It was suddenly more open, as if he had stepped out of a tunnel into a hall.

Courgette silently held up her hand for everyone to stop, peered around the corner and caught her breath. The image of an ancient throne squatting between a vast collection of cobwebbed treasures and dust bedevilled paintings burned into her shocked retina. She shook her head, rubbed her eyes and looked again. Fisk swirled his leather cloak about him and settled into the throne with easy familiarity.

This was Fisk's world. They had strayed into Fisk's domain!

'Time to see what the *Herald* has to say, I think,' sneered Fisk, his voice floating across the treasure-laden cavern. 'I want to read what they have to say about the latest evil doings of the Appropriator! Threatening the King! What a nerve! Oh, naughty, naughty me!' His words dripped with the glistening ooze of far too much relish. 'Fetch!'

Vlad dashed eagerly away from the throne as Fisk laughed long and loud, sneering with evil anticipation of the coming headlines.

Was it Courgette's imagination or had the dashing footsteps of the hunched vampire changed suddenly into the hushed flapping of leathery wings?

As if a warhorse were practising high-velocity dressage upon it, the centuries-old oak table in the centre of the Conference Room of Cranachan resonated to the steady drumming of King Khardeen's impatient fingers.

'They're late!' he bellowed. 'They'd better have a *damned* good reason or, by all that's indecent, their heads will roll!'

He returned to the irritable drumming, the sound bouncing off the bare stone walls and their austere decorations of crossed pikes and maces.

Suddenly he slammed his fist hard on the table and yelled. 'Bring me mead. I need mead! Mead and lampreys!'

A large door creaked open and a terrified attendant vanished, eager to escape the brooding atmosphere within the Conference Room. He knew the King's temper was short but he had *never* seen him this wound up before.

'Where are they?' Khardeen bellowed once more, scowling at Commander Achonite, the only other person currently at table.

'I have no information, Sire,' he replied in as calming a manner as possible. He failed.

'Call yourself the head of the Black Guard? No information? What kind of an idiot do you take me for?'

Careful! Achonite told himself. A head will roll today as sure as eggs is . . . *Don't* mention eggs! Achonite swallowed hard.

'No suggestion as to your shortcomings was intended, your regality. The fault is entirely within my jurisdiction and as soon as is practicable I shall determine its source and rectify it personally, Sire!' crawled Achonite. Now is not the right time to request extra troops to patrol the Foh Pass.

'Well, where are they?' demanded Khardeen.

'I can only surmise that they are between here and Castell Rhyngill, Sire, since I received notification of their departure, by pigeon last night.'

Quietly a door eased open and the attendant returned carrying a flagon of mead and a platter of freshly steaming lampreys. Quivering only very slightly with abject terror, the attendant set the dainty dish before the King, bowed and fled.

'Why are they taking so *long?*' barked Khardeen. 'We're not at war with anyone, are we?'

'No, Sire!' Achonite answered, and was suddenly terrified that Khardeen's next question would be 'Why not?' Instead he simply grinned and rubbed his hands with relish as heavy-booted footfalls echoed down the corridor outside, ending in a barked order and a sharp stamp to attention. The large oak door was struck in request for entry.

Khardeen growled gutturally, sipped his mead and

devoured an entire lamprey, failing to notice the sheen of white powder all over it. He glared at the sundial and took another brooding mouthful of mead. Achonite shifted uncomfortably sensing the build-up of anger within Khardeen.

Outside the door feelings of discomfort were growing. They were late. They knew were late. And they knew the penalty for being late probably decreased their chance of siring offspring to far less than zero.

Suddenly the door was snatched open and King Khardeen stood before them, arms outstretched linking the two doors like an Ammorettan Death Lizard ready to strike, his face gradually exploring all the shades of red that have ever been associated with the word 'fury'.

Eventually settling on a particularly tasteful crimson – love it, darling! That shade speaks volumes. It says anger, rage and tempestuous wrath all at once in *such* a tasteful way. It's you, darling! Just you! Would you like it wrapped? – opened his mouth and bellowed.

'What time do you call this? Where have you *been*? You're *late!*' His handlebar moustache swirled in the tirade of anger. 'You'd better have a damned good excuse!' Then he turned and stomped back to his Conference Throne, Commander in Chief Lappet, Colonel Rachnid and General Bateleur sheepishly in tow, their legs pressed tightly together at the knees.

'Well?' bellowed Khardeen, glaring meaningfully at the sundial.

The three military leaders looked at each other.

'It wasn't our fault,' began Rachnid, his goatee beard twitching as he spoke. 'Set off as soon as we'd checked out Rhyngill . . .'

'. . . hold up on Foh Pass . . .' grunted Lappet. '. . . animals as far as the eye could see . . . hundreds of . . .'

'. . . pairs of 'em coming out of some funny-shaped boat on top of Mount Harrerat . . .' joined Bateleur, his dense black hair belying his eighty years.

203

'. . . sheep and jeeraffs and . . .' added Lappet.

'Never seen it there before!' squawked Bateleur.

'. . . antelopes and bison and . . .'

'Don't know what it was doing there!' added Bateleur shaking his head.

'. . . snakes and ants and . . .'

'Enough!' snapped Khardeen.

'. . . didn't see any fish though . . .'

'Enough! What do you know about boats on Mount Harrerat?' barked Khardeen glaring at Achonite.

'I have received no request for a landing there,' he answered, trying to sound earnest. 'I shall send some men to investigate immediately. And,' he added, suddenly oozing the type of mercenary charm that warmed Khardeen's calculating heart, 'may I suggest the immediate introduction of the Mount Harrerat Mooring Tax and Immigration and Quarantine Charges for all animals, insects and birds, Sire?'

'Excellent, Achonite,' answered the King chewing on another lamprey. 'Make it so!' Then he turned on the trembling threesome before him. 'Your report from Rhyngill? Give it to me!'

Lappet coughed, opened a hastily shuffled mound of parchment and began to read. 'The Independant Investigation into the state of the Kingdom of Rhyngill's seat of power, heretofore known in its entirity as The Castell Rhyngill, has shown that . . .'

'Summarize, man!' shouted Khardeen, spraying a thin film of fish debris across the table, the floor and the three miltary men. 'Give me the bottom line!'

'Fire, Sire!' muttered Lappet, trying to ignore an unidentifiable lump of lamprey as it migrated down his left cheek.

'Fire?'

'Sire,' agreed Lappet, nodding slightly more energetically than he should as he tried to dislodge the glistening glob of fish flesh.

'You trying to be funny?' snarled Khardeen.

'No, Sire,' he denied, shaking his head and breathing a

204

sigh of relief as the piscine particle left his cheek and landed on Bateleur's boot.

'The cause of the fire?' snapped Khardeen.

'Excess organic heat supplied in several sheets of a flammular form by a large aerial saurian of legendary origin, Sire!' answered Colonel Rachnid and immediately wished he hadn't.

Khardeen's jaw dropped open in rage, his handlebar moustache quivering furiously. Achonite cringed.

'What, in the name of sanity, does *that* mean!'

'Er, dragon, Sire!' cringed Rachnid, his goatee beard twitching as it began its goodbyes to his collar and shoulders and all the other parts of his body it would miss.

King Khardeen's facial shading twitched a little more towards the crimson again. 'Are you trying to tell me that you went all the way to Rhyngill and came back with the conclusion that a dragon burnt it down?'

'Yes, Sire!'

'*I* could have told *you* that! It's not too difficult to add plumes of smoke to a whopping great gold flamethrower and work out something similar. Is it?'

They shook their heads.

'Did I or did I not mention something about a conclusion?' he snarled.

'Er, the dragon did it!' blurted Lappet, 'Sire!' he added limply.

'No! No! NO!' yelled Khardeen pounding the table and shooting to his feet. 'Look at the facts! I have a kingdom being destroyed by fire, I have a dragon flying about the place, a creature which up until a *very* short time ago I would have sworn was fictitious. Now, up until the dragon appeared there wasn't any burning, well, except witches and poxy villages that don't pay their tithes on time, but that's different. *That's* professional! It doesn't take a genius to work out that the dragon did it! Even *I* figured *that* one out!' Khardeen paused just long enough to bite the head off another lamprey and swig a flagon of mead.

205

'When I said "conclusion",' continued Khardeen gnawing furiously, 'I meant *stop* the dragon doing it! Get back on your horses and do the job *properly*!'

Any objections the three had were overruled by the angrily chewing face of their King glaring imperiously across the fish-splattered surface of the table.

'And bring back its head!' he yelled after their retreating backs. 'I want to try Dragon-brain Stew!'

Threatening the King! Threatening the King? Firkin's mind seethed in the dark cramped gloom of the tunnel outside Fisk's Throne Room as he stared in and tried to figure out what he could have meant. He knew that if it involved Fisk it was bound to be unpleasant and/or highly extortionate, the stack of nonchalantly ignored treasure lining the cavern was testament to that. Half of Firkin's mind wanted to sneak in, gather a stack of incriminating information, dash out of there and bring the authorities down on him with more force than a whale dropped from fifteen hundred feet; and half was quite happy to content itself with doing what it was doing right now – sitting in the dark, shaking with terror and confusion. What *was* Fisk up to?

Suddenly a hand shot out of the darkness, clamped itself suffocatingly across his mouth and nose and snatched him into a tiny alcove. His eyes wide with luminous panic above the finger he watched as Courgette gestured frantically at him in the dark. With a series of wild flapping movements and fingers pointing down like fangs, she brought Firkin's bewildered attention round to the regular sound of what appeared at first to be a chamois leather being slapped against a wall. It was only as a fruit bat struggled feebly into view with a copy of the *Triumphant Herald* rolled in its mouth that Firkin understood.

Unexpectedly the creature dropped out of the air, landing clumsily on the tunnel floor and started writhing furiously as if some desperate escapologist was trying to free himself from the cartilaginous cuffs of a bat-shaped bag. Somehow, the fur of the bat changed subtly into the faded elegance of a dinner jacket, the wings metamorphosed into arms and the head turned into a mostly humanoid shape. Dawn was swiftly and silently sick.

Vlad, unaware of their presence, brushed off his jacket, picked up the newsparchment and dashed into Fisk's Throne Room.

'Sssspessshial deliffery . . . !' he cried as he hurtled eagerly over the dark stone floor.

'Give it to me, now!' shouted Fisk, gauntlets opening and closing around thin air until the parchment was dropped into his hand.

'You've been flying again, haven't you?' he snapped as his grip slipped on the dribbly parchment.

'It'ssss fassssster . . .'

'It's messier!' he growled, unrolling the *Triumphant Herald* and staring at its front page. He blinked, shook his head and stared again, his lip trembling in an arching sneer of disbelieving anger as he read the headline.

'NO!' he yelled, flinging it to the floor. 'I don't believe it! He cannot deny it!'

'Bad newsssss . . . ?' whispered Vlad cautiously.

'The worst!' came the yelled reply as Fisk thumped the arm of the throne in a wave of surging anger. 'The *worst* thing he could have done! He'll be sorry for that. *Nobody* crosses the Appropriator unscatched. *Nobody* makes fun of me and lives! Nobody, not even the King!'

Fisk, his body twitching with frenzied vehemence, stood and swept out of the hall, kicking a suit of armour to the floor in a crash of metallic annoyance.

Vlad turned to the newsparchment and cringed as he read the tacky headline 'Beyond a yolk!'

'Uh-oh! Dhissss meansssss trrrouble!' he muttered to himself as a hail of frenzied abuse accompanied the sound of a pike-staff plunging through the chest of an innocent suit of armour, a mace decapitating three others and a steel lance being thrust maliciously through the head of a fifth. It went

207

momentarily silent as Fisk admired the freshly kebabed armoury then sparks flew as he applied the sizzling chilli sauce of temper, kicking and pounding in a deep red, harsh rage.

From the peak of the boat-crowned Mount Harrerat, in a swathe along the Foh Pass as far as the eye could see, the evidence that several thousand hungry animals had been suddenly released from enforced captivity was hard to avoid. The footprints of terrified herbivores sprinted down the mountain as they fled the claws of ravenous carnivores. Blood-stained signs of struggle dotted the area. Small bracts of heather twitched and sobbed in botanical woe as they surveyed the damage wreaked by herds of gobbling goats, wiping leafy limbs over tear-stained eyes as they witnessed things a seedling just shouldn't see; shrubs torn swishing and rustling from the ground by insatiable ungulates; willowy sylph-like shoots in the prime of life wrested from the rocky soil to be consumed by camels; or tragically trampled by llamas, squashed by sheep or impacted by impala. Mass herbicide.

But as General Bateleur, Colonel Rachnid, Commander in Chief Lappet and a small contingent of Black Guards picked their way up the mountainside toward the teetering boat it wasn't the sight of this feeding frenzy that caused them acute discomfort. It was the way the relief felt by the ark's passengers at the sudden end of such a difficult sea voyage had been so expertly expressed. In a variety of steaming piles.

'Well done, Dad,' said Spam slapping the old man across the shoulder as he staggered down the gang-plank and onto dry land. 'I didn't think you could do it!'

'Hah! Now *there's* faith!' muttered Nhoer attempting to get used to the ground not moving. Secretly he was wondering how in fact he *had* done it. Wasn't there supposed to be something about a dove and an olive leaf? Not miles of dense black clouds swirling and growing above the ark and then poooof! land-ho!

Oh well, time to start again, he thought, the world has been cleansed of wickedness and is waiting to be repopulated with . . .

'Oi! This your boat, mate?' shouted a voice in the wilderness. 'Well, you can't park it there. Not without permission for mooring, you can't. Have you got permission? Eh, have you?' shouted the figure.

Nhoer looked at Spam and shrugged his shoulders in utter confusion. 'Well, no, I, er . . .' he began.

'Oooooh, dodgy. In contravention of the Shipping and Amphibious Transportation Act of earlier this morning that is!' shouted Sergeant Spline of the Cranachan Black Guard stomping forward, unfurling a small parchment pad and dipping a quill into his ink hip-flask.

'Look, my good man, there seems to be a misunderstanding here. This isn't what it seems . . .' began Nhoer.

'Now, now, sir. None of that "My good man" business. I am an Officer of the Lore.'

'Well, would you be so kind as to inform me where we are?' asked Nhoer. 'Only I seem to be somewhat lost!'

'Do I take it, by that remark, that we must add "Sailing without due care and attention" to my little pad here?' pressed Spline.

'No, no!' protested Nhoer. 'I was sailing in an easterly direction waiting for my little dove to come back when all these black clouds appeared and I, we, er . . . well, here we are.'

'Aha! So these *are* all your pets then, littering the place and causing havoc, eh?'

'I hesitate to use the word "pets". I'm, er, looking after them for someone.'

'Do you have any written documentation for this mass animal-sitting enterprise?' snapped Spline, eager for as many charges as possible. Including rustling.

'No, I, er, just felt the urge to put all these animals on my ark and, er, sail away with them.' Suddenly, Nhoer realised how bad this was all sounding.

209

'I see. I think that you'd better come downtown with me, sonny. You've got quite a lot of explaining to do.' Sergeant Spline grinned as he clipped the leather handcuffs around Nhoer's wrists and began to lead him off, still protesting his innocence.

'In the meantime,' shouted Spline over his shoulder to Spam. 'If you want to avoid being had up before the beak on charges of Illegal and Unauthorised Contravention of the Distribution of Biological Nutrimentary Substances Act (1324c subsection Animal) of OG 1014, rustling and a stack of other criminal charges I'm sure I can think up, I'd round those beasties up and get 'em back on that ship of yours pretty sharpish!'

'Oh no!' muttered Spam to himself as he stared at the scattered acres of footprints. 'Not again!'

With a mood almost as black as the creaking leather armour and eyepatch he wore, Fisk sat in brooding silence on the ancient throne, each bony elbow stable on the armrest, his hands steepled in deep, dark contemptuous contemplation.

'I'm calm,' he insisted for the latest uncountable time since his frenzied armourcidal temper tantrum. 'I am calm.'

A single vein pulsed at his temple, pounding out irritation as surely as if he had been pacing the floor, arms clasped tensely behind his back, steel toe-caps sparking echoes off the stone surroundings. Fisk, despite his claims, was *far* from calm.

Inside his mind an argument was raging, mental voices screaming.

'So what are you going to do about it?' shouted Anger from the top of the Amphitheatre of Emotions, gathering his red robe about him and striding down the cerebral marble steps.

'Kill Khardeen!' yelled Rage, stamping on the floor, raising a puff of smoke.

'No, no!' countered Revenge, shivering in a thick icy-blue robe, his thin bony hands dismissing Rage's statement in a

210

flick of a calculating wrist. '*Far* too straightforward. A childish response.'

'Kill him slowly!' snapped Rage, pounding a smouldering fist into his open palm.

'Old hat!' sniffed Revenge, cleaning the icicles from beneath his dagger-sharp fingernails.

'Steal the entirety of his wealth!' shouted Greed, rubbing his hands with miserly relish.

'That would hurt,' answered Revenge, nodding. 'But not *enough*!'

'Turn him inside out very, very slowly!' growled Rage, glowing crimson as he illustrated his suggestion graphically with a series of expressive arm movements.

'Nice idea! But not this time.' Revenge wagged an icy index finger.

'Well, what are we doing to do?' snapped Anger once more, vying with Rage for the reddest face. 'Pull his arm out and pound him to death with the soggy end!' shrieked Rage attempting to demonstrate this latest idea on Terror.

'No, no!' insisted Revenge. 'As delightfully inventive as your ideas undoubtedly are, my dear Rage, I'm afraid, in this case, they're a little too final. You can't *build* on it.'

'But I hate him!' screamed Rage.

'You hate everybody,' replied Revenge coldly.

'True. But I *really* hate him, he makes me *so* mad my head hurts, I could, I could . . .'

'Not now!'

'I could just kill him a little bit!'

'No!' insisted Revenge.

Taking matters into his viciously flexing hands, Anger lurched up to the ice-blue figure of Revenge, grabbed him in a bone-crushing grip around the throat and lifted him off the marble seat, his biceps bulging in intense irritation.

'What are we going to *do*?' he screamed roaring red-faced fury as Revenge's feet back-pedalled in mid air.

'Cthhuurchkk!' choked Revenge eloquently.

'Yeah? Then what!' snarled Anger.

211

'Put him down!' shrieked Malice from across the Amphi-theatre as she sprinted down the steps, petticoats akimbo. 'You're hurting him! He's turning blue!'

'He's always blue!'

'Not *that* colour!'

Anger screamed, dropped Revenge in a choking heap and stormed off to the other side of the Amphitheatre, muttering and mumbling profusely.

'Oh, my sweet Revenge! Are you all right?' crooned Malice stroking his brow.

'I'll get him!' he muttered, coughed, spluttered and stood up, looking hurt. All eyes were upon him.

'What is the single most important thing in Khardeen's life?' asked Revenge and coughed a little more for Malice's benefit.

'Money!' shouted Greed.

'Food!' yelled Gluttony barely audible around a vast flank of pork.

Revenge shook his head.

'Money *and* Food!' shrieked Greed, rubbing his hands once more. 'Both together, lots and lots of lovely money and gold and treasure and . . .'

'No!' shouted Revenge. 'They're important. But, what's more important? What's going to stop anyone else getting their hands on any of his money? In the future?'

'Swords,' snapped Rage. 'And spears and bows and . . .'

'Klayth!' whispered Malice inside Fisk's head.

'Klayth!' shouted Fisk, smashing his gauntleted fist on to the throne's arm rest startling an already nervous Vlad into complete altertness.

'Vhere, vhere!' squawked the vampire looking around in alarm.

'Why didn't I think of it before!' shrieked Fisk, his one good eye burning with the cold blue of Revenge's cloak. 'Death is too easy! Stab, slice and it's over!'

'Who issss? Vhatt?'

'Let's make him suffer! Let's introduce him to worry!'

Suddenly Fisk was out of his throne and running, his heart pounding with furious energy.

This time it would work. *This* time there could be no denials.

How can you deny the Prince Regent's disappearance?

Vlad stood and sprinted after the wild cackling figure as it vanished into the gloom, shrieks of madness bouncing off the walls in harsh ominousity.

'Did you hear that!' croaked Firkin in the darkness, trying to rage quietly.

'We couldn't exactly fail to!' said Hogshead. 'All that yelling!'

'Come on. Let's get him!' snarled Firkin.

'What wouldst thou do?' asked Courgette, sharply, 'Thou dost not *bristleth* with weaponry!'

'Well, I, we could . . .' grunted Firkin, swiping at the air as if he was beating someone up.

'What? Bite his knees off? Slap his bottom?' snapped Hogshead. 'Just calm down and *think* for a moment!'

'But he's getting away!' protested the writhing Firkin, fury seething through his body.

'We don't know what he's planning, or where he's going, or anything!' said Hogshead.

'I know, I know, we've got to *do* something!' grunted Firkin, 'and do it now!' With an effort he pushed past Courgette, struggled out of Hogshead's grip and sprinted off down the tunnel, his mind seething with vivid images, overflowing with pictures of him, the hero Firkin, leaping in at the last moment to save Klayth from the evil Fisk at swordpoint, swooping across a vast chasm on a rope to land atop a tall tower, metal clashing against sharp metal, hacking, swashing and buckling with a vengeance, driving him back against the parapet, arching his back over the crenellated stone and forcing him to admit defeat.

'He's being silly again, isn't he,' whispered Dawn as he vanished into the dark. She was rapidly learning the myriad complex differences between stealth and stupidity and becoming alarmingly aware that her brother just hadn't a clue. Hogshead nodded, almost apologetically.

'Oh dear,' she said, in the tone of whisper normally reserved for the response to statements such as 'Your pet spider's just been stood on.'

Hogshead almost expected her to say, 'Well, never mind. I can always get another one.' He was immensely relieved that she didn't.

'We can't just sit here, can we?' she asked. 'I mean, he won't come back on his own, will he?' Courgette and Hogshead shook their heads.

'Thought not. Huh, a woman's work is never done!'

The threesome looked at each other, shrugged and dashed off into the dark, undiscovered blackness of a desperate future, hoping that Firkin hadn't done anything *too* stupid yet.

As the sound of dashing footsteps faded into the damp underworld a slight crackling fizzed in the dark as if a mosquito had just crashed into a wire carrying three thousand volts. Then there was another fizz and a tall figure appeared, his conical hat crumpled by the roof of the tunnel and one foot in a dark green puddle of highly dubious cleanliness.

'It's all right!' began the wizard, blinking in the gloom. 'Don't panic, I'm here to . . . Now look, *this* is getting annoying!' He shook his foot with an expression of acute distaste.

'Too true!' snapped the irritable figure of Arbutus as he tapped an angry claw on Merlot's shoulder. 'Losing your touch? Sign of old age, that is!'

'Nonsense, nonsense!' he complained as he brushed vexedly at his squashed and mossy hat. 'They've moved, that's all. Here we go! Third time lucky!'

'That *was* the third time!' insisted Arbutus.

'Details, my feathered irritant. Mere details! Coming?'

Merlot squinted at the grumbling owl, judged the heavily

disguised hoot of less than total disagreement to be a 'yes', held out his right hand, counted three and both of them vanished.

His mind running through the plan of the tunnels with frightening precision, Fisk turned and twisted expertly through the labyrinthine maze. Vlad struggled to keep up as, without pausing to think, Fisk snapped first left after second right, up three levels, fifteenth right, sharp left, and down one in a blinding whirl. His pace only began to slacken as he reached the Royal Sector. Here there was less background noise to cover his steps; here the eyes and ears were ever more vigilant; here was his prize!

Creeping stealthily forward, his breathing only marginally louder than the contained creaking of his leather gauntlets, Fisk eased himself towards the Prince's Chambers. He could hear the tapping of the bored youth's feet above his head as he squirmed cautiously beneath the floor.

Klayth slouched at the window of his chambers killing time before another of his daily lessons. Over the years he had discovered that it didn't pay to be early. The slightest sign of over-keenness and the old tutor was likely to get excited and really load the work on. Extra fencing, three hours more archery a week, even mathematics! This, Klayth had found, was far less preferable to slouching in, looking bored and arriving late. It was one of his teacher's peculiar foibles that tardiness and acute uninterest were treated with a swift clout about the head and fifty times round the courtyard. Klayth's only conclusion was that the old tutor was far more used to boring people to death than he was of inspiring interest. Sad, but true.

Beneath his feet a tiny knot-hole in one of the floor boards vanished and was replaced by a single wild eye.

Idly Klayth broke another fragment of bread from his plate, dosed it liberally with a vast helping of black pepper and mustard and hurled it out of the window to the chirruping flock of eagerly circling sparrows. As he expected it was caught on the wing by a skydiving cock and gulped down in a flash. Three . . . two . . . one. Klayth chuckled loudly as the tiny brown bird smacked its beak in confusion, squawked, then power dived for the cooling bowl of water.

At that same instant a panel was hurled backwards and a wild black shadow, burning with the fires of icy Revenge, erupted from the floor. Klayth turned too late to prevent a large, dusty sack being rammed over his head, pulled down over his torso and tied quickly and expertly around his waist securing his arms in a matter of seconds. Shocked, bewildered and choking, he was dragged down into an unknown world of secret passages and tunnels.

'Firkin, Firkin! Come out of there!' barked Hogshead in an attempted stage whisper.

'I tell you they went this way! Now be quiet and come on!' came the irritable reply from within the narrow passage leading off to the left.

'Are you sure?' he snapped.

'Yes, yes, yes!'

Courgette wrinkled her nose in disbelief. 'How sure are ye?'

'Trust me!' he grunted, squirming a little further up the passage.

'How can we? My leg is still smarting from where you jumped us a minute ago!' protested Hogshead.

'Look, I said I was sorry but you sounded like Fisk and Vlad!' came the muffled answer from the pitch black hole.

'But there were three of us!' moaned Hogshead.

'Could have been an echo. Stop being clever! Now look, we're wasting time. Follow me up here. Trust me, I saw them!'

'I don't like the sound of that!' whimpered Dawn.

The voice from the black passage whispered out once more. 'Have any of you got any better ideas!'

He took the ensuing silence as a 'no' and squirmed on followed with mounting reluctance by Courgette, Hogshead and Dawn.

'Black' Achonite looked across at the King with growing concern. It had been four hours since the three War-Lords had been dismissed, each with several fleas in both ears, and Khardeen hadn't moved.

Well, he had moved, but only to order more mead, more lampreys and sway about a lot, twitching and occasionally dribbling a little. He just hadn't moved from the Conference Room.

And, having not been dismissed himself, neither had Achonite.

He knew the King had taken the loss of Rhyngill badly but he had never seen him in this state.

Suddenly, he sat bolt upright, screamed and began fighting off something huge and invisible. His arms flailed about before him in desperate terror as it swooped and arced above his head. 'Get away. Get away from me!' the King shrieked. 'I haven't got your egg!' Then he grinned stupidly, giggled and slumped face forward into his bowl of mead.

Achonite dashed over to him just as an urgent crashing on the door sounded. In an unprecedented act of either foolishness or bravery, the door was flung open and Klayth's tutor burst in, panting and waving a piece of parchment in breathless terror.

'Sire, Sire!'

'Damn that Dragon! Not *more* burning!' squealed Khardeen as he sat upright once more and shakily looked around him. 'What you staring at? Where's that damn dragon gone now? Where's Bateleur?'

'Would you like those answered in order, Sire?' asked Achonite stepping back a few paces.

'Eh? What you on about?'

'Sire, Sire! It's Klayth!' blurted the tutor.

'No, no! That's Achonite. My old pal, Blacky Achonite!' Khardeen grinned at the trembling Commander. Something was wrong. Well, *two* things, at least, were wrong and he hadn't a clue what either of them were.

'Have you met my old pal Blocky Ichonate?' slurred Khardeen swaying again.

'Yes, your Highness. But, Sire!'

'He's a good chap! Dear old Blicky . . .'

'Sire. Your son . . .'

'No, no! He's my Commander . . .'

'Sire! Your son's gone!' shouted the tutor.

'Gone? Where?' Khardeen shook his head as if trying to struggle out of a deep drug-induced state of confusion. Which he was.

'K . . . kidnapped, Sire!'

Achonite almost collapsed.

Inside the wall to the left of the Conference Room, one of the members of the group of covert invaders was getting acutely claustrophobic.

'If this passage gets any narrower,' protested Hogshead, 'I'll either get stuck, scream or both!'

'We're nearly there!' grunted Firkin. 'I can hear voices!'

'You've been saying that for the last half hour!' complained Hogshead. 'We shouldn't have listened to you. "Round this corner. Just a bit further!" Pah!'

'I *can* hear voices,' insisted Firkin. 'Listen!'

Through the wall, muffled by the thickness of the stone, words were filtering.

'Here's the note I found when I went to fetch him 'cos he was late for lessons, Sire!' whimpered the tutor handing over the parchment.

'Wwwhat!' bellowed the King, staring blearily at the note. 'Is this a joke?' he shouted, standing up suddenly, swaying, then sitting down again quickly. 'I don't believe this!'

'It's true, Your Highness!'

In the blackness the four youngsters stopped and listened to snatches of frantic conversation.

'See? Hear that?' snapped Firkin desperately, 'They said "Your Highness". He's here!' he whispered, 'I *told* you!' Hope launched a plethora of hopeful rockets in his despairing heart, thrilling as they exploded into vast chrysanthemums of glowing confidence. He crawled on towards the Conference Room, his hand touching a wooden panel.

'But, sire! I would tell you if I knew of his whereabouts!' pleaded the tutor.

'Why me?' demanded Khardeen. 'Why now?' he complained. 'As if I haven't got enough on my plate!'

The tutor looked at the tiny fragments of slimy fish and, rather nauseously, agreed.

'Achonite!' commanded the King, rallying remarkably well despite the several hundred milligrams of Ellis Dee's currently mingling with the eight or nine flaggons of mead circulating throughout his body, 'Achonite, I want you to investigate this.'

'Yes, Your highness.'

'I want you to find . . .'

'Klayth!' cried a high-pitched voice as a door burst open six feet up in the wall and a body tumbled out, followed swiftly by a red-haired girl with a large sword, a short fat youth with the appearance of a barrel and a young squealing girl.

Achonite turned in a moment, sword drawn and ready, legs apart guarding the King.

Firkin struggled out from beneath the heap, still yelling. 'Klayth you're in danger. I've . . . uh-oh,' he stopped as he looked into the eyes of a very angry looking Commander Achonite and an impossibly ancient King.

'Seize them!' yelled King Khardeen, pointing to the pile of youths squirming on the floor.

'Oh no!' whimpered Hogshead. 'Not again!'

Afterlife's a bitch

'But we had *nothing* to do with it!' protested Firkin, his hands gripping the door-bars as the cell closed.

'Yeah, yeah. That's one of the two things they all say,' grunted the vast guard sniffing as he locked the door and hung the key back on the belt hitched around his immense midriff. 'You never wanted to alarm the King, did you. Never intended to creep through miles of secret passages that nobody but you knew about. Never once did it cross your mind to kidnap the Prince and hold him to ransom!'

'You're right! We're innocent!' agreed Firkin.

'Yup!' grunted the guard, tutted, spat and turned away from the cell. 'That's the other one. If I could have a pint for every time I've heard that one I wouldn't have a liver by now!'

'Don't say it. Just *don't*!' snapped Firkin as he felt the burning scowls of the other three on the back of his neck.

'Just down here!' mocked Courgette, feeling very naked without Exbenedict and wondering why the urge to chain herself to railings had evaporated. 'Through this passage. I can *hear* him!'

'I didn't hear *you* coming up with any good ideas,' growled Firkin flexing his hands in angry frustration.

'You weren't listening!'

'I was!'

'Wasn't.'

'Was!'

'You just rattled off down the nearest passage that looked right!'

'I didn't!'

'Did!'

Suddenly a seething crackling sound, rather like the noise

you get if you drop a large wet cat into a roiling deep-fat fryer, filled the cell and stopped the argument in mid-denial.

Before the youngsters very eyes a patch of something the colour of E major materialised in the corner of the cell. It expanded vertically, stretching to seemingly fill the air with saxaffron until with a final spitting sound the figure was complete – long beard, owl, tall pointy hat and matching robes covered in stars and stripes, trimmed with C minor 7 collar and cuffs.

'It's all right!' muttered the wizard almost wearily, then perked up as he saw the youngsters' faces. 'Don't panic! I'm here to . . .'

'Merlot!' squeaked Hogshead.

'See?' said the wizard, turning to the owl on his shoulder. 'Third time lucky, what?'

'Fourth,' tutted Arbutus, staring about the cell with a demonstration of almost total neck rotation. 'And I wouldn't say it was particularly lucky!'

'Merlot? It is you, isn't it?' shouted Hogshead.

'What?' growled the wizard, staring at the owl as it folded its wings into the small of its back.

'It does appear to have escaped your notice that we are currently, along with these other four, incarcerated within a high-security cell in the bowels of the Cranachan Imperial Palace Fortress!' answered Arbutus smugly.

'Details! Mere details!' grumbled Merlot. 'You are at risk of becoming tiresomely pedantic, dear feathered friend. Have a mouse!' Merlot lifted his hat and Arbutus cheerfully snatched the petrified rodent from the wizard's off-white head.

'Merlot! Can you hear us!' begged Hogshead, convinced he was hallucinating.

'Yes, yes! No need to shout, young man!' answered Merlot, bending at the waist, staring at him. 'Hah! Hogshead, isn't it! Good, good! Do you like peaches? We have met before, haven't we?'*

'Er, yes,' struggled Hogshead, gasping as he received a handful of fluffy round fruit. 'We have met. Don't you remember!'

'Remember? Course I do! Just get mixed up occasionaly, that's all!' Arbutus hooted with mirth, rolled his eyes idiotically and made small circling gestures at his temple with his index flight-feather.

'What are you doing here?' snapped Firkin, angry at losing control again.

'Aha! Now, that's a very good question, young man, which has a very bad answer,' he answered, crossed his legs and sat on the cold floor of the cell. 'Seen anything strange recently?' he asked.

'Like wizards suddenly appearing in the middle of a cell and *not* offering to get us out to save Klayth!' accused Firkin.

'Yes,' answered Merlot simply.

'Well! Are you going to get us out!' snapped Firkin. 'You can do magic can't you. Only I have to ask, see? We've met a few "sorcerers" who can't.'

'One thing at a time, young Firkin! What *is* this obsession with being locked up!'

'I prefer *not* to be!'

'All in good time, all in good time, dear boy!' said Merlot.

'What's wrong with now!'

'Well, nothing. Apart from the fact that you're safe in here.'

'Safe? What from? Who from?'

'From whooom!' corrected Arbutus.

'Pedant,' snapped Merlot throwing the owl another mouse. Then he fixed the youngsters with a hard stare. 'Are you telling me that you haven't seen anything odd?'

* Mystery and rumour swirled constantly around Merlot; enigmas regarding the source of mice beneath his hat; conundrums such as his ability to remain upright in his cloak despite the combined weight of detritus, junk and wildlife within its pockets (e.g., string, bicycle chains, electric kettles, a colony of field voles and an aquarium), which has been estimated at close to that of a small rhinoceros; and then there was the rumour that he does, in fact, live his life backwards. He distinctly recalled denying that at a press conference six centuries from now.

'No!' barked Firkin, fidgeting impatiently. 'Can we go now, Klayth's in trouble!'

'Shutup!' snapped Courgette, scowling at Firkin and missing a haft to grip. 'Do you mean things like rabbits with pockets watches?'

'Yes.'

'And strange swords?'

'And dragons?' asked Hogshead.

'You've seen all of *them*?' asked Merlot.

The youngsters nodded.

'Ummm,' grunted the wizard, tugging at his beard thoughtfully.

'Is that why you're here?' pressed Hogshead.

'What's going on!' demanded Courgette.

Merlot shook his head grimly and stared at Hogshead's pocket and asked. 'How's Ch'tin?'

Hogshead's face fell. In all the frantic chaos he'd forgotten about the little green bookworm. Apprehensively he pulled 'Lady Challerty's Loofah' out of his pocket, opening it at chapter eighty-five. His jaw dropped as he stared at the hard brown lump pulsing in the corner where Ch'tin should be.

'Eeurgh!' grunted Dawn. 'What's happened?'

'Shame he's pupating,' grunted Merlot. 'He could have given us all the answers!'

'What's going on?' asked Hogshead yet again. 'Where are all these fictitious things coming from?'

'Hazard a guess!' said Merlot.

Hogshead stared at Ch'tin, then at Merlot and Arbutus.

'Beyond the Space-Tome Continuum . . .' he said, awe edging his voice like the atmosphere of a library.

Merlot nodded. 'There's a hole in it. And it's getting bigger. I only ever thought it was a theoretical possibility to have a bookworm-hole in space-tome. But we've got one!'

'How!'

'I don't know!' confessed Merlot. 'But we've got to stop it. If the continuum rips we'll have a Tome Tunnel. Free interchange of reality and fantasy will lead to total chaos.

You've already seen what *can* happen. If it goes on too long, fact will *merge* with fiction. Life in the Chapter Dimensions is in real danger!'

'What can *we* do about it?' squealed a terrified Hogshead.

'Well, you can start by telling me where you've been and what you've done recently!' said Merlot. 'Begin at the beginning!'

Staring out of the window in Klayth's room King Khardeen shook with rage, his fingers angrily clawing stone fragments from the window-sill. Black Guards searched for clues, finding nothing that gave any inkling of what had happened other than the note.

His son had been stolen from under his nose. Stolen!

Roaring with frustration he crashed his fist against the wood of the window-frame, startling the flock of sparrows outside.

He needed his son and heir. Khardeen knew that in a very few years, old age would have sidled up to him and begun taking away the gifts of youth that he had fought so hard to keep. Strength, agility and fleetness of evil thought would desert him, leaving him open to attack. Not even the Physician, Sanaterjen, could cure aging. His kingdom would be snatched from him. Unless he had a son to rule through.

Oh! the humiliation! King Khardeen, ruler of Rhyngill and Cranachan could not control his own child.

For the first time in his life he felt vulnerable. As if someone had stolen his favourite underwear.

He stormed out of Klayth's room barking orders for lampreys and mead to be brought to his chambers. Immediately. If not sooner!

An owl stared between his taloned toes from the disused belfry of Martelloh Tower, boredly watching a group of three tiny men setting up a small stall in the cobbled square far below. They toiled hard, erecting banners and freshly painted boards declaring their business. This time they were sure that the time was right. A groundswell of opinion was rumbling through the aquifers of disbelief, they could smell ripe rumour in the air, catch it in snatched phrases of gossip, even read all about it in the *Triumphant Herald*. Reports of strange happenings filled the newsparchment with odd snippets of mystery, stoking the public's burning interest in the bizarre. Letters flooded in declaring sightings of fictitious creatures stalking the surrounding mountains; early refugees from the burnt-out husk of Rhyngill had brought terrifying reports of the dragon attack. And the High Priests of the Elevated Church of St Lucre the Unwashed were about to, literally, cash in on this chink in the Armour of Denial.

Hundreds of feet below the owl's toes, His Eminence, Bharkleed, the Fervently Exalted, stepped back from the stall admiring their work as His Emmolient, Whedd the Most Lubricious sweated to drive the last spike home.

Bharkleed felt a twinge of excitement wriggle at the base of his spine as he surveyed the altar-like stall. A large wooden trunk stood on the raised platform, covered with an old dark green curtain painted with strangely swirling patterns. Two large poles stood either side supporting a sign, made from several floorboards 'borrowed' for the purpose, which declared;

Afterlife's Mysteries Confusing You? Finding them
A Bit Challenging? Join us before it's Too Late!

His Effulgence, Hirsuit the Very Enpedestalled, joined Bharkleed, watching Whedd scramble down from the sign, cursing as he scuffed his shin.

'Brother Whedd!' declared Bharkleed. 'Language!'

A string of obscene gruntings indicating an extreme hatred of hard work and heights rattled into earshot.

'Be grateful I didn't see that ledge up there before,' Bharkleed pointed to the stone lintel three-quarters of the way up Martelloh Tower.

Whedd looked up and offered another half dozen choice phrases of blasphemy.

In a few short minutes a host of tallow candles had been lit on the trunk, devout-looking books had been strewn about with calculated nonchalance and an immense stack of Certificates of Unquestioning Belief were ready, with quills freshly sharpened nearby, waiting for willing signatories.

Bharkleed stared out from behind the trunk, opened the Red Proselytic Manuscript of St Lucre, turned to Profits and began to read.

'Rely not upon the interest of financial institutions for they are taxed!' he declared. 'I am your spiritual mattress sayeth St Lucre, for I offer security, comfort and a place to hide your fears beneath.'

Several pairs of ears twitched as Bharkleed's words resonated and cavorted around a nearby corner.

'Waste not your pearls by casting them before the swine for they have not pierced ears.'

A group of curious faces appeared around a corner wondering what the fuss was about.

'You, my good people!' shouted Bharkleed, his indigo robe billowing suddenly, 'I know you can sense The End of the World is Nigh! You can feel the The Fabric of Reality tearing at the edges, coming apart at the seams. Tell me what *you* have seen! It may not be too late to be saved!'

In the bowels of the watcher's bowels something stirred; a chord was somehow struck. They had seen things, they had felt things and they'd tried to ignore them, fix the blinkers and look the other way. It hadn't worked. The shaky belief that the flocks of strange scruffy birds building nests in their chimneys were, in fact, hallucinations brought on by excess inebriation had shattered into a million glistening fragments when the damn things had still been there this morning squawking their uniquely borogrovian dawn cacophony. As if this alone had not been enough to destroy the hallucination theory a herd of raths had kept the whole street awake with a serious session of mass nocturnal outgribbing. Undoubtedly something was wrong. And it was getting wronger by the minute!

'*I* can explain the unexplained!' declared Bharkleed gesturing to the group, his hand motions pulling the watching figures out into the square as surely as if they were on strings, each twitch of an ostensibly holy digit tugging, each flick of the wrist gathering them closer to the edge of the slippery slope of St Lucre.

Suddenly a ghostly hungry-looking figure of Famine galloped through the square wielding a polo club and yelling.

In a few moments there was no room to move in the square as crowds of panicking people flooded in, all eager to know the meaning of the basilisk in the bath or the salamander in the sink, or a thousand other happenings. The hum of expectation rose and the noise of yelled questions amplified. As inquiry sparked catechism, and answer ignited redoubled interrogation, an aura grew over the cobbled square. It cast inquisitorial fingers down alleys and ginnels, snatching at the speck of doubt in everyone's heart, winkling out the inklings of fear lodged in their mind's eyes from reading and hearing the inexplicable. The aura sprinkled phosphates, nitrates and essential amino acids on to the germinating seeds of public panic, watering them with the springs of alarm, thrilling as the etiolated shoots of unrest greened and writhed. The Thistles of Hysteria blossomed.

Just as King Khardeen tore the head off another lamprey and anger chewed at his guts, an early barn owl launched itself from the heights of Martelloh Tower. There was still no news of Klayth and it was really beginning to get to him. His mouth worked as he snarled, growled and cursed the inefficiency of the Black Guard. Six hours and *still* nothing. Heads would roll for this, such tardiness would not be allowed to remain unpunished, questions would have to be answered. Like, who first?

As his mind seethed with dark concepts and moods his vision faded, swirled and split in two as if reality were suddenly a reproducing amoeba. Khardeen blinked, rubbed his eyes and stared unbelieving through the double frame of his window. Unheralded and unbidden the cold hard hand of fear snaked across his shoulders, running an osseous digit through the short curly hairs at the back of his neck. He turned, the fear-driven rage of his gaze swomping around the room, the second image slowly catching up and swirling sickeningly round the first. Staggering in disoriented circles he snatched at the wall, missed and collapsed against the window-sill. Floorboards swirled in wild wooden whirl-winds. He stared through Ellis Dee's haze, attempting to focus on anything that would stay still for long enough. All he could see was his future and it didn't look rosy.

High above the Imperial Palace the owl witnessed move-ment at a large window-sill in the royal sector. A Talpine rock-mouse clawed its shaky way up the wall. The owl's eyes locked on, course correcting in a flash, heading for its prey.

The floor suddenly vanished before the King's eyes, turning into a black swirling pool of desperate uncertainty. Below the surface he could sense movement, something rising through the oily liquid, eyes glaring gibbous spheres. A vast mouth broke surface, spewing events of the past few days into the pool, bubbling up through the vast dark hole before him. He screamed – at least he thought he did. It was hard to tell any more.

Dragons swirled before him, trolls spun and destroyed the Market Square. Klayth appeared for a moment before dozens of black-gauntleted hands snatched him away. An indigo-clad figure swirled into view, talking: '. . . burdened with the weight of rulership . . .' cried the grinning image of Bharkleed. 'So many rulers are scared they won't measure up to what the future will hold . . . cowering before destiny as if it were a dragon ready to strike . . .' The words from the chapel flooded back to him.

Behind him a scratching of claws and a squeak signalled the end of the Talpine rock-mouse. The King's attention attempted to snap on to the flurry of flapping wings at his window. His vision blurred, his imagination seethed.

'. . . it's because you believe in the afterlife . . . !' yelled the image of Bharkleed.

The wings battered against the glass, struggling for grip on the rock-mouse and the ledge. The lowering sun glowed orange behind the struggling owl, a heavenly coruscating halo.

'. . . believe in the afterlife . . .' screamed Bharkleed in his head.

The bird snatched the struggling rodent into its beak, turned and soared off into oblivion.

King Khardeen blinked and shook his head as he saw the angel on his window-sill bow, then vanish in a glow of orange. He leapt for the window, shoving it open and screaming 'Wait, take me with you. . .'

Leaning precariously out of the high window, through several hundred times the normal illegal dose of Ellis Dee's he stared in a drugged haze as the angel, his angel, soared off towards Martelloh Tower.

As Merlot sat cross-legged in the bowels of the Imperial Palace, the jagged edges of the tear in the fabric of the Space-Tome Continuum flapped, slapped and grew; expanding as the immeasurable pressure, stoked and maintained by countless storytellers, poets and legend-writers, gushed forth in vast spuming fountains of sheer fantasy. Characters, who for timeless ages had been secure within the boundaries of their storylines, were ripped out, flung into the real world, vanishing from the environs of fiction. Edited.

Firkin tapped his fingers, scowling irritably in the corner of the cell, as Hogshead and Courgette attempted to recount to Merlot where they had been. Or more importantly, when.

Suddenly the wizard leapt upright and stared at them in amazement. Arbutus fluttered and clung on to the saxaffron shoulder.

'That's it!' cried Merlot.

'Eh?' grunted Hogshead in utter bafflement. 'How can Middin being burnt down be the answer?'

'No, no! It's merely a *clue* to the answer. See?' said Merlot.

'Well, in a word: No!' grunted Hogshead, scratching his head.

'Come, come, you just told me that *before* you arrived in Middin you'd been through some Deja Moi field* in all that nonsense about frogs and the two-and-a-half-minute-war,' began Merlot's attempted explanation.

Hogshead and Courgette nodded.

'Surely you *must* see?' said Merlot gravely. 'You've changed history!'

'Yes. That was the whole idea!' nodded Hogshead. 'We averted a disaster! We saved the world!' he added smugly.

'Hmmm,' grumbled Merlot thoughtfully. 'Disaster mayhap. But the world? . . . I'm not so sure.'

'What? Why not?' asked Hogshead, his brain beginning to ache as panic crept into his voice. 'What've we done now?'

'The Tome Tunnel!' groaned Merlot, tutting and tapping an index knuckle on Hogshead's brow. 'Wake up, boy. Pay attention!'

'But . . . I don't understand . . .' he scowled.

Merlot shook his head with despair and tugged his beard. 'Seen Vhintz recently?' he asked out of the blue in the same casual manner as he had just asked if Hogshead liked peaches.

This was too much for Firkin. 'What's Vhintz got to do with anything?' he snapped. 'We've got to get out of here! Merlot, you're a wizard . . .'

'Have you seen Vhintz recently?' repeated Merlot, pointedly ignoring Firkin's question, the cogs in his brain

---

* Deja Moi. The bigger brother of deja vu. Instead of the uncertain feeling that one has 'been there before', deja moi offers the possibility of actually making sure – by going back and visiting wherever it is that you think you might have been. It is practised by Ninth Aeon Deja Moi Masters, one of whom lives in the secret village of Losa Llamas.

whirring audibly, strands of the candy-floss of comprehension whizzing on to the twirling stick of understanding.

Firkin fumed. 'Not since Losa Llamas, no! He was fine then, looked healthy, eating well! Is that enough gossip? Can we go now?' He pointed at the locked cell door.

Merlot, tugging at his beard turned to Hogshead, the pink sugary strands of floss growing. 'And you've had Ch'tin in your pocket all the time?'

'Yes. Why . . . ?' he began, an uneasy feeling rising within.

'Has he been acting a little strange?' asked the wizard.

'Well, apart from turning into something horrid, no. There's nothing wrong . . .'

'Come, come. Are you certain?' snapped Merlot, this answer from Hogshead not fitting his idea.

'He's putting on weight I think. But I don't see how 'cause he's been off his books lately. Bit of stomach-ache, but . . .'

'Aha! That would be it!' declared the wizard. 'Too much magic for such a small body causing acute upper abdominal distension . . .' A mental hand yanked a pink frothy coated stick out of the cognitive silver bowl of reason, waving it joyously. He understood! Ch'tin's raised internal magic quotient from that meal of the appendix from 'Ye Aynshent Almanacke of Conjoorynge, Magycke and Such' was at the root of this. Wasn't it?

Merlot, rubbing his chin where it hurt from too much beard tugging, stepped across to the door of the cell and began rattling his staff across the bars.

'Stoppit!' snapped Firkin. 'That's a terrible noise!'

'The guard'll come!' protested Hogshead.

'Good,' said Merlot, pausing for a second before continuing with greater gusto.

'What?' shrieked Firkin. 'I thought you were trying to get us out of here?'

'Assumptions, dear boy!' chastised Merlot. 'Naughty, naughty!'

'Oh, great! So you come in here for a chat, then naff off again!' shouted Firkin. 'Wonderful!'

From down the corridor a loud bellowed question rattled and roared its way into earshot as the guard stirred his bones. 'What's all that racket?' he yelled. 'Shutup!'

'Come here, my man!' commanded Merlot, his voice echoing strangely through the door. 'This instant!'

Hogshead's ears began to tingle and his teeth tasted as if someone was sharpening a broadsword on them. It meant only one of two things – either someone was sharpening a broadsword on his teeth or there was magic in the air.

Heavy footsteps trudged apathetically to within a few feet of the door and the huge guard stood hands on hips glaring into the cell. 'Now what d'you want?' he barked. Hogshead shook at the booming bass, Dawn squeaked. If this was Merlot's way of breaking out he hadn't a clue how rattling the guard's temper would help.

'I think there's been some mistake!' declared Merlot and stroked his beard, releasing a short crackle of amethyst sparks. Both he and Arbutus focused their combined gaze at the centre of the guard's head, staring into his deep bovine eyes.

'What *you* doin' in there?' he asked unaware of the slight whining sound that Arbutus was making. 'You shunt be in there . . . oooh!' The guard's face, despite its already dull expression, somehow lost several dozen IQ points beneath the concentrated hypnotic gaze.

'You're right, I shouldn't!' said the wizard, his words edged with a strange reverberative tingle. 'Would you be a dear and open the door?' Merlot's pupils wiggled slightly as he cast his thought with increased intensity.

'Uurh, I'm not sure I should . . .' began the guard.

'Oh! Come, come. It's the *only* decent thing you should do! As you said yourself, I shouldn't be in here.'

The guard faltered as Arbutus leant forward and he tried to recall what, indeed, he had said.

'Left hand down a bit,' commanded Merlot tugging

another amthyst fountain from his beard, smiling sagely as the heavy hand followed his wish. 'Lift key-ring.' There was a jangling of metal shapes on a hoop. 'Place key in lock,' continued Merlot, '. . . and turn!'

With a scraping, a grinding and a clunk the door was unlocked. Merlot, holding the guard's gaze firmly in his hypnotic optic barrage, waved the youngsters past him and into the corridor.

'Oh, that's *so* kind of you!' reverberated Merlot at the guard. 'Please do come in and have a seat. I so rarely get visitors these days.' The lumbering warder obeyed, dreamily folding himself on to the floor, cheerfully ignoring the rapidly fleeing wizard and the sound of a slamming cell door.

'Ha! No problem!' whistled Merlot cheerily rubbing his hands. He looked up and down the dark corridor, scratched his head and mumbled, 'Come on, this way!'

'No way!' shrieked Courgette sprinting off in the opposite direction.

Merlot shook his head and raised his eyes to heaven. 'By all that's cartographically challenged where, oh *where* does she think she's going?'

Hogshead shrugged, catching a final flash of calf as the girl bolted round the corner. In a second a series of crashes and bangs rattled into earshot, bouncing and spinning down the corridor – demented decibels on a bid for freedom. Hogshead was running even before he realised it, his heart pounding as he accelerated towards Courgette, ready for anything. Flashing around the corner he came face to face with a whirlwind of slashing metal and whirling limbs – the whole room a million swords filling every inch of the air, spinning and whooshing in deadly limb-rending arcs. A scatter of splinters exploded as the wild sword wielder hacked an ancient oak table into bits. Hogshead's knees suddenly felt weak and he began to dribble as he watched the whirling frenzied female. He could have watched her all day . . . all week! Ooooh, those thighs!

Courgette caught sight of him out of the corner of her eye

and with Exbenedict raised two-handed for another slicing swirl, stopped and turned slightly pink. 'Couldst I abandon my weapon?' she said, looking taller and far more femininely feral than usual. 'Ahem. My joy at feeling Exbenedict's leather hilt between my palms thrilled me more than that for which I was prepared,' she confessed proudly.

'You mean you got carried away?' panted Hogshead, wiping his mouth.

'Ist that not what I said?' she asked as the oak table splintered and crashed to the floor.

'Well, sort of,' he answered despite the slackness of his jaw. 'Er, I *think* we'd better go!'

'Ye tactical withdrawal! Yea, verily!' she exclaimed. 'Come!' She helped Hogshead to his feet and they dashed off to rejoin the others.

'Wait!' screamed Khardeen after the fleeing owl, hauling himself on to the precipitous roof of the Royal Sector of the Palace Fortress. He stood shakily, struggling to remain upright. Away to his left the building dropped sheer for several hundred feet, ending in a jagged mass of rocks before plunging on down the craggy jaw of rock upon which Cranachan squatted. Had he been able to see straight this may have concerned him. All that mattered at present was the single finger of stone pointing skywards, the haunt of angels, Martelloh Tower.

He had hauled himself on to the roof, defying gravity, utilising any handhold available including several tiny plants that had somehow managed to root on this exposed vertical world and now he ran across the grey acres of slate, higher than anybody's kite. Physically *and* narcotically.

Far, far below him, at the base of the tower, the crowd listening to the High Priests of St Lucre had grown way beyond even Bharkleed's optimistic predictions. They were in full voice, extolling the virtues of Belief in their Afterlife. Quoting whole passages from the Red Proselytic Manuscript of St Lucre and still people gathered, including one Turgg

Inyeff, investigative reporter for the *Triumphant Herald*, notebook at the ready, pencil licked and waiting for action.

As a few people began to sign the Certificates of Unquestioning Belief, Khardeen reached the tower and looked up. The solid stone squirmed in two, each image splitting from the other then coming together and knotting around each other like angry spitting cobras hell-bent on strangling its imaginary opponent. Khardeen lurched forward, clinging to the rough stone surface, revelling for a moment in its solid coolness, then began to climb.

'Will you be one of those cast into the turmoil of the inferno,' screamed Bharkleed over the seething throng in the square, 'or will you be one of the *very* few who sit by, feet up with a cold beer, and watch! Sign here for fully furnished apartments with eternal flame open fires. First twenty-five receive free toasting fork!'

With the sun sinking lower on his back and driven on by swirling images of angels Khardeen scrambled up the tower like an arthritic lizard. Pain didn't impinge on him through the surging hallucinatory circulation of his body. Suddenly his hand grasped a ledge, scattering centuries of owl pellets to the four winds. He had reached the top. Grasping a gargoyle by the throat he hauled himself over the ledge and into the tower, his arrival accompanied by a flurry of shocked hoots.

All around he saw pale halo-ed figures, swirling in the heady optic confusion of his drugged haze, perched on rafters and beams as if in conference. This was how he had always imagined angels to be, none of this nonsense about clouds and harps.

Exhausted by the climb, his fingertips bleeding, he fell to his knees and shouted. 'I have come!'

As if the tower had suddenly exploded all the owls took to the air in a blasting of wings. Dust and scattered feathers swirled chaotically in the rarefied atmosphere.

'No, wait!' he cried, lurching desperately for one of the birds. 'Come back!' He ran to the far opening. Misjudging the speed and distance totally, he soared out on a cloak and a curse, arcing earthwards precisely the way his angels didn't.

'Look, you lot!' yelled Bharkleed in the square below, rapidly reaching the end of his tether. He had a rapt audience, but hardly anyone was signing. What did he need to convince them? 'You've seen what the End of the World can bring, the destruction of the Market Square was a sign, a warning! If you don't start believing soon, the whole kingdom will fall about your ears!'

At that precise moment, preceeded by a slight whistling and one or two squeals from the audience, the frantically flapping figure of the very soon to be ex-King of Cranachan and Rhyngill plummeted into the square. In a flash he ripped through the sign, destroying all but the left-hand side, and came to final rest surrounded by awestruck subjects, an ageing green curtain, a pair of candles and a startled spider.

As the dust settled Bharkleed was the first to recover, grabbing the situation in both hands, determined to turn it to his advantage. Just what he needed – a monarch from heaven!

'Er, ahem . . . see? I told you kings will fall about your ears! Own up now, who still isn't believing?'

Turgg Inyeff scribbled furiously, his mind stunned, his hand working almost of its own volition. He was actually there, where the action was!

Rumblings of discontent and shock sounded from the crowd until a woman at the front pointed, screamed, and succumbed to hysteria yelling, 'The sign! It's a sign!' Her hand shot up to the only remaining part of the High Priest's banner. The crowd inhaled as one as they read the message:

> Afterlife's . . .
> A Bit Ch . . .

Bharkleed gulped. 'See? He's suffering already!' he shouted.

In a second the crowd surged forward, clamouring for Certificates of Unquestioning Belief, desperate to join the

236

Elevated Church of St Lucre the Unwashed, totally convinced by the King's last words from beyond the grave.

Turgg Inyeff grinned and mumbled to himself those infamous words which all reporters long to have reason to yell. Adding the final touches to his note pad he smirked and sprinted away.

Hold the front page! he thought gleefully. Hold the front page!

'Look, I'm offering special rates for refugees!' shouted Vhintz, the Travelling Sorcerer, plaintively as he stood at the Gate of Cranachan. 'Surely *somebody* wants their shoes reheeling? It's a long way from Rhyngill. Come on, I'm not charging two groats a pair, I'm not charging one and a half . . . one groat and thruppence a pair. Now I can't say fairer than that!' The downtrodden crowd continued to trudge past him on the final few yards of cliff path, studiously ignoring the soot-splattered robes and the pleading expression. 'Guaranteed good as new. Full Thaumic Warranty valid for three months. At no extra charge!'

On the ground, close to the charred poles and blackened backcloth of his portable stall, a small battered rucksack lay in a crumpled heap.

'You, madam? How about a soothing balm of Aunt Ippodee's Pedal Restorant? Go on, "Give Your Feet a Treat". Only a groat a dozen!'

Behind him three muffled rustlings flopped into Vhintz's attention. He turned quickly, scanning the scene, eyes peeled for burglars. Nothing moved, except the small leaves of a sprig of heather blown by the high Talpine breeze.

'Sir?' he cried, scratching his head and turning back to the river of opportunity escaping before him. 'A Spell of Rest for your weary shoulders?' he asked a shrimpish man struggling beneath an entire hut contents bundled into a sheet. 'Place your burden here, only a ha'penny an hour!'

A blue oath of azure vulgarity lashed out in a definite negative.

'Only asked,' whimpered Vhintz as another three rustlings shuffled into earshot. Snatching a stick from his stall, he wheeled round, ready for any sneak-thieves' shifty moves. The heather shrugged botanical innocence. Suspiciously he eyed the small patch of dirt between him and the solid outer wall of Cranachan. To his right was the path; left a cliff drop. His pack was still there, just where he had left it.

Or was it? Did it look nearer to the heather?

Vhintz shook his head in disbelief and focused his attention back on to grabbing his share of the potential earnings slipping by. A rustle. Question marks flared like spines on a startled Ammorettan Death Lizard. A rustle. His jaw dropped as his rucksack came to a rest. And then hopped again. Reflex kicking his muscles into sudden action he leapt as the pack headed toward the cliff, grabbing as it leapt again, wrestling the old bag to the dusty ground.

Under a hail of curious stares Vhintz pulled the bag to his chest, sat upright and, keeping the neck tight in his hands, warily peered inside. Something was alive in there, something he hadn't put in. He stared into the canvas gloom, looking for rodent eyes glinting above a panting rib-cage. Nothing. Well, nothing *unusual*. Just the run-of-the-mill books, the spare underpants he kept with him (just in case), a random selection of washers, cogs, sundial sails and a whole host of detritus that could never be described as having ever been alive (with the notable exception of a certain pair of particularly aromatic footwear).

Suddenly 'Ye Aynshent Almanacke of Conjoorynge, Magycke and Such' twitched and made a rapid bid for freedom. Vhintz squeaked alarm and snatched the neck of the bag shut. The almanac rattled and fought, flapping its pages angrily and arching its spine in a flurry of frantic effort.

Vhintz's mind whirled as he struggled to control the violently thrashing volume. Something was definitely wrong with it. First, the flapping around his head, then the phoenix incident, what next . . . ?

*

238

'Trust me! I know what I'm doing!'

Courgette and Hogshead stared in unconvinced silence as Merlot tapped and listened with his ear bent against the wall. 'It's here. I'm certain!' Arbutus frowned in irritation trying to keep grip on the wizard's bobbing shoulder.

'Must you dig your claws in *so* deep?' growled Merlot, glaring at the bird on his shoulder.

'Oh no!' snapped Arbutus. 'I'll just slip off and crack my head on the floor and have concussion. I've *always* wanted a fractured skull. Don't mind me!'

'Be reasonable,' began Merlot.

'Be still!' hooted Arbutus.

'Be quick!' snapped Firkin.

'Do you happen to have *any* comprehension of the surface area of the walls in this palace, hmmm?' snarled Merlot in irritable mood. 'Even a one per cent error could mean that one could be several feet away from it!'

'From what!' asked Dawn, totally lost.

'Passageways!' growled Merlot. 'Why do you think they're called "secret passages", hmmm? Don't have flashing signs saying "This way to the hidden Labyrinth!" or "Subterranea straight on!" ' He tapped away at the wall, seeking the tell-tale hollow sound.

Suddenly Hogshead squeaked in alarm. Without any warning something twitched in the depths of his tunic. If he didn't know better he would have sworn that the battered copy of 'Lady Challerty's Loofah' was desperately trying to escape the confines of his pocket. 'That you, Courgette?' he whispered hopefully in the dark.

'What?' she answered.

'Rummaging in my pocket?'

'Nay! Dost thou taketh me for a harlot?' she protested vehemently, tightening her grip upon Exbenedict.

'I, er, only asked.' It twitched again, leaping away from his body in an unmistakable bid for freedom.

'Aha!' declared Merlot as his taps sounded suddenly hollow. 'Here it is!' He bent and stared at the section of wall, ostensibly indistinguishable from anything either side. 'I would guess, by its appearance and position, that it's an old Wyllfrid-type Concealed Egress System,' he mused. 'In which case . . . er, now how did it go? One hand on this stone, sixteen down and five along, one there and push!' he said spread-eagled across the wall.

A grunting, creaking sound filled the corridor as Merlot's ageing muscle fibres scraped impotently. Nothing happened. He stood suddenly, staring at the wall stroking his beard, deep in contemplation. 'Five down, sixteen along, mayhap?'

'Lady Challerty's Loofah', or more precisely the dark brown chrysalid inside it, leapt and writhed a few more times as if it were being prodded with red-hot pokers. Hogshead stared at his animated pocket with rapidly growing concern.

'Could be a Bendyck's Crypto-Ingress Orifice,' mused Merlot. 'Two fingers in *that* hole, one foot there, press here and . . . bum! In that case it's got to be a Gurlyng Voice Activated Cat-flap,' mumbled the wizard staring engrossed at the expanse of stone. 'Now, how did it go . . . "Open poppy seed!" ' he declared addressing the wall.

'Merlot . . .' squeaked Hogshead, as if a vast hairy spider was crawling up his trouser leg.

'Open sugar beet.' The wizard shook his head, deep in thought.

'Merlot?' whispered Dawn, pointing at a small round button on the wall. 'What's that for?'

'Open sssssssss, er, sunflower oil! Nah!' He scratched his head. 'It's *definitely* got something to do with cooking. I'm sure!'

Arbutus shook his head in despair.

'Open . . . seed . . . flour . . . buns . . . sesame!'

Dawn reached out and pressed the little red button marked 'open'.

There was a slight hissing and an entire section of the wall vanished, folding backwards to reveal a black passageway stretching away into sheer gloom.

'Merlot!' whimpered Hogshead trying to contain the writhing romance in his pocket. 'I, er . . .'

'About time tooo!' grumbled Arbutus.

'Hah! I knew I'd get there in the end!' said Merlot happily. 'Easy when you know how, what! Come on, this way!' He stepped into the dark.

As Courgette, hands clasped tightly around the haft of Exbenedict, followed Merlot, Hogshead wrestled with the animated bookworm against forces he could not comprehend and struggled into the passage after Firkin.

Dawn stared at the little red button, then at her finger and then at the hole in the wall. '. . . . ?' she thought.

This changed to '. . . ! Hang on a minute. . . !' a few moments later when she pressed another little red button just inside the passage and the hole slid silently shut behind them.

The volumes of fiction vanishing through the Space-Tome Continuum every second was almost impossible to measure. All across the Chapter Dimensions signs of the losses were beginning to show; lakes of sophistry were drying up; fields of fable were withering and dying; the ships of the imagination that plied the Sea of Tranquillity lay becalmed, their crews growing ever more restless and mutinous.

But, dangerous to all ficton-based life-forms as this was, it was as nothing compared to the new and terrifying happenings on the edge of two dimensions.

In the swirling vortices of fantasy fountaining through the tear in the Space-Tome Continuum, fact mingled with fiction. Cold Hard Truth was winked at across the swirling dance-floor of unreality; beckoned to by the curling red-nailed finger of fancy, gesturing in slow sensual arcs; pouted-at by the glistening lips of whimsy, licked and ready for pleasure; and poured a long intoxicating drink by the lingerie-wrapped exotic vision of seductive beauty that was one of the Maidens of Invention. Cold Hard Truth ran a finger around his stiff collar as the Maiden's silk-skinned toe climbed unashamedly up his calf. He took a nervous swig of the highly aphrodisiac cocktail as she crooned sweet suggestions in his ear and drew tiny little circles on the back of his neck with a dangerously manicured set of nine-inch nails. Her golden eyes flashed wanton lust at his wavering self-control, chipping away chunks of resistance with every wink, arousing with every caress, seducing with every sight of the carnal tip of her lustful tongue . . .

Cold Hard Truth ripped his grey and black striped tie from around his neck and hurled it over his shoulder. He grabbed at his collar and tugged, buttons popping in a fountain of tiny discs as his torso was stripped bare. In a moment a naked Truth and a willing Maiden of Invention had joined, reality's limbs enveloping fantasy's body, fact mingling with fiction.

As they touched, their minds set on the same thoughts, willing and desperate, a sheen grew about them. Their bodies dissolving behind the shower curtain of surreality.

And as fact merged with fiction so was born a new creature; as coldly calculating as truth; as imaginative as fantasy; and as hungry as famine.

A glistening sphere ripped open the shower curtain and rolled out into the maelstrom. It turned, grinned and bounced off towards the Chapter Dimensions, salivating and struggling against the fountainous pressures flooding out through the Space-Tome Continuum.

This was a Faction and it was hungry. Too hungry for mere words. It wanted ficton and literanium, and it wanted them now!

In the high corridors of the Royal Sector of the Palace Fortress 'Black' Achonite ran over how to present the worst report he had ever made.

'Sire,' he mumbled to himself. 'I have the latest progress report on the search for your Son. Klayth. Ahem. After eighteen hours of detailed searching and minute investigation I can safely say that we . . . haven't a clue! And, er, by the way, the prisoners have escaped.' Somehow, he didn't think that tack would work. How about concentrating on the positive. Hmmmm.

'Your Excellent Altitude, Sire,' he whispered against the echoing backdrop of his heavy footsteps. 'We have *increased* the search for the escaped prisoners and after lengthy in-depth inquiries, involving the collation of data from several thousand rooms, we can, without a shadow of doubt, positively exclude the possibility of your Son being in any of them . . . Nah!'

Somehow he felt there was only one alternative.

As he reached the door to the King's Chambers he withdrew his sword, grasped the blade in his gauntlets, knocked and entered. He knelt on the floor, head bowed, sword offered in defeat.

'Sire,' he began, staring at the floorboards, 'Since my head has been utterly useless in the pursuit of any clue as to your Son's whereabouts may I suggest a more profitable use for it might be as the Royal Doorstop. Sire, I resign.'

There was a thick, cold silence.

'Sire . . . ?' he repeated.

No reply.

'Sire, I have willingly come to this decision. Pray, make not this agony last any longer.'

Silence.

'Sire?' Achonite looked up at a room, totally devoid of anything even remotely Kingly. He stood, resheathing his sword hastily, and looked about.

'Sire? Coo-eee, it's me. Achonite.'

Then he saw the plate upended over the remains of a lamprey and above that the open window, the chair pushed next to it and the tell-tale scuffs of bootmarks on the ledge.

'Uh-oh,' he whispered to himself.

This was rapidly turning into one of *those* days.

As Merlot dashed through the maze of labyrinthine passages, twisting and turning with surprising confidence, Hogshead wrestled with the increasingly agitated contents of his pocket, like a struggling mime-artist with a balloon in an imaginary hurricane. With every change in heading, every twist and turn, he had to pull or push the struggling bookworm from a slightly different angle, shoving the stubborn chrysalid with growing frustration. It wasn't long before he realised that he was always applying force in the same direction, irrespective of any wall or other obstacle in the way. It was as if Ch'tin, or something within Ch'tin, was acting as a compass.

Or rather, an anti-compass. Hogshead was struggling *against* a force of repulsion. And it was getting harder to move. Not least because his pocket was becoming heavier, but also because sparks of blue were flashing out in the gloom, swirling and shorting across his fingers – the thaumic equivalent of a ruler across the knuckles.

'Merlot!' shouted Hogshead. 'What's happening?'

The only answer he received was a grunt of, 'Stop whining! We don't have time for that! Oh, and tell me as soon as you can't lift it, er, him, er, the book! It's not far now!'

'What's not far?' snapped Firkin panting from the wild dash. 'Where are we going?'

'Questions, questions!' complained Merlot as he turned a sudden left and began to run up a stone spiral staircase.

'Yes, questions!' snarled Firkin. 'How about some answers?'

Hogshead struggled up the staircase, pulling, lifting and pushing, depending on which side of the staircase he was on.

'What would you like answers to, hmmm?' asked Merlot, the glow from the top of his staff lighting the way.

'Well, how about why Klayth burnt down Middin?'

'Oh, don't be silly!' answered Merlot dashing a ninety-degree to the right and peering behind to make sure everyone was keeping up.

'What?' squeaked Firkin. 'That's not an answer!'

'Shhhh! Not so loud!' stage-whisperd Merlot. 'We're nearly there!'

'Where?'

After a couple of rights and lefts they emerged from a narrow passage and stood in the gloom not far from the drain where they had first encountered Fisk and Vlad in smugly gloating form. Hogshead struggled out from the side passage as if he was attempting to take a thrashing baby rhino to the vet. In his pocket.

'Down there!' whispered Merlot pointing happily, frankly amazed that he had found the way through the twisting and turning passages. It would not have done his ego any good at all to know that the three-and-a-half-mile dash should have only been eight hundred and fifty yards, if one knew the way.

Sending Arbutus ahead to reconnoitre, and warning the youngsters that silence was vital, Merlot and his followers crept towards Fisk's throneroom. Courgette grasped Exbenedict firmly and thrilled with the stealthy advance. They had two main things firmly on their side: 1) Fisk would never expect anyone to find their way into his labyrinth: and, 2) he wouldn't hear them anyway. Well, not at the moment anyhow. Echoed shouts of evil fought with wicked shrieks of malice and rattled down the passage into the approaching ears, as Fisk ranted and gloated over his latest prize. Vlad's sibilant sniggers whirled and cavorted with accomplice relish, sycophantically highlighting the wild ravings.

Firkin stopped, held up his hands and tugged at Merlot's saxaffron robe.

'What, in all of Rhyngill are we doing down here?' he demanded as forcefully as one is able when the luxury of yelling is not allowed. 'I want to see Klayth!'

With a slight beating of wings Arbutus settled back on to the wizard's shoulder. 'Yup. Still got him. Fisk's in a bad mood!' whispered Arbutus. 'And the vampire's just been ordered to fetch the evening parchment.'

Merlot edged forward to within feet of an archway, beckoned to Firkin and pointed.

There, within the treasure-strewn expanses of Fisk's throneroom; among the thousands of encobwebbed paintings of yellow flowers and snakes adrift on rafts; before the dust-dulled golden hoards and the black-stained silver troves humming with collected wealth, a new glittering prize stood motionless. It had little choice.

Bound securely to a vast pillar of stone, almost smothered in swirling coils of rope spiralling from toe to shoulder, Klayth was failing totally to hide his current mood. Yelling and screaming in a very unprincely manner he ranted impotently about the treatment of prisoners under the Gin Ether Convention.

'I have my rights!' he screamed, his thin voice shrill in the gloom. 'Let me call my lawyer.'

'Go ahead,' whispered Fisk cracking a handful of gauntleted knuckles cheerfully. 'Shout as loud as you wish, he won't hear you. Nobody will hear you from here,' he gloated and cracked the other handful percussively.

'You'll pay for this,' shouted Klayth squirming like a maggot super-glued to a stalacmite.

'Tut, tut,' said Fisk oozing smugness. 'Was that a threat?'

'A promise!' he screamed, writhing against his bonds uselessly. 'You will pay!' His blue eyes burned in the dark.

'Ahem. On the contrary, my little treasure. I shall be the last to pay. With you under my "protection" for a few days your father will be only too willing to give me what I want.'

'Never!

'Oh, that is such a shame, I had so set my heart on victory this time,' growled Fisk. His leather creaked ever-so slightly as he stood and stalked across to the shoulder of his latest bargaining chip, casually twirling the glinting blade of a long skinning knife with sinister dexterity. 'You have such nice tender ears,' he observed, his callous breath cold on Klayth's neck. 'I do despise having to separate matching pairs . . .'

Klayth took a long slow breath through clenched terror-filled molars, the back of his head pressed hard against the pillar.

'. . . but . . .'

He froze.

'. . . if extra "encouragement" is required I might have to,' finished Fisk sneering.

Vlad, perched on a tall chair, chuckled sibilantly.

'Of course,' began Klayth's leather-clad captor in a more cheerful way, appearing at the other side of the pillar, 'there are alternative ways, methods of negotiation that will leave your delicate lobes totally untouched, different incentives for negotiation!'

Klayth relaxed to a state of mere abject terror, knowing that he would be told the less bloody alternatives in full gloating technicolour.

'Toes can be just as effective!' shrieked Fisk, sneering with delight, his lip barely able to refrain from twitching in evil pleasure. 'Especially without toenails. It's quite remarkable how the knowledge of a tortured victim can really liven up a dreary discussion!' He howled with black laughter, hurling his head back and revelling in murderous mirth, gauntlets squeaking callous second fiddle to his shrieking cachinnations.

Klayth swallowed and stared at his wild black captor, twirling cloak and dagger in a whirling devilish dance macabre.

Was it ever possible to get used to only having one ear? he thought miserably.

The words rang in Vhintz's head like claxons on a foggy day. '. . . and remember. Where one or more are gathered together for longer than the time taken for a bird to catch a worm, so shall this be an opportunity for selling, spelling or sorcering.'*

It was for this reason that he was following the crowds of Rhyngillian Refugees as they wandered homelessly aimless throughout Cranachan, drifting like clumps of brownian enmotioned gas towards the centre of the town. He waited

* From the book *Sorcery – A Source of Income* published by the Thaumaturgical Board of Philosophers and Psychologists as part of their correspondence course for low-level magic users, 'Myth, Magic and Money'.

This book also contained many other useful aphorisms, such as: 'a ducking stool is a public escapology event horizon', and 'the speed of the foot deceives the long arm of the law', and 'a spell behind bars is cast too late'.

for another chance to ply his thaumic trade amongst the gullible, searching eagerly for a place to set out his wares. At least he would have if it were not for the constant distraction of the incessantly leaping pack upon his back twitching, writhing and spitting blue coruscating sparks at any passers-by. Curiously, and this was something that Vhintz was having terrible trouble trying to fathom, the direction of the leaping always seemed to be in a slightly upward vector. And he was certain that the angle of elevation was increasing. Almost as if the large leather bound copy of 'Ye Aynshent Almanacke of Conjoorynge, Magycke and Such' wanted to be as far away from the ground as possible.

Stepping out of the crowd for a well-earned rest he leant against a wall and tried studiously to ignore the fizzing blast of sparks emanating from his pack. He failed.

In a matter of moments the ancient almanack was pounding at the fastenings in the top of his pack, tugging the straps tight under his armpits, lifting him on to his tip-toes and knocking his hat off.

Fifteen feet directly below him in a dark passageway a rotund figure struggled with the pocket of his tunic as it pulled him down.

'Merlot!' whispered Hogshead in desperate alarm as the stitching on the shoulders of his tunic creaked in oversewn protest and his knees gave out. 'Merlot!' he whimpered as he lay trapped beneath his tunic pocket, repulsive forces from above exerting their invisible load, pressing him into the damp moss-ridden ground.

The wizard turned, saw the almost silent struggle and leapt to his feet, tapping Courgette on the shoulder and pointing. He dashed toward Hogshead, leapt nimbly over the struggling barrel-shaped figure and vanished up a dark set of spiral stairs followed by Courgette.

Fighting against his pack, attempting to stay on the ground and trying to look inconspicuous as the crowds surged by, Vhintz wrestled in choking confusion. His heels lifted off the dusty soil, pulling him back towards the wall behind him.

248

Amongst the dull faces of the refugees filing past, one lit up and stopped to watch the struggle. With attention focused on him Vhintz adopted a pleading expression as his cloak collar tugged harder at his windpipe and the ground pressed ever more lightly against his feet. The watcher in the crowd stared at the fabulous antics, hands on hips, shaking his head in appreciate awe. He rummaged in his pocket and threw a groat into Vhintz's upturned hat.

'You mime artists!' he cried cheerfully. 'Always gets me how you do that. Can you moonwalk?' Three more passers-by hurled coins at a totally baffled Travelling Sorcerer. Vhintz shook his head.

'You learn that! People love it!' said the watcher and walked away, disappearing into the crowd in a second.

Tucked away in the shadow of a small hut a square of earth moved. It trembled for a moment, lifted and placed itself upright against the hut wall. In a second a tall saxaffron-robed wizard sprinted up the remaining few steps, blinked in the light and dashed over to the struggling figure of Vhintz, arms flailing wildly as he fought to stay grounded. Before the flying sorcerer could object Merlot grabbed him by the cloak, tugging him nearer to the waiting Courgette, who started to drag him underground.

Struggling against a rising tide of panic and lack of air, Vhintz choked and pointed to his hat lying in the dust and was amazed to see a crowd of people cheering as he, the star of this impromptu street-theatre spiralled into the ground like a puppet on a music box.

Merlot dashed forward, snatched Vhintz's hat amid a shower of pennies and groats, bowed and vanished down the hole, replacing the cover in a puff of sandy soil.

With Merlot pushing down on Vhintz's sack and Courgette tugging at his feet, the Travelling Sorcerer was bundled down the spiral staircase, into the inchoate black-ness of the labyrinthine maze.

A sweating Merlot, a sword-toting Courgette and a terrified Vhintz wrestled their weary way into the passage,

crackles of blue energy flashing between the pack and
Hogshead's pocket. With a gesture from Courgette, graphic-
ally telegraphed by the tip of Exbenedict, Vhintz removed
his pack, staring in disbelief as it flew from his hand and
pinned itself to the wall opposite Hogshead supported by a
sheet of blue coruscations.

'Look, there's nothing of any value in there!' protested
Vhintz, suddenly unsure. 'So you may as well take the money
from the hat and let me go. That's all I have!'

Merlot shook the nine groats, thruppence and a washer in
the hat and handed it back to Vhintz.

'No, no! You take it!' he whimpered, shaking his hands in
denial. 'I've nothing else of any worth!'

Merlot grinned in the gloom. 'Oh, but you have!'

'Take anything, just don't torture me!' whimpered Vhintz.
'I've never been very good with pain. Especially my own.'

A crackle of blue energy flashed between Hogshead and
the pack, lasering sapphire highlights in the gloom.

'Wh . . . what is that?' spluttered Vhintz, blinking in
shock.

'Acute thaumic energy discharge causing localised atmos-
pheric ionisation phenomena,' answered Merlot smugly.

'Eh?'

'Sparks,' translated Arbutus.

'Thau . . . thaumic? Did you say thaumic?' panicked
Vhintz. 'As in magic type stuff?' his voice rose in semitones
of wild incredulity.

Merlot nodded.

'Magic !. . . but what's it doing in my bag?'

'That's what I'd like to know,' said Merlot moving toward
the pinned and mounted pack. 'Do you mind?' he said
unfastening it.

'Whoa!' protested Vhintz. 'That's private property. I have
my rights!' A sharp whooshing sounded as Courgette spun in
a flash to her feet, legs planted apart, Exbenedict's gleaming
point at the Travelling Sorcerer's adam's apple.

'What thou must recall,' she whispered grinning, 'is that

250

thou art alone, outnumbered and I am horribly beweaponed! Now, dost thou feel generous, punk?'

Vhintz's eyes crossed as he focused on the razor-edged blade. 'Hah, er, feel free!'

Letting the pack drop Merlot pulled a large leather-bound book out, a tome that would have been immensely heavy were it not pressed firmly against the wall of the passage. 'Aha!' he exclaimed as a wave of cerulean sparks fizzed across the surface and ran up his arms. 'This looks promising!'

'No, not that!' protested Vhintz, 'My grandfather gave me that!'

Merlot's long fingers pulled the cover open and stared at the ancient curling script and illuminated letters of 'Ye Aynshent Almanacke of Conjoorynge, Magycke and Such', wishing he had more time. He flicked through to the back, dashing through the acknowledgments, zipping through the bibliography and stopping at the appendices. He was getting close, he could feel it.

He flicked through Appendix I – Controlled Drugs; Propagation and Extraction for Beginners. Through Appendix II – Thaumic Troubleshooting: Fifty-five Common Problems with Magic, and opened Appendix III. With a heart pounding with excitement, he turned the parchment leaf. A flash of sparks zapped out of the page, fizzing and crackling at the brink of overload as Merlot revealed Appendix IIIb, complete and unadulterated.

'Bingo!' whispered Merlot as a hail of blue flames launched themselves from his hat.

Powering its way ravenously against the torrents of fantasy, jaws slavering at the prospect of a feast of literanium, the faction surged forward towards the tear in the Space-Tome Continuum. All around it seethed the vast torrential whale-backs of fable; the bubbling froth of babbling books; the stampeding white-horses of words spilling out through the growing rupture. The faction leapt over waterfalls of wit, dived through pools of prose, struggling on like an assonant salmon with an invite to party. Just one of a steadily growing shoal.

But the closer to the hole, the harder the struggle. Here, at the actual tear, the pressures were immense. Far, far too strong for the factions to break through, yet.

Given time, the pressures between the two dimensions would equalise, reaching a point where they balanced once more. But, long before that the factions would break through. For as the pressure from the Chapter Dimension lessened, so a back-surge from reality would build up, a rebounding factual recoil sending the flow the other way. It would be on this wave that the shoal of factions would enter, catching the turning tide and surfing in for a barbecue on the beach.

So, at the moment they waited, gathering, grouping, warring factions waiting for the kill.

They wouldn't have to wait long.

All the finest magic books have to be printed under the strictest of guidelines using special thaumatin dyes pressed into the very fabric of the book by the inkanting rollers. Once complete, the words act as wave guides, allowing the user to tap into the paracosmic plane, capturing thaumic energy in vast drifting ether nets and channelling it through the spell. Each spell has its recommended thaumic current requirement for optimal casting ease and upper limits controlled by spellcheckers, inherent 'circuit breakers' designed to prevent overload. Once set these cannot be altered.

At least nobody in the Thaumaturgical Board of Philosophers and Psychologists *thought* they could be altered.

It took a certain bookworm's afternoon snack from a specific magical book to stamp all over *that* particular theory. Once the words were free from the page, unleashed from the straight-jacket of two dimensions, they recombined deeper, stronger, more potent than before and, crucially, *without* spellcheckers.

252

'Are you telling me you can *read* that stuff?' spluttered Vhintz incredulously as Merlot stared with mounting horror at the ancient almanack.

'Mmmmm,' he replied, deep in thought, his staff lighting the parchment.

'Gives me a headache as soon as I look at it!' grumbled Vhintz. 'What's it say?'

'. . . ittick phlarr aloe vera . . .'

'No, no! Just the gist of it!' said Vhintz. 'Why are you so interested in it? What's it for? And why's it fizzing?'

'Can it undo ropes?' asked Firkin thinking of Klayth. 'We've got to get him out of there. Who knows what Fisk's planning!'

Merlot turned away from the book. 'It would seem that Appendix IIIb contains all the information and spells to contact the Chapter Dimensions. To talk to characters on the other side!'

'Like a medium?' asked Hogshead eagerly.

'No, they read *between* the lines,' frowned Merlot, his mind whirring as the pieces began to fit together. 'This is the section that Ch'tin ate,' he said, thinking out loud.

'Ate? Nobody ate that. It's still there!' protested Vhintz in confusion.

'Can't you find a spell to save Klayth? snarled Firkin.

A flash of blue spark dashed across the passage and fizzed into Hogshead's pocket, discharging with a tinge of ozone. A retaliatory strike was launched by Ch'tin as he writhed inside the book.

'What about Ch'tin?' snapped Hogshead. 'What's going on, Merlot?'

Suddenly, the wizard's face brightened, the whirling of thoughts having borne fruit. 'Got it!' he exclaimed. 'Appendix IIIb is still there! . . .'

Firkin groaned. 'I just told *you* that!'

'. . . *and* there!' Merlot pointed to the pocket which contained Ch'tin.'

'You just said Ch'tin ate it!' whimpered Hogshead. Vhintz

scratched his head, beginning to see why he had never been able to cast any spells. It was all nonsense!

'He did eat it, once,' said Merlot. 'A chance meeting with Vhintz in the woods not far from here. A meeting that never happened since you changed history with the Deja-Moi field!'

'You trying to blame us?' snapped Firkin. 'We had to do that!'

'But what's that got to do with dragons and swords and . . .?' began Hogshead.

'Too much magic!' frowned Merlot.

'You can't have *too* much . . .' whined Hogshead, desperate for any sort of magic. Vhintz shook his head. This was far too much, and far too close for comfort.

'Too. Much. Magic!' insisted Merlot, his eyebrows arching. 'Two different versions of the same spell. In the same dimension! They're interfering with each other. This time ain't big enough for the both of them!'

Hogshead's mouth fell open. Firkin growled. Vhintz whimpered.

'Can't you feel it?' asked Merlot.

'Like someone sharpening a sword on your teeth?' asked Hogshead.

'Yes! I should have noticed sooner, it's getting worse. I don't think we've got long,' murmured Merlot to himself.

As Firkin took his own matters into his own hands and set off to do something, anything! a flash of sapphire exploded from the surface of the book and collided with a defensive blast from Ch'tin.

Merlot scowled. 'One of them's *got* to go! And before sundown tonight. Any volunteers?'

'Go? Go where?' asked Hogshead.

'The Chapter Dimensions!' said Merlot.

Apart from the rapidly intensifying thaumic arcs of interference zapping and crackling across the passage, total stunned silence fell across the small group.

*

'Well?' snapped Fisk eagerly as Vlad offered him the evening edition of the *Triumphant Herald*. 'Have they reported it right this time? Am I front page news?'

'Not exssssactly,' whistled Vlad.

'What do you mean? There's *nothing* more important than the kidnapping of the Prince of Rhyngill and Cranachan!' Fisk smashed his fist onto the arm of his stolen throne.

'Dhere issss!' answered Vlad, a hint of smugness creeping into his cold voice.

Fisk stared at the vampire holding the headline close to his pale chest and grinning. 'Of course! This is the *Triumphant Herald*, they wouldn't know *real* news if it handed them the story itself! What's the headline – 'Ikhnaton the Assassin – Stripped of Cow-Toppling Championship, Dope Tested Positive'? growled Fisk sarcastically.

'No!'

Fisk roared in frustration and tore the newsparchment from Vlad's grip, turning it over to stare in slack-jawed disbelief. The headline burned its way into his mind like a branding iron on his retina.

'AFTERLIFE'S A BITCH!' Khardeen's opinion of
the Other Side!
Prophet's profits soar – spurred by plunging King.

Fisk's eyes rolled as he read on.

Miracle monarch causes crowd's conversion – Exclusive!

Only seconds after the dust settled on the body
of King Khardeen after mysteriously falling from
Martelloh Tower, this reporter witnessed a message
from the dead monarch . . . .

Throughout Fisk's less than pristinely legal life, he had hardly ever been surprised. Right now he was totally flabbergasted. Shock had sailed up and stolen every scrap of wind from his spinnakers. His jaw hung slackly open, his head drooping; for a second he was utterly at a loss.

But *only* for a second . . . .

With a sound that would put a pack of hyenas to shame Fisk threw back his mane of black hair, shrieked with greed-driven pleasure and slunk toward his captive, his hands rubbing in gloating gauntleted delight.

With his lips curling into his well-practised sneer he stood before the rope-restrained Klayth and bowed a long mocking arc of derision.

'My liege!' he cackled, 'it is my immensely pleasurable duty to inform you of your immediate promotion. It seems that your father has, er, dropped out of the ruling classes! Bet you didn't know he was into sky-diving, eh? . . .'

In the shadows outside the throne room Firkin seethed in raging anger, he'd heard enough. It was time for action!

'Oh, come on!' urged Merlot, 'I just want a volunteer. Any takers? Anybody'll do!'

The silence was solid.

'Look, it's a trip of a lifetime! Opportunities like these only come about once in a blue moon! Hogshead, old chap . . . ?' grinned Merlot. 'How about it, eh?'

Hogshead bit his lip and looked at his feet.

'Why don't *you* do it?' asked Dawn.

'Me?' flustered the wizard, 'Take one of those spells through the rip in the Space-Tome Continuum? Oh, no, no!'

'Why not?' she asked, head on one side.

'Why not? Why not?' muttered Merlot to himself, tapping his chin in a flurry of panicked thought. 'Because, er . . .'

'I mean, you'd know what to do!' added Dawn.

'. . . because, oh . . .'

'You'd be bound to do it right!' she continued.

'No! Er, I mean yes. Ha, got it! I'll tell you why not! Because I have to co-ordinate things!' he proclaimed. 'Timing is actually vital in all matters of interdimensional paracosmic vector realignment, don't you know?'

Arbutus coughed and hooted, 'Coward!' under his breath.

'Well come on!' pleaded the wizard ignoring the owl on his shoulder. 'I need a suggestion! Somebody give me a name!'

Suddenly Firkin dashed around the corner and stood panting in the passage, 'Fisk!' he croaked.

'Possibly!' answered Merlot.

'What?' snapped Firkin. 'No, it's definitely him!'

'Okay, if you insist. I did say anybody would do,' muttered Merlot.

'Where've you been?' asked Dawn, glaring at her brother. 'We've been having important discussions. And you weren't here!'

'I've been round the bend!'

Dawn grinned and stifled a chuckle.

'What's this about Fisk?' asked Hogshead.

'What?' muttered Merlot. 'Objecting are you? All in favour of Firkin's nomination, say "I"?'

'I, I heard him!' panted Firkin.

'Two,' mumbled Merlot.

'He's ready to take over the whole kingdom!' he spluttered. 'I tell you I heard him!'

'Four!' declared Merlot. 'Motion carried! Oh! the power of democracy!'

'Cheat!' hooted Arbutus, glaring at the wizard.

'Look, it was either him or me!'

'Coward!' snapped the owl.

Merlot grinned at Arbutus and turned to the others. 'All right, then . . .'

'Take over the Kingdom!' repeated Hogshead, disbelieving Firkin's words.

'Both of them! Rhyngill and Cranachan!' confirmed Firkin.

'Ahem, pay attention!' grumbled Merlot irritably. 'We haven't got long!'

'*Both* of them?' spluttered Hogshead. 'We've got to stop him!'

'Yes, but we haven't got long!' said Firkin.

257

'Well, now that we've agreed on that,' said Merlot, rummaging in his capacious pockets for a quill, a pot of ink and a stretch of parchment. 'Here's what I want each of you to do . . .'

'Eh?' said Firkin and Hogshead turning and staring at Merlot with the distinct feeling that the shaky grip they had on current affairs had slipped even further out of their hands.

'Charge!' screamed General Bateleur, his eyes sparkling with the thrill of the hunt, his hooked nose slicing the air as he tracked the soaring golden dragon.

'Tally-ho!' yelled Colonel Rachnid, waving his cutlass above his head, joining the charge toward the blazing ruins of Rhyngill.

'Let's grab a flame-grilling whopper!' shouted Lappet, spotting their quarry as it spiralled higher in the rising thermals of hot air.

It was funny, but from this distance he could have sworn the dragon was flying backstroke.

'All right,' whispered Merlot as they crouched at the entrance to Fisk's throneroom. 'Everyone know what to do?'

They all nodded.

Hogshead reluctantly struggled to remove his tunic and handed it to Vhintz.

'Yea, verily ready and willing!' enthused Courgette, grinning as she clutched at Exbenedict, itching for a fight.

'Quill loaded?' Merlot asked Vhintz as the Travelling Sorcerer knelt down on Hogshead's tunic, pinning Ch'tin safely to the floor. Vhintz made a ring of his index finger and thumb and grinned a shaky affirmation. There was magic all around him and he was extremely nervous about it. A lifetime of Travelling Sorcery had *never* prepared him for this.

'Sorry about the pattern on that wallparchment,' said Merlot cringing at the pink flowers and appalling blue humming-birds. 'It was all I could find at such short notice! I really must organise these pockets!'

Vhintz tried a few experimental quill strokes. 'It's fine! Just don't expect calligraphy.' A snake of blue sparks rose cobra-like from Hogshead's tunic pocket and spat at 'Ye Aynshent Almanacke of Conjooryge, Magycke and Such' in Merlot's hand. 'Oh, and . . . hurry up. Please!' whimpered Vhintz, eying the blue phosphorescent serpent with acute alarm.

'We haven't got long, let's do this by numbers. Fifty-three, twenty-four, eighteen, hut, hut, hut! Go!' whispered Merlot wondering what the hell he was on about.

On the other side of the door Fisk snarled and sneered at Klayth, goading the new King, threatening him with a string of tortures, watched by Vlad giggling appreciatively.

In a flash of sprinting heels Firkin and Hogshead dashed into the throneroom, their sights set on their own target, followed a moment later by Courgette swirling Exbenedict, the centre of vast glinting arcs of horribly sharp weaponry.

Hogshead barelled into the open, sprinting angrily for the pale giggling figure in the black mourning suit, accelerating on an unstoppable collision course. Firkin dashed between piles of treasure, circling behind Fisk.

Screaming like a wild badger in a tantrum and yelling a string of choicest mediaeval oaths Courgette streaked towards Fisk, her hair a mane of angry red.

Vlad launched an earpiercing shriek as the steam-roller of Hogshead powered towards him like an angry sentient avalanche, with an attitude problem. The vampire turned and ran a full two paces before Hogshead thudded into the small of his back, flattening him against the floor and knocking all the wind from his anaemic lungs.

Fisk's eyes bulged in shock as Courgette sprinted forward. He backed away in horrified alarm, his arms flailing. Nobody invaded his throneroom!

Almost before he realised what was happening, it was too late. Fisk's horizon plunged toward his feet as he stumbled backwards, tripping over Firkin's outstretched leg, crashing to the hard stone floor in a jumble of thrashing leather-clad

259

limbs. In a flash, Courgette was upon him, her foot on his pounding chest, sword blade at his quivering throat, grinning.

As a surprise attack it was a total success. Much to *everyone's* surprise!

Still within the shadow of the passage Merlot drew a deep breath, took tight hold of the page marked Appendix IIIb and tore it out of the almanac. Sparks flew in a hail of ripping parchment, zapping and crackling in every direction. The wizard cringed – such vandalism! Vhintz squealed as a fountain of blue fire missed him by scant inches.

This is it, thought Merlot with the parchment page in his hand. No turning back now. Sticky tape wouldn't be invented for another three hundred years.

As Vhintz dipped his quill into the pot of ink and began to write on the pink floral wallparchment, Merlot dashed into the throneroom, the hairs on the back of his neck alive with the tension of the building literary pressure. It wouldn't be long before the critical backlash hit. They *had* to be ready for it! Timing would have to be perfect!

'Once upon a time, there was a nasty mean man . . .' wrote Vhintz.

Fisk was screaming his acute displeasure as Merlot approached. 'Get this harlot off me!' he yelled. 'Shouldn't be allowed to play with swords! Definitely *not* ladylike. Go and do some crocheting!'

'Shutup!' squealed Hogshead pinning Vlad to the ground, squirming to avoid his teeth. 'Someone take over here and I'll get him for that!'

'How darest thou besmirch my honour! Hast thou not heard of "Fights for Women!" ' Courgette shouted, digging her heel into Fisk's chest and waggling Exbenedict.

'Fights for Women! Hah! Over my dead body!'

'That canst be readily arranged . . .'

'Wait, wait!' shouted Merlot. 'Let's not get *too* carried away, dear. I'm not very good at communing with the dead!'

'Unlike the King!' squealed Fisk, staring at Klayth. 'Or should that be ex-King!'

260

'Get me *out* of this!' yelled Klayth squirming feebly against the miles of rope. 'Let me at him!'

'. . . and his name was Fisk . . .' continued Vhintz, inky nib scratching on wallparchment.

Merlot stared down at the wild sneering face of Fisk. 'I have the feeling you're not very well liked, what?'

'Who needs to be liked when you have power!' seethed the leather-clad madman writhing on the floor, somehow ignoring the tip of Exbenedict resting menacingly at his thin throat.

Merlot stroked his chin, 'You don't look *that* powerful to me,' he said. 'In fact, phrases regarding large amounts of smelly brown stuff hitting vast air-conditioning systems seem to spring to mind.'

'. . . always dressed in black and nobody really liked him . . .' continued Vhintz's quill.

'Let me at him!' screamed Klayth.

'Dhissss isss all your fault!' screamed Vlad from underneath Hogshead. 'Sssstop bounsssing! It hurtsss!'

'Not very high on the popularity stakes either,' observed Merlot, sensing the growing weight of the turning tide of fiction, surging towards them. Minutes away.

'What is it to you, old man!' snapped Fisk.

'Quite a lot actually. You see, I really don't like violence and fighting and the like, it's such a waste of effort . . .'

'Oh, I quite agree,' sneered Fisk, his hand twitching as he attempted to grab the flick-knife hidden in his gauntlet. 'Get this harlot off me!'

'. . . his armour was made of black leather . . .'

'I've been watching you for a while,' said Merlot, the hairs on his neck wriggling wilder as the back-surge approached, 'and frankly I think you're wasting your time here.'

'What! How dare . . .' he snapped, easing the blade out of the gauntlet.

'You've been fiddling around down here for years, probably decades, and what have you achieved?'

'. . . and he liked power . . .' continued Vhintz slowly but surely, carefully avoiding the one or two sparks of blue that launched themselves from the tunic pocket below him.

'I have treasure beyond your wildest . . .' began Fisk, the blade almost in reach.

'Treasure?' interrupted Merlot, looking down his nose at the heaps of gold, silver and paintings in piles around them.

'This is priceless!' squealed Fisk.

'. . . and loved money . . .' wrote Vhintz.

'This is as bankable as chocolate money compared to the golden hoardes of treasures I know of,' said Merlot dangling a nonchalant carrot.

Firkin stared at Fisk with growing confusion. He felt sure that his armour was, well, fading. He shook his head and rubbed his eyes, it must be all the excitement going to his head. Nobody just fades away. Well, not in reality anyway.

Deep within Hogshead's tunic pocket the hard brown form of Ch'tin wriggled and squirmed in chrysalid anguish. Voices from the Chapter Dimensions screamed throughout his entire body, stomach writhing, blood pounding. Ch'tin could sense the rumbling literal tsunami as it rolled, white-tipped, towards them.

(High above them, at the northern end of the Market Square a group of Black Guards were still searching for any clue as to the whereabouts of Klayth.

'Can you feel something?' asked one of the Guards.

'What?' answered another.

'Rumbling! Like the ground's got indigestion!'

'Don't talk rubbish!' dismissed the other guard and walked on.)

'What treasures?' snapped Fisk, greed sharpening his mind. 'Show me proof!'

Merlot grinned and pulled a fragment of parchment out of his pocket. It fizzed and crackled as he unrolled it. 'Directions!' he declared. 'How to get there!'

Firkin stared in confusion. What was Merlot doing? Bribery?

Fisk had heard enough. Treasure beyond his wildest dreams, eh? Directions! Whatever they were trying, it wouldn't work.

In a sudden flash of movement, Fisk knocked Courgette's foot away from his chest, pulled the flick-knife out of his gauntlet, extending the blade in a split second, and snatched the parchment out from Merlot's hand, stuffing it into his inside pocket amid a crackling of sparks. Before anyone could react he was heading for a pile of armour and weapons.

Courgette screamed in frustration and sprinted after him, Exbenedict whirling, eyebrows a 'v' of madness. Behind her, the rumble of surging fiction increased.

Fisk snatched a two-handed sword from the pile of armour, turned and swung it above his head, barely blocking the wild stroke delivered by Courgette. The sound of metal on metal rang through the throne room like a demented blacksmith's convention as Fisk parried the surging thrusts of Courgette's attack.

Vhintz scribbled away furiously, trying to ignore the clangorous ringing of combat and was almost flattened by a wildly shimmering horseman, sprinting through the wall and brandishing a polo mallet at full gallop. Whether it was terror, or something else, Vhintz would never know, but just for a split second he felt hungrier than he ever had in all his life.

(In the Market Square, the Black Guard put his ear to the ground and listened. 'Sounds like a fight going on down there. Something's going on, I tell you! I can hear horses now!')

The backsurge of fiction flooded onwards, frothing at Famine's heels, closing rapidly with every sword stroke, the base of the wave seething in as a mist around everyone's ankles.

'What's happening!' squealed Firkin at Merlot over the low-rumbling. 'He's got the parchment! You can't bribe him now!'

'Bribery? Who said anything about bribery?' yelled Merlot.

' "Treasure beyond your wildest dreams!" you said. I heard you!'

'That's not bribery. Just a bit of incentive!'

'Incentive? So what's *that*?' squealed Firkin as the vast stone column of an ankle plunged through the far wall.

'Success, I should think!' bawled Merlot, wincing as Arbutus clung to his shoulder with very sharp claws.

Fisk parried another stroke aimed at his head, turned and dashed away, leaping over a chair, totally oblivious of the ninety-foot stone troll wading through his throneroom. Fisk bounded into the air and . . . hung there, thrashing and cursing, fizzing blue sparks pulling him upwards from his translucent shoulders. The mist swirled around Courgette's calves.

('You telling me you *can't* feel that rumbling?' said the Guard as two of them lay ears to the ground in the Market Square.

'Does feel a bit weird, but I can't hear any swords!')

Courgette screamed as she waved Exbenedict impotently at Fisk's ankles, baffled by the sword's sudden urge to fly. 'Cometh ye back down here! Canst thou not fight like a man!' she yelled, tightening her grip and hooking her feet under a vast stone slab. 'Coward!'

Fisk stared about him in terror, eyes bulging. He felt lightheaded. Come to that he felt lightbodied, too. Alarm bells ringing at full volume, he stared through a ghostly vision of his hand. Right into the face of a hundred-foot-long golden dragon exploding translucently through the far wall.

Vhintz scribbled away. Each added word loosening Fisk's grip on reality, prising his fingers from this dimension; each added flap of the dragon's wing breaking his hold on sanity.

Hogshead clawed at the back of his neck. He felt as if he was in the middle of a raging tropical storm. Words battered at him like malaria-crazed mosquitos in the rainy season, sentences sliced through him as they surged towards the tear in the Space-Tome Continuum. His scream was lost

in the swirling, deafening tumult of the dragon's vast wing
soaring about his head.

'. . . wore a n eyyedpatch . . .' Vhintz was finding it
harder to write as the parchment flapped. The tunic he was
kneeling on was bucking and writhing and sparkling madly as
Ch'tin thrashed about inside the pocket. Ch'tin could feel the
rumble, sense the wall of words curling upwards into the
horizon of the imagination, closer, unstoppable.

('Definitely rumbling!' said the first Guard. Fifteen reclin-
ing guards grunted their agreement. 'What should we do?'

'Leave it. That's a problem for the drainage department!')

'Come ye back, chicken!' squealed Courgette at the
gibbering Fisk as she thrust, slashed and clung to
Exbenedict, up to her thighs in swirling fiction.

'. . . eyepadtch whych wa s aslo black . . .' continued
Vhintz, scribbling down the events, fictionalising Fisk,
levering his body out of reality helped by the kilothaums of
magic supplied by the copy of Appendix IIIb in Fisk's
pocket. Famine galloped towards him, polo mallet wind-
milling above his head.

A buzzing, rumbling cacophany raced towards the throne-
room. Hogshead turned to look as a critical mass tidal wave
surge of backpressure crashed through the wall behind him.
The wild white horses of fantasy riding the surf, galloping
atop the grey, horizon-filling expanse of words and ideas,
chasing Famine's heels.

Fisk spun on aerials of sparks, his head thrown back,
clutching his sword, shrieking defiance, screaming terror as
the dragon homed in.

Ch'tin's chrysalid skin split down his back as he struggled
in the turmoil, thrashing in confusion, baffled as he saw legs.
And wings.

Then the backsurge hit. Concentrated and forced between
the thaumic pillars of the two copies of Appendix IIIb, the
pressure built, surging through the throneroom with ear-
splitting force, snatching Fisk upwards with increasing
velocity. The dragon tucked a wing, arced sideways, bent its

reptilian knees and surfed across the curling wall of fiction, claws out in front, eyes on the hovering black insect with the sword.

As all the characters from all the books, poems and songs he had ever read, heard or sang surged through the wall at him, Hogshead screamed. Faces, weapons, animals, fabled beasts rushed through him, unicorns kebabed his kidneys and were gone, disorienting, unnerving. A carpet beneath the thrashing vampire bucked and cavorted, tossing Hogshead in an arcing curve across the crackling throne room. Vlad sprinted in the opposite direction, fleeing the swirling, chaotic tumult, ducking out of sight through a tiny doorway. Something else, naturally red in tooth and claw, ran screaming at Hogshead . . . The wave hit. Pressure surging through, blasting manhole covers from the ceiling in a sudden silver burst of explosive energy, shattering paintings and exploding vases as it crashed and roared in, seething and whirling in a wild tumult.

('Run away!' screamed the Guard as a snowstorm of spinning manhole covers exploded upwards, each turning end over end ahead of columns of seething mist.

'Alright! So maybe it's not the drains!' squealed the other Guard sprinting for cover as the force of gravity took over and began to tug the manhole covers back to earth, shaking his head in an attempt to dislodge the glimpsed image of a vast wooden boat packed with pairs of animals hot on the tail of a hundred foot gold dragon carrying a writhing black figure in its enormous claws.)

The wave ripped through the thoneroom like a whirling drug-crazed hurricane. And in an instant was gone.

Fisk's sword hung in mid-air for a moment, then crashed noisily to the wreckage-strewn floor.

As the last of the latest converts to the Elevated Church of St Lucre the Unwashed signed his Certificate of Unquestioning Belief, blew on the inky scribble and drifted off with a heady feeling of having a future not only secure but bound in chains and riveted to the walls of fortune, Bharkleed collapsed with exhaustion. A dull explosion sounded under the northern end of the Market Square.

'Cor, what a signing session!' exclaimed His Effulgence, Hirsuit the very Enpedestalled. 'I'm knackered!'

'I know you wanted to get the King on our side,' said Whedd, glaring at the ex-Monarch, 'but is that what you had in mind?'

A swirl of dark clouds grew above them.

'Well, I must confess, Brother Whedd,' began Bharkleed smirking, 'I didn't envisage him getting *so* personally involved. But I do appreciate him throwing himself into our support with such whole-hearted dedication!'

Hirsuit chuckled, blissfully unaware of the growing inchoate mass of cumuli.

'I didn't expect such body *and* soul cooperation!' added Bharkleed.

'It was nice of him to drop in!' spluttered Whedd.

'Yeah, dead nice!' cackled Hirsuit, staring at the piles of Certificates. A single stab of blue lightning flashed.

And while they were still talking about their latest haul a figure came and stood amongst them, and said, 'Greed be with you!'

'Oh, come back tomorrow, mate. We're closed!' grunted Whedd as Bharkleed mused on the day's success. 'You know,' said the Most Exalted One, his hands folded behind his head, 'It's always so nice to present a body of evidence for your theories. Especially a King's! Such is the power of body language!'

'I wonder what his epitaph'll be?' said Hirsuit. 'How about "King gone – died of Surfeit's lamprey's"?'

The slightly glowing figure stepped forward, 'Good day, Apostles!'

'Who're you called a Possle, eh?'

'You, dear Whedd,' said the figure. 'Nice to see your devotion is increasing your waistline!'

'Eh?' Whedd stared at the slightly translucent figure and

then at his own belly. It was true: since embarking on this, their lastest fund-raising scam, his toes had become a memory.

'And you, dear Hirsuit,' said the figure. 'Better than robbing banks, eh?'

'Don't know what you mean!' flustered His Effulgence, panic crossing his face followed quickly by a streak of guilt.

'Come, come,' said the figure. 'Don't be troubled by the past. I can forget *all* about your seedy backgrounds of desperate depravity as busking bank raiders – robbery with violins? grievous bodily harmonicas? What were you *thinking* of! I can erase it *all* from my capacious memory, forgive every misdemeanour. Just as soon as you hand over the dosh!'

Bharkleed stood suddenly and stared at the figure. 'Who the hell are you?'

'Tut, tut, Bharkleed! Language!' said the figure wagging a finger. 'Do you not recognise me? It is I, me, myself, yours truly, the unwashed one . . . need I go on?'

'Are you standing there claiming to be St Lucre the Unwashed?' shrieked Bharkleed.

'Yup, that's me!'

'But you don't exist!' protested Bharkleed.

'Who d'you think wrote the Red Proselytic Manuscript of St Lucre, eh?'

'Well, I thought that was a pseudonym . . .'

'Idiot! Now, give me what is mine!' demanded St Lucre with a filthy laugh. 'Give me all the tons of lovely loot, the acres of land, the estates and kingdoms, limpet mines and all else which you have *so* generously collected for me!'

'Unless I see the Fiddled Expense Sheets of Faith, the Holy Loops of Taxation and the Theologically Totalled Year End Figures, I will not believe it!'

'You always did like poking your fingers where they don't belong!' scowled St Lucre. 'All right! I've tried the easy way. Suck on this, punk!' He clicked his finger and a rain of expense sheets fell from the sky, tumbling profit and loss forecasts swirled as they plummeted towards the three

268

not-so-High Priests. A blizzard of odd and even figures, a forest of columns, the weight of evidence was crushing.

As Bharkleed, Hirsuit and Whedd struggled beneath the mountains of evidence the mysterious figure of St Lucre vanished. Along with a satisfyingly bulging offertory plate.

Carried by the claws of a hundred-foot gold dragon on the surging, swirling forefront of the literary wave, Fisk, or rather Fisk's fictional double, was tossed and bounced about as he was swept helplessly towards the tear in the Space-Tome Continuum.

Ahead of him, a host of silver spheres licked their expectant lips and began to paddle, building up speed, ready to run in upon the wave of phrases. The factions were waiting.

Behind them, Famine (currently galloping outrider next to the soaring saurian) was affecting the giant lizard's massive appetite. A vast tongue slurped at its huge maw, savouring the prospect of flash barbecued factions.

The tear yawned wider as the factions surged towards the curving grey arc, their excitement rising with every closing foot.

Suddenly the tear was upon them, the wave curling in all directions, wrapping around to force its way in, funnelling everything through the vast gap. Into the other side.

The only warning the factions had that perhaps they weren't going to make it intact was a deep saurian belly-rumble, a sort of hiccupping sound and a blast of searing flame.

As Famine, the dragon, Fisk and the ark screamed through the hole and crossed the Space-Tome Continuum, enormous flaps of dark matter knitted together, sealing the breach. It was almost as if the Great Projectionist in the Sky was running a vast slow-motion rewind of a magic bullet blasting through a giant black peach at point blank range. Almost.

Courgette waved the tip of Exbenedict dazedly through a host of shafts of light gleaming through the blasted manhole covers. She shook the sword at where Fisk had been, thrusting at nothing, baffled at the fact that it now felt so inert. She blinked in bewildered disbelief. Then in acute anger. He'd gone! Escaped.

'Come on! Get me *out* of here!' shouted Klayth yet again, pleading profusely from every winding of rope. 'You *can* use that sword, can't you?'

Courgette screamed, turning angry frustration into feisty action, raising Exbenedict above her head, bringing it down in a sweeping stroke that would make an ageing Mongol warrior weak with pride. Fragments of rope flew in every conceivable direction, exploding like a hail of kamikaze kapok snakes, wriggling and spinning. Sparks flew from Exbenedict's tip as it struck the stone of the pillar and buried itself eighteen inches into the living igneous rock.

'I only asked!' squeaked Klayth, picking himself up off the floor.

Courgette pulled a face as she struggled with both hands on the haft, feet either side of Exbenedict, arching her back, straining and failing to remove the sword from the stone. 'Feast thine eyes on what thou hast maketh me do, you prat!' she screamed. 'It budgeth not!'

'Temper, temper!' said Klayth.

Courgette snarled at him. 'Hast thou had thine tonsils removed yet?'

'He . . . he's gone!' spluttered Firkin crawling out from beneath a pile of paintings and dusting himself off. He stared at the spot, eighteen feet in the air where Fisk had been moments before. 'He just van . . . vanished.'

Merlot stood in the middle of the alternative throneroom and grinned, rubbing his hands as if he'd just finished working on a particularly messy and complex alchemical apparatus before dusting off his shoulders and Arbutus. 'Yes, yes,' he said to the owl. 'That seems splendid, what? Absolutely super!'

'What?' squealed Firkin, 'but Fisk's escaped!'

'Don't worry your young head about such concerns,' said Merlot, 'There's Klayth!'

'Yes, yes, but Fisk, he's . . .'

'People!' tutted Arbutus rolling his eyes. 'Never happy!'

'Well, we can't stand about chatting all day,' said Merlot looking about. 'Must dash, things to do. Dimensions to save!'

'Hold thy departure!' squealed Courgette turning on Merlot. 'Loose my weapon with thy powers!'

'Ahh, yes! Nearly forgot about that,' muttered Merlot walking across to the pillar. He grasped Exbenedict's hilt, whispered a few soft words and pulled the sword out with only a slight flurry of sparks. 'Anyway, must be off now . . .'

'Returneth to me by blade!' demanded Courgette, standing proud, legs apart, chest heaving arrogantly, holding out her hand.

Just behind her Hogshead hauled himself out from a pile of armour and several large boxes of gold goblets. He stood gazing at her, weak at the knees, heart pounding, tongue hanging limply.

Merlot stared at Courgette. 'Magic word?' he said.

She thought for a second, 'Now!'

Merlot shook his head.

'Please!' whispered Hogshead staring at her.

'Returneth to me my blade, please!' demanded Courgette.

'No,' said Merlot.

'What?'

'It's not yours,' he explained. 'There's a certain stone and anvil waiting to have this pulled out of it. Something to do with choosing monarchy. Sounds a bit fairy-taly to me, but there you are! Anyhow, must dash. Can't keep King Halva waiting . . . oops, I'm telling you the plot!' He strolled nonchalantly behind the pillar and disappeared.

Courgette squealed with wild red-haired fury and dashed around the pillar, 'Come back! Stop thief!'

'Too late,' said Hogshead. 'He's gone back to . . .' Suddenly his mind waved a bookworm-shaped memory neuron. 'Ch'tin,' he recalled and dashed towards Vhintz and his tunic.

'Back to Ch'tin?' said Dawn pulling a face.

Vhintz's mouth hung open as he looked alternately from the length of pink floral wallparchment, to the space where Fisk had been and to the crumpled heap of 'Ye Aynshent Almanacke of Conjoorynge, Magycke and Such'. He couldn't believe what he had just witnessed. He had actually been present when some *real* magic was cast. In fact, he had played a part in it! At least, he thought he had. Me? he spluttered mentally. Do magic? Nah, surely not!

Hogshead tugged his tunic out from beneath the stunned Sorcerer and yanked the copy of 'Lady Challerty's Loofah' out of his pocket. Immediately, he noticed two things about the battered romance. It was far lighter than it should have been and it looked as if a small explosive charge had been planted inside. The cover came off in his hand and a snowstorm of shattered pages fell like headbanger's dandruff as he picked it up. 'Ch'tin,' he whispered as what looked like the remains of a small brown leather inner tube after a high speed blow-out fell on to the remains of the gutted book.

'Hey, Merlot,' said Arbutus, tapping the wizard's saxaffron shoulder as they soared off, heading toward the Chapter Dimensions. 'You're not just going to leave them like that are you?'

'They don't require us any more. It won't take them long to sort everything out now,' mused Merlot. 'You know, I bet if we went back there in a few months' time it will feel like a whole new kingdom, peace will have settled, it'll be spring, the daffodils will be blooming on the slopes of . . .'

'Gahhhg! *Spare* me, please!' squawked Arbutus, his index flight-feather half-way down his throat. 'I meant you're not going to *leave* like that!'

'What?'

Arbutus tutted. 'Left-hand side of your cloak, third pocket down, fifth compartment. Remember?'

Merlot rummaged about near his left pectoral, his eyebrow raising as he felt the small hard cylinder.

'You're not going to waste it, are you?' pressed Arbutus.

Merlot grinned as he changed course and headed back.

'You certain it went this way?' asked General Bateleur as he and Colonel Rachnid galloped around the back of one of Castell Rhyngill's smoking towers.

'I saw it!' answered Rachnid, drawing his sword. 'It soared down here. I'm sure!'

'Well, I can't see it!' snapped Bateleur, his arrow finger getting very itchy.

'Must be perched somewhere.'

'Perched!' shrieked Bateleur. 'Perched? Ninety-foot fire-breathing dragons don't perch. They're not blinking sparrows!'

'Well, vultures perch,' said Rachnid defensively.

'I don't care what it's doing. I just want to know where it is!'

'Funny, isn't it?' said Rachnid as they had spied all the way around the tower. 'It can't be hiding. It's too big. It's almost as if it's just vanished into thin air!'

'Don't talk rubbish! Something that big can't just vanish. Can it?'

'Who *are* you lot?' asked Klayth, staring at the group of youngsters standing in the wreckage-littered throneroom. 'Some sort of undercover secret team? Like Interking-domnal Rescue, or something?'

'No, no,' said Firkin. 'We're your friends.'

Way above their heads, each open manhole began to sprout tiny growths of rope.

'Friends?' said Klayth. 'But I've never seen you before!'

'You sure?' asked Firkin rolling his eyes as he thought about this.

'Think about it!' said Dawn, staring at her brother. 'Have you been hit on the head, or something?'

Suddenly, all around them lengths of rope tumbled out of the manholes followed seconds later by a host of abseiling

273

Black Guards, screaming in to save Klayth, like a thousand overgrown task force spiders. They landed in an avalanche of heavy boots, unhooked themselves from the ropes, fanning out, surrounding everyone and covering all exits in seconds. Commander 'Black' Achonite was yelling orders in double time even before he touched down, stabbing his index finger from above with deadly accuracy. 'Arrest them . . . and him . . . and her . . .'

Suddenly, with a sound like a herd of wild-cats in a sack, Courgette leapt from behind a stack of paintings, whirling the biggest stick she couldn't find at such short notice and ran at Achonite. The Black Guards took a step forward, totally unsure what to do. They couldn't strike a defenceless woman . . .

'Fights for Women!' she screamed.

'Courgette! No. Stop!' shouted Hogshead. 'They're on our side. You'll be arrested!'

The Black Guards drew their swords and stood instantly ready for action. Defenceless women were one thing . . . she was different!

'I don't care!' squealed Courgette, still on an adrenalin high, whirling the stick above her head. 'I've done time before. This is something I believe in. Fights for . . .'

'Someone else!' shouted Hogshead as he grabbed her purple, green and white decorated ankle. 'They're on our side!' he pleaded as he was dragged along the floor.

'But, they're *men*!'

'And they're bigger than you!'

'You men are all alike . . . size isn't important! It's what you *do* that matters!'

Suddenly a saxaffron-clad wizard stepped out from behind the pillar of stone. 'Oh, Courgette, have you not calmed down yet? Shame on you!'

'You!' screamed Courgette, turning on Merlot. The Black Guards, forgotten for a moment, breathed a sigh of relief as the tirade turned and ebbed towards the wizard. 'Give me back my sword!' She headed forward dragging Hogshead from her ankle.

274

'Klayth, er, Your Highness!' spluttered Merlot, backing away from the feral female. 'May I suggest that your first action . . . no, Courgette, stop it . . . as King of Rhyngill and Cranachan . . . look be careful with that, I'm trying to help . . . is to give this girl . . .'

'Woman! Fights for girls doesn't *sound* right!'

'. . . er, woman. Give her a blinking sword!'

'Hear that, Courgette?' asked Hogshead from her ankles. 'Put the stick down and you can have a sword!'

Courgette stopped and stared at Klayth her mind whirring. 'And an axe?' she said.

'Yes! Now, put the stick down!'

'And one of those spiky things on the end of a chain that whizz round your head and scream and . . .'

'Yes. Now, shutup, Miss!' said Klayth firmly.

'It's Miz,' snarled Courgette.

Achonite and the Black Guards, taken aback at all the treasures strewn everywhere and the fact that Klayth seemed to be all right and have the situation under control, began to fidget, feeling almost embarrassed. As if they'd stormed a private party, sirens blazing.

'Come on!' urged Arbutus on Merlot's shoulder. 'Do it now before they all start to go! They'll love it! You'll see!'

'Er, ahem!' said Merlot. 'Don't like to interrupt now everything's all right, so I'll just sneak off quietly, if that's OK with everyone?'

Various grunts and nods of baffled approval came from the Guards as they stared mistrustfully at the now unarmed Courgette.

Underneath the ruined debris of 'Lady Challerty's Loofah' a creature struggled to comprehend the concept of limbs. If it was some kind of practical joke, it thought, it was in really bad taste! Whilst it had been asleep, someone had glued six spindly legs and four wings on to its body. It was sick! Wriggling its mandibles in irritation it spat and cursed.

'Got a lot of clearing up to do, see?' added the wizard.

275

'There's bound to be a few factions to zap!' he added tapping his staff.

'Get on with it,' hissed Arbutus out of the side of his beak.

'Well, I'll see you all around I expect. If ever you find yourselves in the Chapter Dimensions, look me up. I'm in the Index, under . . .'

Arbutus snatched the little cylinder from Merlot's hand and hurled it on to the floor. It exploded in a thunderflash of silver sparks, blue fountains and crimson sky-rockets, clouds of smoke billowed around them in plumes of grey and yellow.

'Merlot?' shouted Hogshead from the floor.

'Wow!' exclaimed Klayth through a cloud of cordite and magnesium. 'Neat trick, I thought it was good seeing a borogrove last week, but *that* . . .'

'You've seen a borogrove?' asked Firkin.

'Oh, yeah. It was unreal!'

'Is *that* all?'

The creature pumped blood through its crumpled wings, straightening them out into four seemingly vast emerald flight surfaces.

'Oh? And I suppose you've seen better?' grumbled Klayth.

'How about eight-foot frogs with teeth as big as your arm, have your head off as soon as look at you!' said Firkin smugly.

'Oh, come on . . .' said Klayth dripping disbelief. 'Where have you seen that?'

'Er, those. A whole army of them!'

'Where?'

'Oh. I'm sorry I'm not at liberty to divulge any information regarding the whereabouts of such a creature or creatures. Official secret!'

Suddenly out of the gloom of the passageway, a bright green winged creature lurched unsteadily as it tried to come to terms with the complexity of flight. It stalled, crashed, picked itself up on its six spindly legs and headed determinedly for Hogshead.

'And dragons . . .' added Firkin.

'Sounds like a fairy-tale to me,' said Klayth as they headed off out of the labyrinth escorted by the Black Guards.

Vhintz didn't know where to look or which conversation to listen to. There was suddenly *far* too much magic around. Didn't anyone just want a tap mending or a shoe reheeling?

'Get off!' squawked Hogshead as he struggled up off the floor beneath the furious emerald flapping of beautiful wings.

'Swat me not!' piped a strangely familiar voice.

'Help!' whimpered Hogshead as the verdant shimmering wings crashed about his head.

Courgette and Dawn stood and watched, smirking.

'Stop flapping, get off!'

'Land on floor if so I do!' whistled Ch'tin as he settled on Hogshead's shoulder and held his glistening wings up.

'Ch'tin? What's happened to you!'

'Changed I am!'

'I can see that! But, *what* are you?'

'You remember me not, mmmmh?'

'Course I do, but . . .'

'Bookerfly, I think! Hungry I am, slushy romance have you? Mmmmh?'

Hogshead pointed at Vhintz's right hand, still holding 'Ye Aynshent Almanacke of Conjoorynge, Magycke and Such'. 'How about a brief snack of that?' he asked Ch'tin, smirking.

The bookerfly rolled his eyes and shook his head in denial. 'No! No! Too dangerous it is! Romance of slushiness, please!'

'Don't worry, Ch'tin. I wouldn't let you!'

With the bookerfly balanced on his shoulder, Hogshead accelerated to catch up with everyone else. 'Er, Your Highness? Hello . . . Got any books you don't want?'

As the throne room emptied, two whispered voices floated from behind the pillar.

'Too soon!' said Merlot.

'You would have been there all night! "If ever you're in

277

the Chapter Dimensions, look me up"! Pah!' exclaimed Arbutus. 'I've told you before about milking an audience's response!'

'I wasn't prepared! You should know it takes a while to get a spell ready!'

'That's obvious. That's why we're still here I suppose, skulking behind pillars like common magicians!'

'Sometimes, my dear feathered friend, you are *far* too theatrical for your own good!' Merlot raised his right hand, counted three and the two of them vanished with only the slightest of silver shimmers.

'But I *like* explosions!' protested Arbutus' disembodied voice.

'Arsonist!' grumbled Merlot.

'Wimp!'